Nietzsche's Mirror

Nietzsche's Mirror

The World as Will to Power

Linda L. Williams

ROWMAN & LITTLEFIELD PUBLISHERS, INC.
Lanham • Boulder • New York • Oxford

ROWMAN & LITTLEFIELD PUBLISHERS, INC.

Published in the United States of America
by Rowman & Littlefield Publishers, Inc.
4720 Boston Way, Lanham, Maryland 20706
http://www.rowmanlittlefield.com

12 Hid's Copse Road
Cumnor Hill, Oxford OX2 9JJ, England

British Library Cataloguing in Publication Information Available

Library of Congress Cataloging-in-Publication Data

Williams, Linda L., 1953–
    Nietzsche's mirror : the world as will to power / Linda L. Williams.
      p. cm.
    Includes bibliographical references and index.
    ISBN 0-8476-9794-0 (alk. paper) — ISBN 0-8476-9795-9 (pbk. : alk. paper)
    1. Nietzsche, Friedrich Wilhelm, 1844–1900—Contributions to the philosophy
of power. 2. Power (Philosophy)—History—19th century. I. Title.
B3318.P68 W55 2001
193—dc21   00-038701

Printed in the United States of America

♾™ The paper used in this publication meets the minimum requirements of American
National Standard for Information Sciences—Permanence of Paper for Printed Library
Materials, ANSI/NISO Z39.48-1992.

To Ross

Contents

Foreword

I first encountered Friedrich Nietzsche when I was an undergraduate philosophy major. I immediately was intrigued by his phrase "will to power." It was provocative and mysterious. What could Nietzsche have meant by it? Initially, it seemed to suggest what most first-time readers infer from it—some draconian lust for physical or military power. Luckily, my professor was well versed in Nietzsche interpretation and quickly dispelled these leanings, but what replaced them was rather vague. After that brief first undergraduate fling, I encountered Nietzsche again in graduate school. I knew exactly what I wanted to concentrate on in the graduate seminar on Nietzsche—will to power. Although the seminar proved to be a thorough grounding in Nietzsche's later texts, what Nietzsche meant by "will to power" remained for the most part a mystery; however, the cause of the mystery seemed to belong more to Nietzsche's writing than to the reader. As I continued to delve not only into Nietzsche's texts but into the commentaries on the texts, it became clear that while everyone agreed that will to power was a central, if not the central, idea of Nietzsche's, not everyone agreed on what will to power was.

The purpose of this book is to attempt to sort through this mystery. Quite frankly, what I hope to do is write the kind of book that I would have wanted to read when I first was taken with Nietzsche's famous phrase. Why is it so hard to figure out what Nietzsche meant by it? Why are there conflicting interpretations of it? How did Nietzsche come to invent it? Why is the book *The Will to Power* unhelpful in answering these questions? While some of the answers to these questions are rather straightforward, they do not seem to be presented all in one place. Some commentaries do not discuss the history of the idea at all, while others discuss only the psychological aspects of it. Some interpreters ignore Nietzsche's unpublished writings, while others focus exclusively on them. Who is right and who is wrong? Instead of pointing fingers, I will show why these splits have occurred, as well as what is gained and lost by going one way rather than an-

other, and direct the reader to more sustained examinations than this one book
can offer. For example, there may be some connection between Nietzsche's life
and his conception of will to power, but I do not have the time in this book to do
a detailed analysis of Nietzsche's life, especially when there are several excellent biographies of Nietzsche already available. In such cases, I will direct the
reader to other books on the topic, if the reader wants to explore Nietzsche's life
or philosophical ideas from other viewpoints.

So this book becomes, in essence, what a Nietzsche reader might want to know
about will to power from both a commentary on Nietzsche's own texts and an
analysis of the myriad of interpretations will to power has generated. It is my
hope that it will provide a solid introduction to the phrase that will enable the
reader to begin to develop an enlightened interpretation of will to power and to
have some understanding of the current commentary on it.

The book is divided into five chapters. The first chapter introduces the reader
to questions and problems surrounding will to power and addresses the evolution of the phrase in Nietzsche's early texts. How will to power is presented con-
textually in the works Nietzsche published within his lifetime or authorized to
be published before his mental breakdown is the subject of chapter 2. Here I focus on will to power within the context of master and slave morality. Chapter 3
discusses will to power in Nietzsche's unpublished notes and the status of the
Nachlass, the unpublished material, and addresses whether will to power is a
metaphysical principle. I shall argue that it is not. Chapter 4 attempts to resolve
some apparent paradoxes between will to power and Nietzsche's views on truth.
The book concludes with some of my speculations on the effects of my interpretation of will to power on other themes of Nietzsche's work, such as eternal
recurrence and *amor fati* (love of fate).

Ultimately, if my reading of Nietzsche's texts is even in the ball park, a wholly
univocal answer to the question "What is will to power?" is not only impossible
but also undesirable. Each reader must grapple with Nietzsche's thoughts individually; yet Nietzsche also warns that his writings will be misunderstood. Despite the discrepancies among commentators, there is a growing sense that at least
some of the more recent work on Nietzsche and on will to power are less mistaken than others—that we can get to a certain, enlightened point before we must
give way to the unique individuality of personal experience. But we cannot start
there. Nietzsche did not believe that all interpretations are equivalent, and that
holds true, too, for interpretations of his will to power. Why are some interpretations better than others? Let's find out.

Acknowledgments

I wish to thank, first of all, John Arras and Bernd Magnus, who encouraged me to love philosophy in general and Friedrich Nietzsche in particular. Special thanks go to Richard Schacht and his 1989 National Endowment for the Humanities seminar on Nietzsche and to all the "Nietzsche campers" involved in that seminar. In addition, I would like to thank my colleagues at Kent State University, who have listened to my ideas on Nietzsche with great patience, good humor, and helpful advice, particularly Dan Silber, whose insightful comments on chapter 4 were greatly appreciated. The Kent State University Research Council generously provided funds for the completion of this project.

Further thanks are due to all the editors at Rowman and Littlefield, who have been so helpful and patient with my questions. Finally, I wish to let my family know how much their love and support have meant to me and have sustained me throughout my research and writing of this book, and a big hug goes to Mike Halliday-Williams, who helped proofread the German and organize the notes.

The following publishers have granted permission for their material to be reprinted in this book:

- Selections from the *Kritische Gesamtausgabe Werke* by Friedrich Nietzsche, ed. Giorgio Colli and Mazzino Montinari. Copyright © 1967–71 by Walter de Gruyter and Co. Reprinted by permission of Walter de Gruyter and Co.
- Selections from *The Portable Nietzsche,* ed. Walter Kaufmann, trans. Walter Kaufmann. Translation copyright © 1954 by Viking Press, renewed © 1982 by Viking Penguin Inc. Reprinted by permission of Viking Penguin, a division of Penguin Putnam, Inc.
- Selections from *Daybreak* and *Human, All-Too-Human* by Friedrich Nietzsche, trans. R. J. Hollingdale. Copyright © 1982 and 1986 by Cambridge University Press. Reprinted by permission of Cambridge University Press.

- Selections from *The Basic Writings of Nietzsche* by Friedrich Nietzsche, trans. Walter Kaufmann. Copyright © 1967 by Walter Kaufmann. Reprinted by permission of Random House, Inc.
- Selections from *The Gay Science* by Friedrich Nietzsche, trans. Walter Kaufmann. Copyright © 1974 by Random House, Inc. Reprinted by permission of Random House, Inc.
- Selections from *The Basic Writings of Nietzsche* by Friedrich Nietzsche, trans. Walter Kaufmann. Copyright © 1966 by Walter Kaufmann. Reprinted by permission of Random House, Inc.
- Selections from *The Will to Power* by Friedrich Nietzsche, trans. Walter Kaufmann and R. J. Hollingdale. Copyright © 1967 by Walter Kaufmann. Reprinted by permission of Random House, Inc.

Key to the Abbreviations

For those who would like to compare the translation to the German, I have placed the German text immediately following the English. At the end of each quote, English translations are marked with the abbreviation of the English title followed by either the aphorism number or, when there is no aphorism number, the page number of the English translation. German passage is cited by its place in the *Kritische Gesamtausgabe Werke.*

All of the following were written by Friedrich Nietzsche.

AC   *The Antichrist.* In *The Portable Nietzsche,* trans. Walter Kaufmann (New York: Viking Press, 1968).

BGE   *Beyond Good and Evil.* Trans. Walter Kaufmann (New York: Random House, 1966).

BT   *The Birth of Tragedy out of the Spirit of Music.* In *The Basic Writings of Nietzsche,* trans. Walter Kaufmann (New York: Modern Library, 1968).

D   *Daybreak.* Trans. R. J. Hollingdale (Cambridge: Cambridge University Press, 1982).

EH   *Ecce Homo.* Trans. Walter Kaufmann (New York: Random House, 1969).

GM   *On the Genealogy of Morals.* Trans. Walter Kaufmann (New York: Random House, 1969).

GS   *The Gay Science.* Trans. Walter Kaufmann (New York: Vintage Books, 1974).

HAH   *Human, All-Too-Human.* Trans. R. J. Hollingdale (Cambridge: Cambridge University Press, 1986).

KGW   *Kritische Gesamtausgabe Werke.* Ed. Giorgio Colli and Mazzino Montinari (New York: Walter de Gruyter and Co., 1967–71), 8 volumes. The volume number is in roman numerals, followed by the band number and the page number, except in the case of the *Nachlass* notes, when the note number is indicated before the page number.

KSA   *Sämtliche Werke, Kritische Studienausgabe.* Ed. Giorgio Colli and Mazzino Montinari (New York: Walter de Gruyter, 1980), 15 Bandes.

TI   *Twilight of the Idols.* In *The Portable Nietzsche,* trans. Walter Kaufmann (New York: Viking Press, 1968).

TSZ   *Thus Spoke Zarathustra.* In *The Portable Nietzsche,* trans. Walter Kaufmann (New York: Viking Press, 1968).

WP   *The Will to Power.* Trans. Walter Kaufmann and R. J. Hollingdale (New York: Random House, 1967).

Breazeale   *Philosophy and Truth: Selections from Nietzsche's Notebooks of the Early 1870's.* Trans. and ed. Daniel Breazeale (Atlantic Highlands, N.J.: Humanities Press International, 1979).

1

The Development of Will to Power

What is will to power? A century after Nietzsche wrote the phrase, we are still asking ourselves this question. At one time, Nietzsche thought about writing an entire book concerning it. However, the book, *The Will to Power*, that we can purchase today is not the book he envisioned; it is merely a collection of unpublished notes put together by his sister and editors after his debilitating collapse in Turin. So we have no lengthy exposition by Nietzsche himself as to how he conceived will to power. As a result, will to power is still an enigmatic and often misunderstood notion. Even today there are those who think Nietzsche's writings on will to power spawned the Third Reich.[1] While Adolf Hitler's propaganda machine used writings from Nietzsche (as did competing German social and political groups),[2] the idea that Nietzsche's philosophy by itself formed the ideological basis of Hitler's regime is completely erroneous.

I would like to say that this book is an attempt to separate fact from fiction about will to power, but for reasons that will become clear through the course of this book, I cannot say this. Instead, this book is more an attempt to "corral" Nietzsche's notion of will to power by tracing its development throughout Nietzsche's writings, by preserving the contexts in which the phrase appears, and by sorting out which interpretations of will to power are textually supported and faithful to Nietzsche's overall concerns.[3] Although this method has its problems, it is a starting place and a context from which I hope to make clear where the problems with the method arise. Will to power is an integral part of Nietzsche's critique on culture and morality, and how it is interpreted affects other key and central concepts, such as eternal recurrence, perspectivism, *amor fati*, and the *Übermensch* (the "overman").

There is something seductive about the phrase. *Will to power (Wille zur Macht)* conjures up all sorts of images from sadomasochism to "ethnic cleansing" and global conquests. But is that all there is to it—"Übermensch, Übermensch über alles"? If so, will to power would not seem to be very interesting or original. But

1

Nietzsche himself writes that sheer physical power is only one instance, and a very crude one at that, of will to power.[4] There are other instances of it, and these are often the more intriguing and original. Nietzsche speaks of will to power in relation to values, truth, psychology, and the world, which span the traditional categories of ethics, epistemology, and metaphysics in philosophy. Will to power permeates every aspect of Nietzsche's philosophy.

So what *is* will to power? It is difficult to answer this question for several reasons. First, Nietzsche's own style works against easily answering this kind of question. Nietzsche rarely if ever defines his terms. He never says, "This is what I mean by . . . ," and the closest he comes to doing this with will to power is followed by a spate of metaphors.[5] He writes in aphorisms and short passages designed to provoke active thought and consideration of his positions rather than passive intake of them. He even recognizes that much of his writings will be misunderstood and misapplied. In many ways, his style is altogether appropriate for and contributes to his philosophy, but it can be terribly frustrating for the beginning reader.

Second, much of his writings are in the form of unpublished notes left in notebooks or on slips of paper. Many of these notes, and some that are quite relevant to our discussion of will to power, are dated rather early in relation to when the majority of his published works were written. This, it has been suggested,[6] gave Nietzsche ample opportunity to include these thoughts in some published form, but Nietzsche chose not to include them. Some commentators have then inferred that Nietzsche was only experimenting with these ideas,[7] and some believe that he found them unsatisfactory in some way.[8] The question then becomes how much weight should be given those ideas that Nietzsche decided not to publish. Was he going to use them but never got the chance because he became ill rather suddenly and at a relatively early age? That question will never be answered definitively.

Finally, an answer to what will to power is poses problems because it assumes that there is *one answer* to this question. As you may have noticed already, I do not refer to will to power as "the" will to power, as many other commentators do. Nietzsche, of course, wrote in German, and proper German places the definite article in front of the noun. Translating German into English, however, is a bit trickier. Sometimes the definite article is omitted to render the sentence into everyday English. In the case of *der Wille zur Macht,* I think it would be better to omit *der.* Including the definite article in the English translation grammatically seduces the reader to think of will to power as a thing—one unified thing at that. It tempts one to start an answer to our question with, "It is. . . . " If I make my case successfully enough, referring to will to power by *it* is an error. I find the singular verb *is* problematic as well. Again, it already suggests that an answer to the question will be in the singular, but, as Nietzsche himself contends, language is limiting because of its arbitrarily imposed linguistic and grammatical structures.[9] Perhaps a better way to put the question is, "Will to power—??" But because this is being written in English, I am constrained within English grammar. The best I can hope for is to mark these places where the marriage between Nietzsche's thoughts and the rules of language become strained to the point of divorce.

Nietzsche's writings, like Plato's, can be divided into three periods—early, middle, and late.[10] The early period encompasses the works up to and including *The Birth of Tragedy out of the Spirit of Music*. The middle period begins with *Untimely Meditations* and ends with the first four parts of *The Gay Science*. The late period is everything from *Thus Spoke Zarathustra* on. Each period has a distinguishing feature. The early writings include his juvenilia, his philological writings, and his earliest philosophical writings, which are heavily influenced by Arthur Schopenhauer and Richard Wagner. The middle period is characterized by Nietzsche's supposed "positivism" and use of science to criticize metaphysics. Finally, the late period is Nietzsche's "mature" thought: Nietzsche abandons his "faith" in science, and the ideas of eternal recurrence, the *Übermensch,* and will to power are expressed. In the late period, certain strands of the earlier works can still be found. But here they are no longer lifted rather straightforwardly from other thinkers, for example, Wagner and Schopenhauer in the early writings, or influenced by the scientific movements of the time, as is the case with the middle period. Instead, ideas gathered through other sources, albeit scientific or philosophic, are transformed by Nietzsche's own insights on the world. Thus, Nietzsche's mature thoughts are an amalgamation of some of the ideas he encountered with his unique, personal stamp upon them. Thus, they are not wholly original, in the sense that his ideas were never affected by any other idea he read—if this is even possible; yet they are completely original in the way he thought them through and modified them in order to make his sense out of them. This is certainly true of "eternal recurrence," a phrase that first appears in Nietzsche's late period. As it has been persuasively shown elsewhere,[11] eternal recurrence is not a wholly original idea. A form of it had been professed by the Stoics and others, and Nietzsche as a classics professor was certainly well steeped in Stoic writings. He had to have been familiar with at least the Stoic rendition of eternal recurrence. But Nietzsche's eternal recurrence is not that of the Stoics. There may be similarities, but there is not identity.

So, too, will to power is not wholly original. There are places in other nineteenth-century writings, philosophical and scientific, as well as earlier writings, where we can find similar themes, but they are not identical to Nietzsche's. They may have exerted some influence on him, but he did not simply relocate them. Whatever scientific theories appropriated by Nietzsche that may have affected or supported his idea of will to power, they subsequently appeared in areas decidedly unscientific. Whatever philosophical readings that may have started Nietzsche thinking in a certain direction, the destination was clearly Nietzsche's own by the 1880s. So as we proceed to determine what will to power means and why, we cannot say that will to power is simply rehashed Schopenhauer, Wagner, Friedrich Lange, or Ruggiero Boscovich.

Although the phrase *will to power* first appears in published form in *Thus Spoke Zarathustra,* it did not suddenly pop into Nietzsche's thought like he claimed eternal recurrence did. It evolved from philosophical and scientific writings Nietzsche read, and the idea can be found in pubescent form in his own writings prior to *Zarathustra.* The development of will to power does not seem to follow any clear linear progression. There seem to be two concurrent strains in the development of will to power: one consisting of discussions of "will" and "willing" and another linking power to different modes of being. It is difficult to discuss the two strains together, so I will concentrate on the latter strain in this chapter and switch to the former in the next chapter. What follows is an exceedingly brief introduction to Nietzsche and his thought. I hope only to get us to a place where we can discuss the evolution of Nietzsche's use of *power.* For more detailed discussions of Nietzsche's life and early influences, I direct the reader to the end of this chapter, where I recommend several books for additional information.

It was taken for granted that Friedrich Nietzsche would follow in his family's occupational tradition. His father had been a Lutheran minister, as had his grandfather, and his mother was the daughter of a Lutheran minister. His early training was in those skills helpful to preaching—oration and music. But in high school, Nietzsche's interests changed to philology, what today we call "classics." He was a classics major throughout college, and his first teaching position at Basel University was as a classics professor. While in college, however, he read Schopenhauer's *The World as Will and Representation,* which was to influence him in some way throughout his productive life.

The largest effect Schopenhauer had on Nietzsche was simply to interest him in philosophy itself. As a classicist, Nietzsche had encountered the writings of Plato and Aristotle, as well as the pre-Socratic and post-Socratic Greek and Roman philosophers. Philosophical thinking was not wholly new to him, but Schopenhauer's book seems to have fanned the flame of Nietzsche's philosophical fascinations. He began to read other philosophers, not just the ancient ones.

Schopenhauer saw *The World as Will and Representation* as an advancement on Immanuel Kant's work in *The Critique of Pure Reason.* Schopenhauer was a steadfast defender of Kant in a time when it was unfashionable to be one. Schopenhauer had been a colleague of George Hegel at the University of Berlin. Hegel was at the height of his success and popularity, partly because of his criticism of Kant's work. Schopenhauer deliberately scheduled his classes at the same time as Hegel's, and while Hegel's classes were always standing room only, Schopenhauer managed only a handful of students at best. Schopenhauer soon resigned from his teaching position and lived a rather solitary life in the country, continuing to write and publish. It was no secret that he was bitterly envious and resentful of Hegel's philosophy and popularity. The conclusions that Schopenhauer reaches in his own writings—that the world is fundamentally meaningless and human life likewise—could be seen as a rationalization of Schopenhauer's own depressing outlook on life.

What was it about Schopenhauer's work that attracted Nietzsche? In *The World as Will and Representation,* Schopenhauer basically accepts Kant's bifurcation of experience into noumena and phenomena. The world the human mind encounters is purely phenomenal. What constitutes the noumenal realm is not entirely clear. While Kant posits the existence of a noumenal world, it is unknowable, for as soon as we encounter anything with our minds, it immediately is in the phenomenal realm. Thus, Kant says nothing about the noumenal world because it is theoretically impossible for him to say anything about the noumenal world, except that it "gives rise to" or "supports" the phenomenal one. The noumenal world, according to his philosophy, is unknowable.

For Schopenhauer, however, the noumenal world is not completely unknowable. According to Schopenhauer, the noumenal world is a world of complete chaos, of which the human mind attempts to grab hold and make sense. It does so by categorization and delineation, by trying to make something stable out of the instability. The mind must do this in order for us to function amid the chaos. But any order that the world seems to have is order our minds have imposed phenomenally on it, not order we discover in it. As the noumenal world is unknowable, in principle, for Kant, why does Schopenhauer think that he can say anything about it? Schopenhauer believes that human beings, being part of the world, are chaotic, too. Thus, we can have a glimpse of the noumenal world through our own noumenal aspect—our will.

Will, for Schopenhauer, is the ultimate metaphysical substance of the world. Will is essentially chaotic, and it is our minds that create any order and stability. Even our own will can be tamed and directed by our minds through reason. Also, will can express itself through a medium that is entirely transcultural—music. Music is the representation of the chaotic noumenal world bursting into the ordered phenomenal one.

Music plays an important role in both Schopenhauer's and Nietzsche's philosophies. Nietzsche studied piano in his youth and had dreams at one time of becoming a famous composer. He had flirted with majoring in music before settling on philology. During his days at Basel University, he met and then spent weekends with Richard Wagner, who exerted considerable influence over Nietzsche at that time. Perhaps Nietzsche saw Wagner as a father figure, but beyond that psychologism, both men seemed to recognize the other's creative genius. The influences of both Schopenhauer and Wagner were converging on and greatly influencing Nietzsche. It comes as no surprise that the ideas of both men are prominent in *The Birth of Tragedy out of the Spirit of Music,* in which Nietzsche explicitly praises them. Schopenhauer's valorization of music would appeal to Wagner, too, and Nietzsche saw music as a way to induce cultural change. At one time he believed that Wagner's music might usher in a whole new era of German culture, the grandeur of which would rival or surpass Greece's Golden Age. This is the stuff of youthful dreams, and while Nietzsche abandoned his uncritical infatuation with both Schopenhauer and Wagner, he never completely abandoned his vision of a Golden Age. However, he did abandon his ideas

that it would be a German Golden Age and that music would be the primary cata-
lyst of it.

"POWER" IN THE EARLY PERIOD

As previously mentioned, Nietzsche's "early period" comprises Nietzsche's
juvenilia, some more or less polished but unpublished pieces (such as "Homer's
Contest" and "Truth and Lie in the Extra-Moral Sense"), and *The Birth of Tragedy out of the Spirit of Music* and finally culminates with *Untimely Meditations.*
One of the characteristics of this stage of Nietzsche's writings is Nietzsche's preoccupation with Greek culture, although this is not universally the case. As we
shall see, there is no univocal characteristic of any of Nietzsche's "periods," but
traditionally Nietzsche scholarship has divided them in these general ways.

In *The Birth of Tragedy out of the Spirit of Music* Nietzsche divides the world
of art into two parts, just as Schopenhauer did with his metaphysical worlds, with
Nietzsche's "Dionysian" art nicely corresponding to Schopenhauer's chaotic
noumena, and Nietzsche's "Apollonian" art corresponding to the more ordered
and "artificial" phenomenal realm. Nietzsche basically says as much when he
writes,

> In contrast to all those who are intent on deriving the arts from one exclusive prin-
> ciple, as the necessary vital source of every work of art, I shall keep my eyes fixed
> on the two artistic deities of the Greeks, Apollo and Dionysus, and recognize in them
> the living and conspicuous representatives of two worlds of art differing in their
> intrinsic essence and in their highest aims. I see Apollo as the transfiguring genius
> of the principii individuationis through which alone the redemption in illusion is truly
> to be obtained; while by the mystical triumphant cry of Dionysus the spell of indi-
> viduation is broken, and the way lies open to the Mothers of Being, to the inner-
> most heart of things. This extraordinary contrast, which stretches like a yawning gulf
> between plastic art as the Apollonian, and music as the Dionysian art, has revealed
> itself to only one of the great thinkers, to such an extent that, even without this clue
> to the symbolism of Hellenic divinities, he conceded to music a character and an
> origin different from all the other arts, because, unlike them, it is not a copy of a
> phenomenon, but an immediate copy of the will itself, and therefore compliments
> *everything physical in the world* and every phenomenon by representing *what is
> metaphysical,* the thing in itself. (Schopenhauer, *The World as Will and Represen-
> tation* I, 310) (BT, 16)

> Im Gegensatz zu allen denen, welche beflissen sind, die Künste aus einem einzigen
> Princip, als dem nothwendigen Lebensquell jedes Kunstwerks abzuleiten, halte ich
> den Blick auf jene beiden künstlerischen Gottheiten der Griechen, Apollo und
> Dionysus, geheftet und erkenne in ihnen die lebendigen und ansschaulichen
> Repräsentanten *zweier* in ihrem tiefsten Wesen und ihren höchsten Zielen
> verschiedenen Kunstwelten. Apollo steht vor mir, als der verklärende Genius des
> principii individuationis, durch den allein die Erlösung im Scheine wahrhaft zu

erlangen ist: während unter dem mystischen Jubelruf des Dionysus der Bann der Individuation zersprent wird und der Weg zu den Müttern des Sein's, zu dem innersten Kern der Dinge offen liegt. Dieser ungeheuere Gegensatz, der sich zwischen der plastischen Kunst als der apollinischen und der Musik als der dionysischen Kunst klaffend aufthut, ist einem Einzigen der grossen Denker in dem Maasse offenbar geworden, dass er, selbst ohne jene Anleitung der Hellenischen Göttersymbolik, der Musik einen verschiedenen Charackter und Ursprung vor allen anderen Künsten zuerkannte, weil sie nicht, wie jene alle, Abbild der Erscheinung, sondern unmittelbar Abbild des Willens selbst sei und also *zu allem Physischen der Welt das Metaphysische,* zu aller Erscheinung das Ding an sich darstelle. [Schopenhauer, *Die Welt als Wille und Vorstellung* I, 310] [KGW III/1, 99–100]

Thus we can see that Nietzsche's division of the art world self-consciously parallels Schopenhauer's division of the real world. The plastic arts are part of the phenomenal world because they are representations of representations. Music originates from the noumenal world because it is a representation of will. Thus, music shares a unique and esteemed place in both Schopenhauer's and Nietzsche's philosophies at this rather early stage in Nietzsche's writings. Music is transcultural because it is translingual. Native American flute music or Zulu drumming can move a person as profoundly as Beethoven's Ninth Symphony. But that is not to say that music cannot be Apollonian. We can take the more primitive and chaotic Dionysian music and make a representation of it by structuring it into particular forms, for example, sonata or concerto forms, and by emphasizing only the harmonic sounds and discarding any dissonance.

But Dionysian music has a power that the plastic arts and Apollonian music lack—it has the power to evoke dithyrambs in us in a way that paintings and sculpture cannot. Parents never object to their children attending an art museum, but attending a rock concert is another story. Things can get "out of control" at a rock concert and "go too far." Rock concerts have been known to induce people to shed their inhibitions and self-consciousness and become "one with the music." The individual loses her or his sense of individuality, identity, and becomes an undifferentiated part of the whole. This loss of consciousness of the self is the criterion for being in Nietzsche's Dionysian state, which is described as "ecstatic," "primeval," and "intoxicating." Apollonian music is all structure and harmony; Dionysian music is all frenzy and beat—if there is harmony, it is unplanned. Greek choruses had the power to evoke dithyrambs in the ancient Greeks; some rock bands can do the same for their fans.

Thus we can see that even in Nietzsche's first book the ideas of chaos and power are joined; however, they are united only in the case of music. While Nietzsche takes Schopenhauer's ideas on the world and music and expands on them as he applies them to Greek tragedy, chaos and power themselves are not critically discussed. Schopenhauer's metaphysics and the association with Wagner combined to indelibly stamp upon Nietzsche the power of the interaction between art and chaos. Although the later Nietzsche found serious, irreconcilable problems with both Schopenhauer's and Wagner's ideas, he continued to address their beliefs throughout his productive life. Nietzsche believed the Schopenhauerian idea that the apparent stability of the world we experience is a deception, and Schopenhauer's notion of a primordial will resonates throughout Nietzsche's notion of will to power.

"POWER FEELINGS" IN THE MIDDLE PERIOD

In the works prior to will to power's debut in *Thus Spoke Zarathustra,* we can see an increase in Nietzsche's use of the term *power* and an increase in the areas in which this term is employed. The middle period is supposedly Nietzsche's "positivistic" stage, generally characterized by Nietzsche's estimation of science. Scientific positivism is a valuable tool for criticizing metaphysics during this period. In *Human, All-Too-Human,* Nietzsche's use of the word *power (Macht)* is quite conventional: he uses it to describe the state's or government's ability to act. A typical example is as follows:

> *Resurrection of the Spirit*—A nation usually rejuvenates itself on the political sickbed and rediscovers its spirit, which it gradually lost in its seeking for and assertion of power. Culture owes this above all to the ages of political weakness. (HAH, 465)

> *Auferstehung des Geistes*—Auf dem politischen Krankenbette verjüngt ein Volk gewöhnlich sich selbst und findet seinen Geist wieder, den es im Suchen und Behaupten der Macht allmählich verlor. Die Cultur verdankt das Allerhöchste den politisch geschwächten Zeiten. [KGW IV/2, 310]

This aphorism juxtaposes political power and weakness with politics and culture, so that political power is cultural weakness and vice versa. Here Nietzsche is using *power* in a way that fits nicely in our everyday connotations of power—sheer physical authority or control over others.

In the last part of *Human, All-Too-Human,* entitled "The Wanderer and His Shadow," Nietzsche begins using the phrase *the lust for power.* This change seems rather abrupt and extraordinary until we remember that "The Wanderer and His Shadow" was written sometime after the original chapters of *Human, All-Too-Human.* What is now known as "volume 1" was the entire book *Human, All-Too-Human: A Book for Free Spirits* when it was first published in 1878. It was reissued in 1886 with the addition of "volume 2," which is composed of two previously published pieces, *Assorted Opinions and Maxims* (originally published in 1878) and *The Wanderer and His Shadow* (originally published in 1880).

The dates are important because in 1880 Nietzsche also published *Daybreak: Thoughts on the Prejudices of Morality.* In *Daybreak,* Nietzsche uses *Machtgelust* (which Hollingdale rather titillatingly translates as "lust for power" but which can be rendered as "desire for power") quite often, so it is no surprise that *The*

Wanderer and His Shadow includes it as well. The difference between the first volume of *Human, All-Too-Human* and *The Wanderer and His Shadow* and *Daybreak* is that the word *Machtgelust* is now used usually to connote a psychological motivation.

In *Human, All-Too-Human,* Nietzsche's first chapter is devoted entirely to a critique of traditional metaphysics along positivistic lines—there is no empirical or scientific proof of any metaphysics, whether it be Plato's Forms or Kant's noumena. Much of the rest of *Human, All-Too-Human* is taken up with a discussion of the impact on the nature of truth and morality if one abandons metaphysics. Again, Nietzsche's main concern throughout his writings is the cultural and spiritual health of humankind. Nietzsche saw the European culture as stifling to some individuals, and he thought that the cause was the metaphysical underpinnings of the European culture. If he could show the errors of the underpinnings, then many other areas of the culture are affected, especially European morality.

In this phase it seems that Nietzsche does hold science in high regard and that he thinks that, with science's help, a true picture of the world can be attained. That there could be a true picture of the world is also a differentiation between this period in Nietzsche's writings and his later period. Nietzsche is against traditional Western metaphysics, and science allows him ammunition for his attack on what he sees as transcendental philosophy, so at this point science is an ally.

The natural sciences flourished in the nineteenth century, but they had their detractors, too. It is hard to say that any one event in the sciences was the focal point for that century, although Charles Darwin's *The Origin of the Species* seems to be the culmination of a trend toward nihilism that Nietzsche believes started with Copernicus. Nietzsche cites the astronomer as having a profound impact on Western culture. With Copernicus's "revolutionary" arrangement of the solar system, the earth and humankind were no longer the center of the universe, which severely undermined religious theory and authority:

> Since Copernicus, man seems to have got himself on an inclined plane—now he is slipping faster and faster away from the center into—what? into nothingness? into a *"penetrating* sense of his nothingness?"* (GM III, 25)

> Seit Kopernikus scheint der Mensch auf eine schiefe Ebene gerathen,—er rollt immer schneller nunmehr aus dem Mittlepunkt weg—wohin? in's Nichts? in's *"durch-bohrende* Gefühl seines Nichts"? [KGW VI/2, 422]

The advances in the microscope were also important. Naive realism, the idea that humans perceive exactly what is going on, was shattered. Boyle's corpuscular theory was but one example of the blows to naive realism. To find that blood was not simply a red liquid, that it actually contained solid, microscopic "corpuscles," opened up a huge wave of scientific speculation and imagination. If blood was not exactly as it looked, what else in the world was other than it seemed? Of course, there had been theories that everything was composed of small "stuff" since the ancient Greeks. Heraclitus had talked about everything being composed of elementary "atoms." But these kinds of theories had been just that—theories—abstract and debatable. Now there was the prospect of scientific "proof," and as microscopes became more powerful, more and more data were being gathered to support the burgeoning theories of the microscopic world. This world was never directly experienced by humans; yet its workings could greatly affect humans. The microscopic world established certain parameters for humans; yet humans had little or no control over it.

As science continued to inspect and dissect the world, the place of humans in the cosmic scheme became less and less significant. Theologically, humans had been placed on earth to have dominion over it, but as the scientific studies showed, humans looked less dominating than dominated by forces unseen, and for many centuries unknown, by them. Then with the publication of *The Origin of the Species,* Darwin suggests a plausible alternative to the "divine plan" explanation as to why there are humans at all. Instead of a loving God designing humans and the world and placing them in the world, the cause of human existence was postulated as evolution, a value-blind happenstance of favorable biological factors. As science progressed, the absolute authority of the Bible as an accurate historical document was questioned, and religious leaders were quick to denounce Darwin's and other scientists' ideas.

Science also invaded the realm of morality. As more and more of the world was seen strictly in terms of cause and effect, people's behavior and, indeed, people themselves were seen as mechanisms—their actions determined by preceding causes. That people are conscious is only a complicating factor. It makes people more complex than other living organisms, but it does not alter the underlying assumption—that human actions are the products of physical causes even if those causes are quite complex. A social scientist, Charles Fourier, began "scientifically" cataloging every human emotion and the causes that determined each one with the hope that "negative" emotions could be avoided by cutting off the environmental and biological causes that lead to them. In that way, vices could be eliminated and virtues could be more scientifically encouraged by arranging society in such a way as to favor the "positive" emotional causes. "Social realism" became quite popular in the mid–nineteenth century as people looked to science to create a utopian society where the causes of immorality and unhappiness never arose.

Daybreak continues Nietzsche's high estimation of science, although some cracks in this position are beginning to appear. Nietzsche explicitly criticizes authoritarian thinking in morality, although at this point science is not seen as authoritarian. As its subtitle, "Thoughts on the Prejudices of Morality," suggests, *Daybreak* is more concerned with exposing the "imaginary" foundations of morality. Most of Nietzsche's writings on science in this book, as science is at this point seen as value neutral, are favorably disposed. But even so, there are passages in *Daybreak* that make it clear that Nietzsche does not see science as the last word, as the sole creator of knowledge.[12]

It is in *Daybreak* that Nietzsche begins to speak of "desire for power" (Machtgelust) and "feeling of power" *(Gefühl der Macht)* as psychological motivation:

> But because the feeling of impotence and fear was in a state of almost continuous stimulation so strongly and for so long, the *feeling of power* has evolved to such a degree of *subtlety* that in this respect man is now a match for the most delicate gold-balance. It has become his strongest propensity; the means discovered for creating this feeling almost constitute the history of culture. (D, 23)

> Aber weil das Gefühl der Ohnmacht und der Furcht so stark und so lange fast fortwährend in Reizung war, hat sich das *Gefühl der Macht* in solcher *Feinheit* entwickelt, dass es jetzt hierin der Mensch mit der delicatesten Goldwage aufnehmen kann. Es ist sein stärkster Hang geworden; die Mittel, welche man entdeckte, sich dieses Gefühl zu schaffen, sind beinahe die Geschichte der Cultur. [KGW V/1, 30–31]

> When a man possesses the feeling of power he feels and calls himself *good*: and it is precisely then that the others upon whom he has to *discharge* his power feel and call him *evil*! (D, 189)

> Wenn der Mensch im Gefühle der Macht ist, so fühlt und nennt er sich *gut*: und gerade dann fühlen und nennen ihn die Anderen, an denen er seinen Macht *auslassen* muss, *böse*! [KGW V/1, 162]

> *Feeling of power.*—Be sure you mark the difference: he who wants to acquire the feeling of power resorts to any means and disdains nothing that will nourish it. He who has it, however, has become very noble in his tastes; he now finds few things to satisfy him. (D, 348)

> *Gefühl der Macht.*—Man unterscheide wohl: wer das Gefühl der Macht erst gewinnen will, greift nach allen Mitteln und verschmäht keine Nahrung desselben. Wer es aber hat, der ist sehr wählerisch und vornehm in seinem Geschmack geworden; selten, dass ihm Etwas noch genugthut. [KGW V/1, 240]

> *Effect of happiness.*—The first effect of happiness is the *feeling of power*: this wants to *express itself,* either to us ourselves, or to other men, or to ideas or imaginary beings. The most common modes of expression are: to bestow, to mock, to destroy—all three out of a common basic drive. (D, 356)

> *Wirkung des Glückes.*—die erste Wirkung des Gluckes ist das *Gefühl der Macht*: diese will *sich äussern,* sei es gegen uns selber oder gegen andere Menschen oder gegen Vorstellungen oder gegen eingebildete Wesen. Die gewöhnlichsten Arten, sich zu äussern, sind: Beschenken, Verspotten, Vernichten,—alle drei mit einem gemeinsamen Grundtriebe. [KGW V/1, 242]

These passages illustrate the change that occurs from *Human, All-Too-Human* to *Daybreak*. When Nietzsche uses the word *power (Macht)* in the first volume of *Human, All-Too-Human,* the contexts are always about some physical control or social authority, usually in connection with the state. In *Daybreak* Nietzsche discusses power in the context of feelings, drives, and desires—a more subtle rendering of power than merely physical power. Power becomes a psychological motive; it explains actions, whether those actions are individual or collective. But Machtgelust is not identical to Wille zur Macht. When does Nietzsche make the transition to will to power, and what is gained or lost by doing so?

We can find the phrase *will to power* in *The Gay Science,* book 5, aphorism 349, so it might be reasonable to assume that Nietzsche introduced this phrase publicly around 1881–82 when he was writing *The Gay Science.* This would be a mistake, however, because the fifth book was written at a later time—1886—in between *Beyond Good and Evil* and *On the Genealogy of Morals.* In the first book of *The Gay Science,* Nietzsche is still discussing Gefühl der Macht, although in this section he calls it a *Lehre* (teaching/doctrine):

> *On the doctrine of the feeling of power.*—Benefitting and hurting others are ways of exercising one's power upon others; that is all one desires in such cases. One hurts those whom one wants to feel one's power, for pain is a much more efficient means to that end than pleasure; pain always raises the question about its origin while pleasure is inclined to stop with itself without looking back. (GS, 13)

> *Zur Lehre vom Machtgefühl.*—Mit Wohlthun und Wehethun übt man seine Macht an Andern aus—mehr will man dabei nicht! Mit Wehethun an Solchen, denen wir unsere Macht erst fühlbar machen müssen; denn der Schmerz ist ein viel empfindlicheres Mittel dazu als die Lust:—der Schmerz fragt immer nach der Ursache, während die Lust geneigt ist, bei sich selber stehen zu bleiben und nicht rückwärts zu schauen. [KGW V/2, 58]

This passage echoes those in *Daybreak* with its treatment of power. Here again power seems to be equated with physical power and the hurt equivalent to physical pain, although psychological power and pain should not be discounted. Indeed, psychological power may be more prominent in the latter part of the aphorism where Nietzsche associates truth with power. When one feels that he or she possesses the absolute Truth, one feels powerful and willing to do anything to retain the powerful feeling. According to Nietzsche's Lehre, those who possess the absolute Truth believe they are more powerful and hence more valuable than those who believe differently from them.

Nietzsche makes two important points in this lengthy aphorism. The first is that brute physical force over others is a lack or poverty of power. This is the only aphorism that explicitly states that physical power over others is a lower form of power than power over oneself. Personal power is tenuous if it is solely dependent on others to achieve. If one is able to generate and control one's own power, then one has more power than those who derive it from others' pleasure or pain, for one does not need to rely on others to have it.

The second important point of aphorism 13 of *The Gay Science* is that compassion *(Mitleid),* normally considered one of the most virtuous traits, can be thought of in terms of power. At this point, Nietzsche says only that pity is a sentiment for the weak, but he reiterates and expands on this theme in future books. Those who possess great power harden themselves against compassion; they reserve it only for those who are capable of becoming their enemies. On the other hand, as he writes of those who possess little or no power,

> Pity is the most agreeable feeling among those who have little pride and no prospects of great conquests: for them easy prey—and that is what all who suffer are—is enchanting. (GS, 13)

> Mitleid ist das angenehmste Gefühl bei solchen, welche wenig stolz sind und keine Aussicht auf grosse Eroberungen haben: für sie ist die leichte Beute—und das ist jeder Leidende—etwas Entzückendes. [KGW V/2, 60]

Eventually, pity will become an expression of power for the strong over the weak—by expressing sympathy toward weak people, one expresses one's difference and superiority over them. Extending compassion shows others that you are not in their sorry circumstances, that you are "wealthy" enough to expend some of your power toward them. This is only one instantiation of the concept in Nietzsche's Lehre of power.

Sometime in between the publication of the first edition of *The Gay Science* and *Thus Spoke Zarathustra*, *Machtgefühl* is replaced by *Wille zur Macht*. Why? There are really no clues in the published writings as to why Nietzsche makes this seemingly sudden switch, so this looks like the perfect place to investigate the unpublished notes, called the *Nachlass*. Nietzsche's notes are little help here. The first instance of the phrase *Wille zur Macht* is found during a period of writing that *Nachlass* editors Giorgio Colli and Mazzino Montinari label as the end of 1876 to the summer of 1877. Walter Kaufmann translates this initial reference in his book on Nietzsche: "Fear (negative) and will to power (positive) explain our strong consideration for the opinions of men."[13] This sentence is part of a longer notebook entry that deals with ambition and the desire for power *(Lust an der Macht)* arising from the dislike of dependency and powerlessness. Here Nietzsche is talking about power in terms of psychological motivations and explanations at precisely the time when he moves to the more psychological aspects of power designated by *Gefühl der Macht* in *Human, All-Too-Human* and *Daybreak*.

What is interesting is that the second occurrence of *Wille zur Macht* was written in the summer of 1880, at least three full years and 1,485 notebook entries later, according to the *Kritische Gesamtausgabe Werke*. In fact, the aphorisms containing *Wille zur Macht* are quite few and far between until the spring/summer of 1885. There are another 1,041 notebook entries between the second and third citings of *Wille zur Macht*, 450 entries between the third and fourth citings, and 898 entries between the fourth and fifth entries, the fifth one written between November 1882 and February 1883. Clearly, will to power was not an all-consuming concept at first. Interspersed among these spotty references of will to power are a spate of "will to"s. During the last six years of his productive life,

Nietzsche attached *will to* to over 150 different nouns.[14] There are the ones that appear in his published works, such as "will to truth" and "will to life." But Nietzsche also paired less common nouns with *will to*: creation, destruction, misunderstanding, faith, pleasure, cruelty, self-overcoming, and death. Finally, there are obscure pairings with *will to*: victory, hibernation, urination, and "the lowland."

So there is no decisive moment when "will to power" bursts on Nietzsche's writings and becomes a dominant theme. In fact, *will to power* is in only a tiny minority of aphorisms or phrases. It is found only thirty-two times in the published works and 147 times in the unpublished entries, and about twenty-five of these latter entries are simply book titles or brief outlines for his book *The Will to Power*. This means that less than 5 percent of Nietzsche's entries in the *Nachlass* contains the phrase *Wille zur Macht*. Of that paltry amount, one-fifth of the occurrences of *Wille zur Macht* have to do with variously lengthed outlines of the projected but ultimately abandoned book of the same title rather than with aphorisms that would be helpful in understanding what Nietzsche means by the term. Given the small percentage of references, one would think that will to power would not have gained the prominence it currently enjoys had not Nietzsche talked about writing a book with that as the title, as well as exalting the phrase in *Ecce Homo*. Nevertheless, will to power has garnered more notoriety, perhaps, unfortunately, from the Third Reich associations than "will to truth," which has more entries in the *Nachlass*.

The Gay Science is more than just a transitional book to *Thus Spoke Zarathustra. The Gay Science* is a definite break from the previous books in Nietzsche's "positivism" stage. In book 3 of *The Gay Science* Nietzsche argues that his problem with morality is not that God is not the right foundation but, rather, that the entire notion of a foundation *at all* is erroneous. Thus, science can be no better foundation for anything, truth and morality included, than God. Like Christianity, science is built on faith, except in the case of science, the faith is in the notion of cause and effect rather than a supreme being.[15] In *The Gay Science* the idea of cause and effect is a "necessary error" that helps the human species to survive. Whatever positive status science holds in *Human, All-Too-Human* and *Daybreak,* it has disappeared by the time *The Gay Science* is published.

In the famous aphorism in which the madman announces the death of God (GS, 125), it is not just the Christian God's elegy. The shadow of God, which Nietzsche refers to in the first aphorism of book 3 (GS, 108), supposedly casts its shadow for thousands of years. But this shadow takes many different forms, including science. Immediately preceding the madman aphorism, Nietzsche writes metaphorically of leaving the land, indeed, "burning" the land like burning bridges behind us, and being on an infinite sea. We may get homesick for land—we may invent foundations—but, as Nietzsche informs us, "there is no longer any 'land'" (GS, 124). As a foundation for objective truth or knowledge, science is as dead as God, although the longing for an objective base for truth and knowledge may "cast its shadow" over humankind for centuries, so great is our "will to truth."

Finally, in book 4 Nietzsche introduces us to the idea of eternal recurrence and to the character Zarathustra, which erases any notion that there is a clean break between Nietzsche's middle and late periods. The walks Nietzsche took in the winter of 1881–82, while he was in the middle of writing the first four books of *The Gay Science,* inspired the plan and many of the ideas of *Thus Spoke Zarathustra.*

But if there is no moment of epiphany for his idea of will to power, like he reported there was for the idea of eternal recurrence, then why does Nietzsche change terms from *Machtgelust* and *Machtgefühl* to *Wille zur Macht*? There may be several explanations. First, the phrase *Wille zur Macht* appears in the *Nachlass* at a time when Nietzsche was attaching *Wille zur* to many different nouns. Attaching it to *Macht,* then, would be much less surprising than attaching it to *Niederung* (the lowland), which he does as well. Nietzsche could have become more taken with the new phrase once he saw it attached to *will to.* However, *Machtgefühl* continues to be used in *Nachlass* entries postdating the appearance of *Wille zur Macht*'s published debut. This suggests that the two terms are not synonymous to Nietzsche and cannot be thought of as interchangeable.

As I have suggested, *Machtgefühl* is used in those contexts in which Nietzsche is emphasizing psychological motivations. In these contexts, it is the *gefühl* (feeling) part that is crucial. Many times people behave in certain ways to engender or avoid particular feelings. So, as a psychological observation, *Machtgefühl* is an apt description of human behavior. In *Daybreak* Nietzsche describes humans as composed of drives *(Triebe).* The first part of this extremely interesting aphorism begins as follows:

> *Experience and invention*—However far a man may go in self-knowledge, nothing however can be more incomplete than his image of the totality of *drives* which constitute his being. He can scarcely name even the cruder ones: their number and strength, their ebb and flow, their play and counterplay among one another, and above all the laws of their *nutriment* remain wholly unknown to him. This nutriment is therefore a work of chance: our daily experiences throw some prey in the way of now this, now that drive, and the drive seizes it eagerly; but the coming and going of these events as a whole stands in no rational relationship to the nutritional requirements of the totality of the drives: so that the outcome will always be two-fold—the starvation and stunting of some and the overfeeding of others. (D, 119)

> *Erleben und Erdichten*—Wie weit Einer seine Selbstkenntniss auch treiben mag, Nichts kann doch unvollständiger sein, als das Bild der gesammten *Triebe,* die sein Wesen constituiren. Kaum dass er die gröberen beim Namen nennen kann: ihre Zahl und Stärke, ihre Ebbe und Fluth, ihr Spiel und Widerspiel unter einander, und vor Allem die Gesetze ihrer *Ernährung* bleiben ihm ganz unbekannt. Diese Ernährung wird also ein Werk des Zufalls: unsere täglichen Erlebnisse werfen bald diesem, bald jenem Triebe eine Beute zu, die er gierig erfasst, aber das ganze Kommen und Gehen dieser Ereignisse steht ausser allem vernünftigen Zusammenhang mit den Nahrungsbedürfnissen der gesammten Triebe: sodass immer Zweierlei eintreten

wird, das Verhungern und Verkümmern der einen und die Überfütterung der anderen. [KGW V/1, 109]

Conceiving humans to be constituted by drives was not a wholly original idea on Nietzsche's part. Several German thinkers had described the human psyche as being composed of drives, Johann Herder and Johann Fichte most notably. Nietzsche begins using *Machtgefühl* and *Triebe* at the same time in his writing. This suggests that during this period Nietzsche was thinking primarily in psychological terms. *Machtgefühl* certainly conveys a more psychological connotation than simply *Macht* alone.

However, *Wille zur Macht* has certain advantages over *Machtgefühl* for Nietzsche. First, because *Machtgefühl* does stress feelings, Nietzsche may have become less comfortable with it. Feelings are by no means primary or foundational human states for Nietzsche; they are parts of many other states, such as willing, thinking, wishing, dreaming, and so on. To associate power with only one of these human states would too severely limit the role of power. Second, because *Machtgefühl* stresses the psychological aspect of human behavior, it describes what motivates human behavior. This assumes that human beings have motivations and that these motives are causally efficient. Both these assumptions are questioned in Nietzsche's later works. Thus, Nietzsche may have seen the more ambiguous *Wille zur Macht* as a better term than *Machtgefühl* because it does not beg either of these questions. At any rate, the use of *Machtgefühl* decreases, although it does not entirely disappear, as the use of *Wille zur Macht* increases in both the published and unpublished writings (keeping in mind, of course, that Nietzsche's use of either term is extremely sparse given the entire corpus of writings).

We now turn to Nietzsche's later works, in which *Wille zur Macht* makes its first appearance in the books that Nietzsche authorized for publication. What do the contexts in which *Wille zur Macht* appears tell us about the meaning of the phrase? Are there any conflicting or contradictory uses of *Wille zur Macht*? The major question for the next chapter is how and in what directions does Nietzsche expand the notion of power.

FURTHER READING

For biographical information, see the following:

Hayman, Ronald. *Nietzsche: A Critical Life*. London: Weidenfield and Nicolson, 1980.
Hollingdale, R. J. *Nietzsche*. Boston: Routledge and Kegan Paul, 1973.
Pletsch, Carl. *Young Nietzsche*. New York: The Free Press, 1991.

For Nietzsche's early writings, see the following:

Nietzsche, Friedrich. *Philosophy and Truth: Selections from Nietzsche's Notebooks of the Early 1870's*. Trans. and ed. Daniel Breazeale. Atlantic Heights, N.J.: Humanities Press International, 1979.

For Schopenhauer's philosophy, see the following:

Janaway, Christopher. *Schopenhauer.* New York: Oxford University Press, 1994.
Schopenhauer, Arthur. *The World as Will and Representation.* Trans. and ed. E. F. J. Payne. New York: Dover Publications, Inc., 1969.
Zimmern, Helen. *Arthur Schopenhauer: His Life and Philosophy.* London: G. Allen and Unwin Ltd., 1932.

2

Will to Power in the Published Works

As noted in the preceding chapter, the term *will to power* first appears in the works Nietzsche authorized for publication in *Thus Spoke Zarathustra* in the passage "One Thousand and One Goals":

> Much that was good to one people was scorn and infamy to another: thus I found it. Much I found called evil here, and decked out with purple honors there.
>
> Never did one neighbor understand the other: ever was his soul amazed at the neighbor's delusion and wickedness.
>
> A tablet of the good hangs over every people. Behold, it is the tablet of their overcomings; behold, it is the voice of their will to power. (Z, 170)

> Vieles, das diesem Volke gut heiss, heiss einem andern Hohn und Schmach: also fand ich's. Vieles fand ich hier böse genannt und dort mit purpurnen Ehren geputzt.
>
> Nie verstand ein Nachbar den andern: stets verwunderte sich seine Seele ob des Nachbarn Wahn und Bosheit.
>
> Eine Tafel der Güter hängt über jedem Volke. Siehe, es ist seiner Überwindungen Tafel; siehe, es ist die Stimme seines Willens zur Macht. [KGW VI/1, 70]

The context of this passage concerns human behavior and morality. What people deem "good" and "evil" are manifestations of their will to power. "A tablet of the good" is a metaphor for a moral system that members of a given society or community of people share. Whatever moral system a community has is "the voice of their will to power." In other words, a people's will to power is expressed by their moral system, and the kind of moral system a society has will reflect or inform us about the kind of will to power of that society. Fortunately for us in our attempt to understand will to power, Nietzsche does discuss different types of moralities. He bifurcates moral systems into two typologies—"master" and "slave" moralities. Nietzsche explicitly states that these two classifications are generally heuristic devices and are rarely found in "pure" form in either a community or even a single individual.[1]

19

In order to understand what Nietzsche means by "master" and "slave" morality, we will examine Nietzsche's genealogy, or "family history," of morals as presented in his later works—*On the Genealogy of Morals* and *Beyond Good and Evil*. He describes the purpose of *On the Genealogy of Morals* as a "psychological analysis of the counter-concepts of a *noble* morality and a morality of *ressentiment*."[2] In this book Nietzsche seeks to uncover the sources of morality which would reveal the "value of these values themselves."[3]

Nietzsche juxtaposes the notions of good and evil with the notions of good (noble) and bad (base). From an etymological review of the word *good,* Nietzsche finds that

> everywhere "noble," "aristocratic," in the social sense, is the basic concept from which "good" in the sense of "with aristocratic soul," "noble," "with a soul of high order," with a "privileged soul" necessarily developed. (GM I, 4)

> dass überall "vornehm," "edel" im ständischen Sinne der Grundbegriff ist, aus dem sich "gut" im Sinne von "seelisch-vornehm," "edel," von "seelisch-hochgeartet," "seelisch-privilegirt" mit Nothwendigkeit heraus entwickelt. [KGW VI/2, 275]

Here Nietzsche suggests that the idea "good" describes a certain class of people—namely, the aristocrats. "Good" designates a certain class of people and not what "ought to be done." Actions are judged good because aristocratic people perform them and not because those actions were "good in themselves." As Nietzsche writes in *Beyond Good and Evil,*

> It is obvious that moral designations were everywhere first applied to *human beings* and only later, derivatively, to actions. (BGE, 260)

> Es liegt auf der Hand, dass die moralischen Werthbezeichnungen überall zuerst auf *Menschen* und erst abgeleitet und spät auf *Handlungen* gelegt worden sind. [KGW V1/2, 219]

Conversely, *bad* is etymologically derived from such words as *common, plebeian,* and *low,* which also applied to a class of human beings and not to actions.[4] Thus, according to Nietzsche, "good" and "bad" merely denote what class of person performed the action with no judgment whether one class is *morally* better than the other.[5] This is changed, however, by the "common folk." They see the disparity in power (e.g., monetary, military, personal, and political power) between themselves and the aristocracy.

Unable to overcome directly the aristocrat's power, resentment begins to build in the common people from their powerlessness. This is Nietzsche's insight of *ressentiment*.[6] The common people's resentment of the aristocrats motivates the creation of their own meanings of *good* and *bad*. Having neither the external, physical strength to confront the aristocracy, they use the only avenue open to them—moral condemnation. As Nietzsche states in *On the Genealogy of Morals,*

The slave revolt in morality begins when *ressentiment* itself becomes creative and gives birth to values. (GM I, 10)

Der Sklavenaufstand in der Moral beginnt damit, dass das *Ressentiment* selbst schöpferisch wird und Werthe gebiert. [KGW VI/2, 284]

The traits and deeds of the common people become "good"—not in the sense of being *descriptive* of actions of the aristocracy but in the *prescriptive* sense of what they ought to do—and the traits and deeds of the aristocracy become not just "bad"—in the sense of a description of what common people do—but "evil" in the moral sense created by the resentful common people. The term *evil* connotes an immorality, a sinfulness, that the more descriptive term *bad* (of the aristocracy) lacks. Only in this way can the common people feel superior to the aristocracy. But this way of creating a moral system is reactionary—it devolves from the reaction of the common people to the aristocracy. On the other hand, the aristocratic values do not take the common people into consideration at all. The aristocracy's values simply stem from whatever the aristocracy chooses to affirm or condemn:

Every noble morality develops from a triumphant affirmation of itself. (GM I, 10)

Alle vornehme Moral aus einem triumphirenden Ja-sagen zu sich selber herauswächst. [KGW VI/2, 284]

Aristocratic morality is "active"—it originates from itself, and its values are determined from within the aristocracy. What is "good" enhances the aristocracy; what is "bad" does not. Conversely, the common people's morality is reactive—it originates from outside itself, namely, from their reaction to the aristocracy.[7] Thus, slave-type morality is derivative.

Nietzsche designates an active, "good and bad" moral system as "master" morality and a reactive, "good and evil" moral system as "slave" morality. What is meant by *good* in master morality is quite different from what is meant by *good* in slave morality owing to the differences in the origins of each morality. That is why Nietzsche thinks it is important to investigate the history, the *genealogy,* of morals. Slave morality not only inverts the values of the nobility, it invests them with a moral invective—it is not simply "other" or "different" but "evil" or "sinful." What the aristocracy would deem "good," slave morality deems "evil." Master morality and slave morality designate types of morality, not actual, historical moralities; however, Nietzsche considers Christianity an example of a slave-type morality. In *The Antichrist* Nietzsche writes,

In my *Genealogy of Morals* I offered the first psychological analysis of the counter-concepts of a *noble* morality and a morality of *ressentiment*—the latter born of the No to the former: but this is the Judeo-Christian morality pure and simple. So that it could say No to everything on earth that represents the ascending tendency of life, to that which has turned out well, to power, to beauty, to self-affirmation, the instinct

of *ressentiment,* which had here become genius, had to invent *another* world from whose point of view this affirmation of life appeared as evil, as the reprehensible as such. (AC, 24)

Ich habe in meiner "Genealogie der Moral" zum ersten Male den Gegensatz-Begriff einer vornehmen Moral und einer ressentiment-Moral psychologisch vorgeführt, letztere *aus dem Nein* gegen die erstere entsprungen: aber dies ist die jüdisch-christliche Moral ganz und gar. Um Nein sagen zu können zu Allem, was die *aufsteigende* Bewegung des Lebens, die Wohlgerathenheit, die Macht, die Schönheit, die Selbstejahung auf Erden darstellt, musste hier sich der Genie gewordne Instinkt des ressentiment eine *andre* Welt erfinden, von wo aus jene *Lebens-Bejahung* als das Böse, als das Verwerfliche an sich erschien. [KGW VI/3, 190]

The Judeo-Christian slave-type morality creates an entire cosmology where an omnipotent being can determine eternal bliss or damnation. The cosmology includes a God who not only creates the laws and moral standards but also is powerful enough to enforce punishments for eternity. By making master-type traits "evil" or sins, believers of slave-type morality ensure their own eternal happiness and the nonbelievers' eternal doom. In this way, slave-type morality believers transform their resentment into an entire system that prefers the slave traits. The morality has the added advantage that, by being based on a transcendent cosmology, it cannot be disproved by empirical means. For Nietzsche, Christianity is a huge fiction or myth created out of *ressentiment* by slave-type people in order to diminish the master-type people's dominion.

Nietzsche believes that the slave-type believer does not knowingly manufacture this cosmology with the express purpose of retaliation against the master type. Rather, Christianity is the result of nonconscious or subconscious resentment. Nietzsche refers to this as "sublimated" resentment—or *ressentiment.* Consciously, Christians sincerely believe that Christianity is the "true picture" of the universe and is not a myth. Subconsciously, slave-type people realize that they are in too weak a position to directly express their anger, so their resentment becomes suppressed, and the suppression or sublimation eventually expresses itself in an indirect and reactive manner. It is Nietzsche's contention that Christianity is the product of *ressentiment* because it is based on a powerful supreme being who values and rewards the virtues of the meek and disenfranchised and damns and punishes the virtues-turned-to-sins of the aristocracy. By creating an otherworldly God who sees and knows everything, even our inner thoughts, and who administers praise and damnation, the slave-type individual is not making any overt moves against those individuals of the master type. It is God who has created the moral code, not the common people. It is God who judges the goodness of individuals, not the common people. It is God who determines what punishments or rewards are given, not the common people. The common people are as subordinated to this absolute moral code as the aristocrats, so the aristocrats cannot blame or be aggressive against the common people. It is pure "luck" that the traits of the common people "naturally" coincide with what God deems virtuous. No wonder Christianity is so appealing to the powerless.

According to Nietzsche, another indication of slave-type morality (and so Christianity) is that it attempts to equalize everyone. Everyone is as deserving or as culpable as the next person with respect to rights and responsibilities, whether they are political rights or the religious "right" to enter heaven:

> The poison of the doctrine of "equal rights for all"—it was Christianity that spread it most fundamentally. Out of the most secret nooks of bad instincts, Christianity has waged war unto death against all sense of respect and feeling of distance between man and man, that is to say, against the *presupposition* of every elevation, of every growth of culture, out of the *ressentiment* of the masses it forged its chief weapon against *us,* against all that is noble, gay, high-minded on earth, against our happiness on earth. "Immortality" conceded to every Peter and Paul has so far been the greatest, the most malignant attempt to assassinate *noble* humanity.
>
> And let us not underestimate the calamity which crept out of Christianity into politics. Today nobody has the courage any longer for privileges, for masters' rights, for a sense of respect for oneself and one's peers—for a *pathos of distance.* Our politics is *sick* from this lack of courage. (AC, 43)

> Das Gift der Lehre "*gleiche* Rechte für Alle"—das Christenthum hat es am grundsätzlichsten ausgesät; das Christenthum hat jedem Ehrfurchts—und Distanz—Gefühl zwischen Mensch und Mensch, das heisst der *Voraussetzung* zu jeder Erhöhung, zu jedem Wachsthum der Cultur einen Todkrieg aus den heimlichsten Winkeln schlechter Instinkte gemacht,—es hat aus dem Ressentiment der Massen sich seine *Hauptwaffe* geschmiedet gegen *uns,* gegen alles Vornehme, Frohe, Hochherzige auf Erden, gegen unser Glück auf Erden. . . . Die "Unsterblichkeit" jedem Petrus und Paulus zugestanden war bisher das grösste, das bösartigste Attentat auf die *vornehme* Menschlichkeit.—Und unterschätzen wir das Verhänginiss nicht, das vom Christenthum aus sich bis in die Politik eingeschlichen hat! Niemand hat heute mehr den Muth zu Sonderrechten, zu Herrschafts-Rechten, zu einem Ehrfurchts-Gefühl vor sich und seines Gleichen,—zu einem *Pathos der Distanz.* . . . Unsere Politik is *krank* an diesem Mangel an Muth! [KGW VI/3, 215–16]

In terms of deserving respect, or, in the case of Christianity, deserving to get into heaven, no one has inherently a greater claim than anyone else. Nietzsche sees this leveling maneuver as unnatural:

> That little prigs and three-quarter madmen may have the conceit that the laws of nature are constantly broken for their sakes—such an intensification of every kind of selfishness into the infinite, into the *impertinent,* cannot be branded with too much contempt. And yet Christianity owes its triumph to this miserable flattery of personal vanity: it was precisely all the failures, all the rebellious-minded, all the less favored, the whole scum and refuse of humanity who were thus won over to it. (AC, 43)

> Dass kleine Mucker und Dreiviertels-Verückte sich einbilden dürfen, dass um ihretwillen die Gesetze der Natur beständig *durchbrochen* werden—eine solche Steigerung jeder Art Selbstsucht ins Unendliche, ins *unverschämte* kann man nicht genug Verachtung brandmarken. Und doch verdankt das Christenthum *dieser* erbarmungswürdigen Schmeichelei vor Personal-Eitelkeit seinen Sieg,—gerade alles

Missrathene, Aufständisch-Gesinnte, Schlechtweggekommene, den ganzen Auswurf und Abhub der Menschheit hat es damit zu sich überredet. [KGW VI/3, 215]

That "little prigs and three-quarter madmen" should be equally deserving of respect as, say, Goethe, sickens Nietzsche. Equality is unnatural because, from Nietzsche's observations, people are very different—with different traits, abilities, and personalities. These observations suggest to Nietzsche that people should be accorded differing amounts of respect. This amounts to "ranking" individuals and moralities as well:

> The difference among men becomes manifest . . . in the difference between their tablets of goods—in the fact that they consider different goods worth striving for and also disagree about what is more or less valuable, about the order of rank of the goods they recognize in common. (BGE, 194)

> Die Verschiedenheit der Menschen zeigt sich . . . in der Verscheidenheit ihrer Gütertafeln, also darin, dass sic verschiedene Güter für erstrebenswerth halten und auch über das Mehr und Weniger des Werthes, über die Rangordnung der gemeinsam anerkannten Güter mit einander uneins sind. [KGW VI/2, 117]

But what are the criteria for ranking individuals or moralities? Nietzsche never explicitly states these criteria, so trying to cull out possible criteria for ranking is difficult. However, in *Beyond Good and Evil* Nietzsche provides us with some clues to how *he* might rank moralities. At one point he says that having an instinct for rank is one clue that one is of a higher rank—a self-serving criterion at best![8] In aphorism 259 he gives more helpful clues for ranking moralities. In this aphorism he is criticizing those moral and political theories that advocate equality:

> Refraining mutually from injury, violence, and exploitation and placing one's will on a par with that of someone else—this may become, in a certain rough sense, good manners among individuals if the appropriate conditions are present (namely, if these men are actually similar in strength and value standards and belong together in *one* body). But as soon as this principle is extended, and possibly even accepted as the *fundamental principle of society,* it immediately proves to be what it really is—a will to the *denial* of life, a principle of disintegration and decay. (BGE, 259)

> Sich gegenseitig der Verletzung, der Gewalt, der Ausbeutung enthalten, seinen Willen dem des Andern gleich setzen: dies kann in einem gewissen groben Sinne zwischen Individuen zur guten Sitte werden, wenn die Bedingungen dazu gegeben sind (nämlich deren thatsächliche Ähnlichkeit in Kraftmengen und Werthmaassen und ihre Zusammengehörigkeit innerhalb Eines Körpers). Sobald man aber dies Princip weiter nehmen wollte und womöglich gar als *Grund princip der Gesellschaft,* so würde es sich sofort erweisen als Das, was es ist: als Wille zur *Verneinung* des Lebens, als Auflösungsund Verfalls-Princip. [KGW VI/2, 217]

Anything that "denies life" would deserve a low ranking. If we were to discover what Nietzsche considers "life" to be, we would be in a better position to know what would count as "denying life." Nietzsche presents his perspective of "life" in the immediately succeeding passages:

> Life is *essentially* appropriation, injury, overpowering of what is alien and weaker, suppression, hardness, imposition of one's own forms, incorporation and at least, at its mildest, exploitation. (BGE, 259)

> Leben selbst ist *wesentlich* Aneignung, Verletzung, Überwältigung des Fremden und Schwächeren, Unterdrückung, Härte, Aufzwängung eigner Formen, Einverleibung und mindestens, mildestens, Ausbeutung. [KGW VI/2, 217]

This is not a rosy picture of the world, but Nietzsche warns us at the same time not to feel sentimental about life and not to think pejoratively of these descriptive words. It is only because we have been raised in a culture that puts negative values on these words that we find them deprecatory. We might instead regard these descriptions as evaluatively neutral descriptions, to be taken as no more value laden than scientific "facts" about the world. Thus, we should consider "Life is exploitation" to be as value laden a sentence as "Koala bears eat eucalyptus leaves." We consider it neither good nor bad that koalas eat eucalyptus leaves; they merely do. Analogously, it is neither good nor bad that life is exploitation; it merely is. Again, "Life is exploitation" merely describes the way the world is for Nietzsche; it is not to be taken prescriptively, as how the world should be.

It is not such an impossible task to view these words neutrally, for there are many contexts in which the words do not have pejorative connotations. We can suppress laughter, exploit a mine for its ore, and incorporate new ideas into a belief system. Suppressing a laugh in a certain social situation may be prudent on your part, but no one would accuse you of doing something evil or immoral to your laughter.[9]

Nietzsche believes equality denies life because it leads to mediocrity. Individuals would be encouraged to be like everyone else and not to pursue their own individual excesses and excellences. We need only to read the prologue of *Thus Spoke Zarathustra* and Nietzsche's description of the last man to understand where he thinks equality will lead:

> No shepherd and one herd! Everybody wants the same, everybody is the same: whoever feels different goes voluntarily into a madhouse. (TSZ, 130)

> Kein Hirt und Eine Heerde! Jeder will das Gleiche, Jeder ist gleich: wer anders fühlt, geht freiwillig in's Irrenhaus. [KGW VI/1, 14]

In this scenario even uniquely excellent people are forced to "settle" for equality, for the "happiness" of the mediocre in a society that demands equality. But this manufactured "happiness" is a kind of death for humans who are not mediocre. It denies the unique and authentic individual existence humans at either end of the spectrum would live if not subjected to live up or down to the middle.

If all moralities, ranked high or low, are expressions of will to power, then this one term must account for both master-type and slave-type moralities. Because these moralities are in opposition to each other, we are left with two ways of interpreting the role will to power plays in moralities. Either will to power has within it two distinguishable, but not metaphysically distinct, aspects, or pure slave morality is the complete negation or absence of will to power.

Is there any evidence in Nietzsche's texts as to which interpretation is correct? It is here that I suggest we turn our attention to the "will to" part of *will to power* in order to answer this question. If we are to talk about "will," we must be sure of what we are discussing, for there are many places where Nietzsche claims that there is no such thing as "will":

> In the beginning there is that great calamity of error that the will is something which is effective, that it is a capacity. Today we know that it is only a word. (TI, "Reason in Philosophy," 5)

> Am Anfang steht das grosse Verhängniss von Irrthum, dass der Wille Etwas ist, das *wirkt,*—dass Wille ein *Vermögen* ist. . . . Heute wissen wir, dass er bloss ein Wort ist. [KGW VI/3, 71]

The "will" in this passage refers to our usual, "everyday" notion of will—as a capacity humans have that enables them to effect change according to their wishes. The slightest human introspection supposedly reveals this will, and for Nietzsche, many philosophers, most notably Descartes and Schopenhauer, fail to consider the matter any further; they believe the will is wholly self-evident through direct introspection of their "inner" selves.

It is this supposedly transparent, "self-evident" will that Nietzsche believes does not exist. Nietzsche believes that what we usually take *will* to denote is neither self-evident nor singular. *Will* is a word we use to denote the outcome of a very complex and obscured series of operations of which we have severely limited knowledge, if indeed we have any knowledge of it at all. We like to think that our "will" is something over which we have complete control. But according to Nietzsche's characterization, it seems we are under "its" control, and there really is no one "thing" that controls us; *it* stands for many drives that are constantly competing with one another to actualize their impulses. We are not conscious of many of these operations. Thus, *will* does not denote a single entity or capacity for Nietzsche. *Will* is shorthand, a linguistic "economy," for many internal operations—recall the competing drives (Triebe) Nietzsche describes in *Daybreak*—going on that cannot be, or at least are not, known by us.

Our experience of ourselves, our self-knowledge, is not wholly clear and immediate (or as Descartes puts it, "clear and distinct"), according to Nietzsche. Our experience of ourselves may be only a part of a whole dynamic and complex interplay of drives. For Nietzsche, we are aware only of the "winning" drives, the drives that manage to subvert or overpower other ones. What we are conscious of may be just a small part of this:

> For we could think, feel, will, and remember, and we could also "act" in every sense of that word, and yet none of all this would have to "enter our consciousness" (as

one says metaphorically). The whole of life would be possible without, as it were, seeing itself in a mirror. Even now, for that matter, by far the greatest portion of our life actually takes place without this mirror effect. (GS, 354)

Wir könnten nämlich denken, fühlen, wollen, uns erinnern, wir könnten ebenfalls "handeln" in jedem Sinne des Wortes: und trotzdem brauchte das Alles nicht uns "in's Bewusstsein zu treten" (wie man im Bilde sagt). Das ganze Leben wäre möglich, ohne dass es sich gleichsam im Spiegel sahe: wie ja thatsächlich auch jetzt noch bei uns der bei weitem überwiegende Theil dieses Lebens sich ohne diese Spiegelung abspielt. [KGW V/2, 272]

We might not be conscious of our entire experience, which may be much more complicated than we realize. The feelings, thoughts, and volitions that we are aware of may be only a portion, and perhaps a very small portion, of the chaotic drives and impulses of which we are composed.

Similarly, Nietzsche suggests that "will" is more complex than we are aware. There is no such thing as a self-evident, efficient capacity that we set in motion— "will"—for Nietzsche. That "will" does not exist except as a simplifying term in our language. Hence, when we try to account for things by appeal to this "everyday" notion of the "will," we are mistaken.

I believe the crucial passage is aphorism 19 of *Beyond Good and Evil*. Here Nietzsche is doing something akin to a conceptual analysis of "will" and "willing." The first move Nietzsche makes is to persuade us that "will" is not what we commonly think it is:

Philosophers are accustomed to speak of the will as if it were the best-known thing in the world: indeed, Schopenhauer has given us to understand that the will alone is really known to us, absolutely and completely known, without subtraction or addition. But again and again it seems to me that in this case, too, Schopenhauer only did what philosophers are in a habit of doing—he adopted a *popular prejudice* and exaggerated it. Willing seems to me to be above all something *complicated,* something that is a unit only as a word—and it is precisely in this one word that the popular prejudice lurks, which has defeated the always inadequate caution of philosophers. (BGE, 19)

Die Philosophen pflegen vom Willen zu reden, wie als ob er die bekannteste Sache von der Welt sei; ja Schopenhauer gab zu verstehen, der Wille allain sei uns eigentlich bekannt, ganz und gar bekannt, ohne Abzug und Zuthat bekannt. Aber es dünkt mich immer wieder, dass Schopenhauer auch in diesem Falle nur gethan hat, was Philosophen eben zu thun pflegen: dass er ein *Volk-Vorurtheil* übernommen und übertrieben hat. Wollen scheint mir vor Allem etwas *Complicirtes,* Etwas, das nur als Wort eine Einheit ist,—und eben in Einem Worte steckt das Volk-Vorurtheil, das über die allzeit nur geringe Vorsicht der Philosophen Herr geworden ist. [KGW VI/2, 25–26]

The first thing we may notice in this passage is that by this time (1886) Nietzsche's uncritical affection for Schopenhauer has vanished. In chapter 1 it is said that "will" was Schopenhauer's metaphysics, the one constituent of the noumenal world to which everything could be reduced. Now Nietzsche questions, What, precisely, is denoted by that word? Nietzsche suggests it is merely "popular prejudice" that *will* denotes one indivisible and self-evident thing. And philosophers, too, have used the word *will* as if everyone knew to what it referred and no further discussion was warranted. Nietzsche, however, regards "will" as not so clear and unitary. What is "will" for Nietzsche? He writes,

> So let us for once be more cautious, let us be "unphilosophical": let us say that in all willing there is, first, a plurality of sensations, namely, the sensation of the state *"away from which,"* the sensation of the state *"towards which,"* the sensations of this *"from"* and *"towards"* themselves, and then also an accompanying muscular sensation, which, even without our putting into motion "arms and legs," begins its action by force of habit as soon as we "will" anything. (BGE, 19)

> Seien wir also einmal vorsichtiger, seien wir "unphilosophisch"—, sagen wir: in jedem Wollen ist erstens eine Mehrheit von Gefühlen, nämlich das Gefühl des Zustandes, von dem *weg,* das Gefühl des Zustandes zu dem *hin,* das Gefühl von diesem "weg" und "hin" selbst, dann noch ein begleitendes Muskelgefühl, welches, auch ohne dass wir, "Arme und Beine" in Bewegung setzen, durch eine Art Gewohnheit, sobald wir "wollen" sein Spiel beginnt. [KGW VI/2, 26]

This passage suggests that Nietzsche regards "will" as internally dualistic. "Will," although linguistically denoted by a single word, is first, according to Nietzsche, a complex operation consisting of many sensations or feelings of two states, "toward which" and "away from which," accompanied by sensations of muscular activity (whether or not any particular arm or leg moves). Along with these various sensations are associated thoughts:

> Therefore, just as sensations (and indeed many kinds of sensations) are to be recognized as ingredients of the will, so, secondly, should thinking also: in every act of the will there is a ruling thought—let us not imagine it possible to sever this thought from the "willing," as if any will would then remain over! (BGE, 19)

> Wie also Fühlen und zwar vielerlei Fühlen als Ingredienz des Willens anzuerkennen ist, so zweitens auch noch Denken: in jedem Willensakte giebt es einen commandirenden Gedanken;—und man soll ja nicht glauben, diesen Gedanken von dem "Wollen" abscheiden zu können, wie als ob dann noch Wille übrig bleibe! [KGW VI, 26]

When we think of human "will," we can understand Nietzsche's analysis. Our "popular prejudice" about our will is that, first, we have a conscious desire to do something and, second, that our desire communicates itself to the will, which then moves the appropriate muscles to accomplish the task. But Nietzsche notices the enormity of this scenario: How do conscious desires relate to the will? How do they communicate this desire to the will? How does the will relate to the physical body? How does "it" know what the appropriate muscles to activate are? How is the will effective? For Nietzsche, there is no separate entity called "will" that interacts with thoughts and desires and is the "middleman" between our desires and our muscles. Nietzsche continues,

Third, the will is not only a complex of sensation and thinking, but it is above all an *affect,* and specifically the affect of the command. That which is termed "freedom of the will" is essentially the affect of superiority in relation to him who must obey: "I am free, 'he' must obey"—this consciousness is inherent in every will; and equally so the straining of the attention, the straight look that fixes itself exclusively on one aim, the unconditional evaluation that "this and nothing else is necessary now," the inward certainty that obedience will be rendered—and whatever else belongs to the position of the commander. A man who *wills* commands something within himself that renders obedience, or that he believes renders obedience. But now let us notice what is strangest about the will—this manifold thing for which the people have only one word: inasmuch as in the given circumstances we are at the same time the commanding *and* the obeying parties, and as the obeying party we know the sensations of constraint, impulsion, pressure, resistance, and motion, which usually begin immediately after the act of will; inasmuch as, on the other hand, we are accustomed to disregard this duality, and to deceive ourselves about it by means of the synthetic concept "I," a whole series of erroneous conclusions, and consequently of false evaluations of the will itself, has become attached to the act of willing—to such a degree that he who wills believes sincerely that willing *suffices* for action. Since in the great majority of cases there has been exercise of will only when the effect of the command—that is, obedience; that is, the action— was to be *expected,* the *appearance* has translated itself into the feeling, as if there were a *necessity of effect.* In short, he who wills believes with a fair amount of certainty that will and action are somehow one; he ascribes the success, the carrying out of the willing, to the will itself, and thereby enjoys an increase of the sensation of power which accompanies all success. "Freedom of the will"—that is the expression for the complex state of delight of the person exercising volition, who commands and at the same time identifies himself with the executor of the order—who, as such, enjoys also the triumph over obstacles, but thinks within himself that it was really his will itself that overcame them. (BGE, 19)

Drittens ist der Wille nicht nur ein Complex von Fühlen und Denken, sondern vor Allem noch ein *Affect*: und zwar jener Affect des Commando's. Das, "Freiheit des Willens" gennant wird, ist wesentlich der Überlegenheits-Affect in Hinsicht auf Den, der gehorchen muss: "ich bin frei, 'er' muss gehorchen"—dies Bewusstsein steckt in jedem Willen, und ebenso jene Spannung der Aufmerksamkeit, jener gerade Blick, der ausschliesslich Eins fixirt, jene unbedingte Werthschätzung "jetzt thut dies und nichts Anderes Noth," jene innere Gewissheit darüber, dass gehorcht werden wird, und was Alles noch zum Zustande des Befehlenden gehört. Ein Mensch, der *will*—, befiehlt einem Etwas in sich, das gehorcht oder von dem er glaubt, dass es gehorcht. Nun aber beachte man, was das Wunderlichste am Willen ist,—an diesem so vielfachen Dinge, für welches das Volk nur Ein Wort hat: insofern wir im gegebenen Falle zugleich die Befehlenden *und* Gehorchenden sind, und als Gehorchende die Gefühle des Zwingens, Drängens, Drückens, Widerstehens, Bewegens kennen, welche sofort nach dem Akte des Willens zu beginnen pflegen; insofern wir anderseits die Gewohnheit haben, uns über diese Zweiheit vermöge des

synthetischen Begriffs "ich" hinwegzusetzen, hinwegzutäuschen, hat sich an das
Wollen noch eine ganze Kette von irrthümlichen Schlüssen und folglich von falschen
Werthschätzungen des Willens selbst angehängt,—dergestalt, dass der Wollende mit
gutem Glauben glaubt, Wollen *genüge* zur Aktion. Weil in den allermeisten Fällen
nur gewollt worden ist, wo auch die Wirkung des Befehls, also der Gehorsam, also
die Aktion *erwartet* werden durfte, so hat sich der *Anschein* in das Gefühl übersetzt,
als ob es da eine *Nothwendigkeit von Wirkung* gäbe; genug, der Wollende glaubt,
mit einem ziemlichen Grad von Sicherheit, dass Wille und Aktion irgendwie Eins
seien—, er rechnet das Gelingen, die Ausführung des Wollens noch dem Willem
selbst zu und geniesst dabei einen Zuwachs jenes Machtgefühls, welches alles
Gelingen mit sich bringt."Freiheit des Willens"—das ist das Wort für jenen
vielfachen Lust-Zustand des Wollenden, der befiehlt und sich zugleich mit dem
Ausführenden als Eins setzt,—der als solcher den Triumph über Widerstände mit
geniesst, aber bei sich urtheilt, sein Wille selbst sei es, der eigentlich die Widerstände
überwinde. [KGW VI, 26–27]

Essentially this passage informs us that Nietzsche believes there is no simple,
unitary, and indivisible thing called the "will." Instead, the "will" of which we
are conscious is the conclusion of a complex struggle of drives "toward which"
or "away from which." We think we initiate action and the action occurs. But
exactly which impulses must go out, which muscles must remain slack and which
must tighten, are never truly in our control. We are cognizant of only our commands. That is because commanding gives us a feeling of power that obedience
does not. By focusing solely on the "command" aspect of "will" as the executor
of "will," we are led to the "popular prejudice" of "free will." But, as Nietzsche
reminds us, there can be no "commanding" without "obeying"; there cannot be
resistance without something resisting and something that must be resisted. A
myriad of feelings are fighting for expression. Some of those feelings will "win
out" over others; some feelings will "command" and others "obey." Some
thoughts about what to do next, what to go toward or away from, will be suppressed; others, pursued. For Nietzsche, intentions do not arise ex nihilo and
"cause" actions. It only seems that way because we do not choose to focus on
the "obeying" sensations. They do not give us a sensation of power.

These "dualistic" aspects of willing I believe provide the main clue to interpreting *will* to power as pluralistic—that is, there are two states of will to power,
"toward which" and "away from which." I interpret these dual states to correspond to master and slave morality, respectively, if the state "toward which" is
considered active and life affirming and the state "away from which" is considered reactive and life denying.[10]

The third essay of *On the Genealogy of Morals* also supports the view that will
to power is inherently pluralistic. Here Nietzsche discusses the meaning of ascetic ideals. As we saw earlier, Nietzsche believed Christianity was an example
of a slave-type morality. Thus, the ascetic, the height of the religious practitio-
ner, represents individual slave-type traits to a high degree. Of the ascetic priest
Nietzsche says,

We can no longer conceal from ourselves what is expressed by all the willing which has taken its direction from the ascetic ideal: this hatred of the human, and even more of the animal, and more still of the material, this horror of the senses, of reason itself, this fear of happiness and beauty, this longing to get away from all appearance, change, becoming, death, wishing, from longing itself—all this means— let us dare to grasp it—*a will to nothingness,* an aversion to life, but it is and remains a *will*! . . . And to repeat in conclusion what I said at the beginning: man would rather will *nothingness* than *not* will. (GM III, 28)

Man kann sich schlechterdings nicht verbergen, *was* eigentlich jenes ganze Wollen ausdrückt, das vom asketischen Ideale her seine Richtung bekommen hat: dieser Hass gegen das Menschliche, mehr noch gegen das Thierische, mehr noch gegen das Stoffliche, dieser Abscheu vor den Sinnen, vor der Vernunft selbst, diese Furcht vor dem Glück und der Schönheit, dieses Verlangen hinweg aus allem Schein, Weschel, Werden, Tod, Wunsch, Verlangen selsbst—das Alles bedeutet, wagen wir es, dies zu begreifen, einen *Willen zum Nichts,* einen Widerwillen gegen das Leben, eine Auflehnung gegen die grundsätzlichsten Voraussetzungen des Lebens, aber es ist und bleibt ein *Wille.* . . . Und, um es noch zum Schluss zu sagen, was ich Anfangs sagte: lieber will Noch der Mensch *das Nichts* wollen, als *nicht* wollen. [KGW VI/ 2, 430]

The ascetic priest, who perpetuates and preaches the ascetic ideal, eschews this world and devotes time, actions, and thoughts toward the eternal, spiritual world— heaven. He or she pities and even despises the material world and its concerns, all of which are trifling and petty when compared with heaven and its rewards. But even this "slavish" ascetic wills, although what the ascetic wills is nothingness—the negation of everything Nietzsche considers life to be. One could will nothingness to the same degree as one could will something life enhancing. Given the intensity of some ascetics' religious fervor, to say they are willing to a lesser extent than other, life-affirming people would seem clearly false.

To support the view that slave willing is not a lesser degree but, rather, a different kind of willing, it will be helpful to return to *Beyond Good and Evil* 19, where Nietzsche is analyzing "will." After discussing the states "toward which" and "away from which" and the thoughts that accompany them, Nietzsche writes,

The will is not only a complex of sensation and thinking, but it is above all an affect, and specifically the affect of command. That which is termed "freedom of the will" is essentially the affect of superiority in relation to him who must obey: "I am free, 'he' must obey"—this consciousness is inherent in every will. . . . A man who *wills* commands something within himself that renders obedience, or that he believes renders obedience. But now let us notice what is strangest about the will— this manifold thing for which the people have only one word: inasmuch as in the given circumstances we are at the same time the commanding *and* obeying parties. (BGE, 19)

Drittens ist der Wille nicht nur ein Complex von Fühlen und Denken, sondern vor Allem noch ein *Affekt*: und zwar jener Affeckt des Commando's. Das, was "Freiheit des Willens" genannt wird, ist wesentlich der Überlegenheits-Affect in Hinsicht auf

Den, der gehorchen muss: "ich bin frei, 'er' muss gehorchen"—dies Bewusstein
steckt in jedem Willen. . . . Ein Mensch, der *will*—, befiehlt einem Etwas in sich,
das gehort oder von dem er glaubt, das es gehorcht. Nun aber beachte man, was das
Wunderlichste am Willen ist,—an diesem so vielfachen Dinge, für welches das Volk
nur Ein Wort hat: insofern wir im gegebenen Falle zugleich die Befehlenden *und*
Gehorchenden sind. [KGW VI/2, 26–27]

It is apparent from this passage that the very act of willing involves a struggle
for superiority within oneself. The states "toward which" and "away from which"
vie for command. The "victor" commands and the "loser" obeys, and either state
may become the victor. All will inherently involves a struggle for superiority.
"Willing" (in our everyday sense of human free will) is not the *initiation* of an
action, according to Nietzsche, but already the *outcome* of a complex struggle
within oneself to determine what will command and what will obey.

Nietzsche discusses "the weak" having will to power in other passages in his
writings. He describes "the weak" as being those people who inspire or preach
pity of humankind, which is indicative of slave morality:

> They are all men of *ressentiment,* physiologically unfortunate and worm-eaten, a
> whole tremendous realm of subterranean revenge, inexhaustible and insatiable in
> outbursts against the fortunate and happy and in masquerades of revenge and pre-
> texts for revenge; when would they achieve the ultimate, subtlest, sublimest triumph
> of revenge? Undoubtably if they succeeded in *poisoning the consciences* of the for-
> tunate with their own misery, so that one day the fortunate began to be ashamed of
> their good fortune and perhaps said one to another: "it is disgraceful to be fortu-
> nate: *there is too much misery!"* (GM III, 14)

> Das sind alles Menschen des Ressentiment, diese physiologisch Verunglückten und
> Wurmstichigen, ein ganzes zitterndes Erdreich unterirdischer Rache, unerschöpflich,
> unersättlich in Ausbrüchen gegen die Glücklichen und ebenso in Maskeraden der
> Rache, in Vorwänden zur Rache: wann würden sie eigentlich zu ihrem letzten,
> feinsten, sublimsten Triumph der Rache kommen? Dann unzweifelhaft, wenn es
> ihnen gelänge, ihr eignes Elend, alles Elend überhaupt den Glücklichen *in's
> Gewissen zu schieben*: so dass diese sich eines Tags ihres Glücks zu schämen
> begönnen und vielleicht unter einandersich sagen: "es ist eine Schande, glücklich
> zu sein! *es giebt zu viel Elend!"* [KGW VI/2, 388–89]

These weak, unfortunate people resent the strong, fortunate people, so they pa-
rade their weaknesses and unhappiness in order to make the fortunate people feel
guilty about their good fortune. And the weak do even more, according to
Nietzsche. They attempt to turn their weakness (Nietzsche also calls it their "sickness") into an asset. They reserve the title "good" for themselves:

> At least to *represent* justice, love, wisdom, superiority—that is the ambition of the
> "lowest", the sick. . . . They monopolize virtue, these weak, hopelessly sick people,
> there is no doubt of it: "we alone are the good and just" they say, "we alone are

homines Bonae voluntatis." They walk among us as embodied reproaches, as warnings to us. . . . There are among them an abundance of the vengeful disguised as judges, who constantly bear the word "justice" in their mouths like poisonous spittle, always with pursed lips, always ready to spit upon all who are not discontented but go their way in good spirits. . . . The will of the weak to represent *some* tyranny over the healthy—where can it not be discovered, this will to power of the weakest! (GM III, 14)

Die Gerechtigkeit, die Liebe, die Weisheit, die Überlegenheit wenigstens *darstellen*—das ist der Ehrgeiz dieser "untersten", dieser Kranken! . . . Sie haben die Tugend jetzt ganz und gar für sich in Pacht genommen, diese Schwachen und Heillos-Krankhaften, daran ist kein Zweifel: "wir allein sind die Guten, die Gerechten, so sprechen sie, wir allein sind die homines bonae voluntatis." Sie wandeln unter uns herum als leibhafte Vorwürfe, als Warnungen an uns. . . . Unter ihnen giebt es in Fülle die zu Richtern verkleideten Rachsüchtigen, welche beständig das Wort "Gerechtigkeit" wie einen giftigen Speichel im Munde tragen, immer gespitzten Mundes, immer bereit, Alles anzuspeien, was nicht unzufrieden blickt und guten Muths seine Strasse zieht. . . . Der Wille der Kranken, *irgend* eine Form der Überlegenheit darzustellen, ihr Instinkt für Schleichwege, die zu einer Tyrannei über die Gesunden führen,—wo fände er sich nicht, dieser Wille gerade der Schwächsten zur Macht! [KGW VI/2, 387–88]

It is evident from this passage that the weak, the "sick," can express will to power. Some of the reasons "sick" will to power differs from "healthy" will to power are that the weak express their will to power by devious methods and that their objective—the downfall or equalization of the strong—is reactive and unnatural according to Nietzsche's view of man. Nietzsche wants to promote strength of character. The weak use different means, such as indirect, covert, surreptitious ways, and have a different end, such as the reduction of the noble to the level of the base to express their will to power. This suggests that it is not a difference in degree but, rather, in kind—determined by the ends and means of will to power— that differentiates sick will to power from healthy will to power.

The weak express their will to power in an underhanded way. They try to "trick" the strong people into feeling guilty for their strength of character. And if the weak are successful in obtaining their goal, as Nietzsche is convinced they had been in nineteenth-century Europe through Christianity, it would certainly seem that the weak would exhibit a greater degree of will to power than the master-type people. In Christianity-based societies, the "weak" have a great deal of social, political, and moral power. It would seem absurd to assert that in these societies there is a very small amount of will to power. It would seem more reasonable to say that in these societies a different kind of will to power, a reactive, life-denying, *ressentiment*-based will to power, was operating.

However, there are two passages that provide textual evidence for the competing interpretation that slave morality might merely be a lesser degree, or smaller amount, of will to power. In *On the Genealogy of Morals* Nietzsche writes,

By prescribing "love of the neighbor," the ascetic priest prescribes fundamentally an excitement of the strongest, most life-affirming drive, even if in the most cautious doses—namely, of the *will to power*. The happiness of "slight superiority" involved in all doing good, being useful, helping and rewarding, is the most effective means of consolation for the physiologically inhibited, and widely employed by them when they are well advised: otherwise they hurt one another, obedient of course, to the same basic instinct. (GM III, 18)

Der asketische Priester verordnet damit, dass er "Nächstenliebe" verodnet, im Grunde eine Erregung des stärksten, lebenbejahendsten Triebes, wenn auch in der vorsichtigsten Dosirung,—des *Willens zur Macht*. Das Glück der "kleinsten Überlegenheit," wie es alles Wohlthun, Nützen, Helfen, Auszeichnen mit sich bringt, ist das reichlichste Trostmittel, dessen sich die Physiologisch-Gehemmten zu bedienen pflegen, gesetzt dass sie gut berathen sind: im andern Falle thun sie einander weh, natürlich im Gehorsam gegen den gleichen Grundinstinkt. [KGW VI/2, 401]

In this passage, the ascetic is prescribing small "doses" of will to power, so it seems that there are amounts of will to power, which would not contradict our first interpretation of two different kinds of will to power. But the above passage implies that will to power has only to do with striving for superiority, and, for Nietzsche, being able to give anything—love, aid, money, even harm or pain—reflects the giver's superiority over the recipient. This would mean that, for Nietzsche, giving money to charities and inflicting pain on someone weaker express the same basic kind of act—a demonstration of superiority over someone else. The only difference would be that the former has monetary power to give and the latter an excess of physical power to "give." The ascetic, by encouraging followers to give love, is encouraging the congregation to express will to power, even though this "loving superiority" is only a small dose of will to power. So it would appear from this passage that will to power is only one kind of act or will—the life-affirming striving for superiority—and people express differing amounts or degrees of this striving.

Later in this aphorism, Nietzsche again implies that will to power is only one certain kind, that of gaining superiority:

The "will to mutual aid," to the formation of a herd, to "community," to "congregation" called up early in this was (as a remedy for depression) is bound to lead to fresh and far more fundamental outbursts of that will to power which it has, even if only to a small extent, aroused: the *formation of a herd* is a significant victory and advance in the struggle against depression. . . . All the sick and sickly instinctively strive after a herd organization as a means of shaking off their dull displeasure and feeling of weakness. (GM III, 18)

In einem dergestalt hervorgerufnen "Willen zur Gegenseitigkeit," zur Heerdenbildung, zur "Gemeinde," zum "Cönakel" muss nun wiederum jener damit, wenn auch im Kleinsten, erregte Wille zur Macht, zu einem neuen und viel volleren Ausbruch kommen: die *Heerdenbildung* ist im Kampf mit der Depression ein wesentlicher Schritt un Sieg. . . . Alle Kranken, Krankhaften streben instinktiv, aus einem Verlangen nach Abschüttelung der dumpfen Unlust und des Schwächegefühls, nach einer Heerden-Organisation. [KGW VI/2, 401–02]

According to this passage, "sick" people band together not only to find solace in one another's company but also to increase their will to power. It would seem that their individually small doses of will to power can become a considerable force as a collective will. Like the Russian army of World War I, where the sheer number of ill-equipped and untrained soldiers produced victories because their enemies ran out of ammunition, so it seems the magnitude of the herd could create a collective amount of will to power that could overcome the individually more powerful, but far fewer numbered, master-type aristocrats. Banding together to create a collective, stronger will to power is the only way individually weak, "sick" people can gain power.

The other passage that suggests that will to power is only one kind of will-ing—life-affirming willing—is in *Twilight of the Idols*. Here Nietzsche equates liberalism with the herd:

Liberal institutions cease to be liberal as soon as they are attained: later on, there are no worse and no more thorough injurers of freedom than liberal institutions. Their effects are known well enough: they undermine the will to power, they level mountain and valley and call that morality, they make men small, cowardly and hedonistic—every time it is the herd animal that triumphs with them. (TI, "Skir-mishes," 38)

Die liberalen Institutionen hören alsbald auf, liberal zu sein, sobald sie erreicht sind: es giebt später keine ärgeren und gründlicheren Schädiger der Freiheit, als liberale Institutionen. Man weiss ja, *was* sie zu Wege bringen: sie unterminiren den Wille zur Macht, sie sind die zur Moral erhobene Nivellirung von Berg und Tal, sie machen klein, feige und genüsslich,—mit ihnen triumphirt jedesmal das Heerdenthier. [KGW VI/3, 133]

Because anything that is herdlike "undermines" will to power, Nietzsche seems to be associating the term *will to power* with only life-affirming, "masterly" ac-tions.

However, the bulk of the will to power aphorisms in the works Nietzsche him-self authorized for publication supports the pluralistic interpretation.[11] Many of the aphorisms containing the phrase *will to power* are incomprehensible unless they are interpreted pluralistically. The best example of this is *Beyond Good and Evil* 51. I reproduce it in full:

So far the most powerful human beings have still bowed worshipfully before the saint as the riddle of self-conquest and deliberate final renunciation. Why did they bow? In him—and as it were behind the question mark of his fragile and miserable appearance—they sensed the superior force that sought to test itself in such a con-quest, the strength of the will in which they recognized and honored their own strength and delight in dominion: they honored something in themselves when they honored the saint. Moreover, the sight of the saint awakened a suspicion in them: such an enormity of denial, of anti-nature will not have been desired for nothing, they said to and asked themselves. There may be a reason for it, some very great danger about which the ascetic, thanks to his secret comforters and visitors, might have inside information. In short, the powerful of the world learned a new fear before him; they sensed a new power, a strange, as yet unconquered enemy—it was the "will to power" that made them stop before the saint. They had to ask him. (BGE, 51)

Bisher haben sich die mächtigsten Menschen immer noch verehrend vor dem Heiligen gebeugt, als dem Räthsel der Selbstbezwingung und absichtlichen letzten Entbehrung: warum beugten sie sich? Sie ahnten in ihm—und gleichsam hinter dem Fragezeichen seines gebrechlichen und kläglichen Anscheins—die überlegene Kraft, welche sich an einer solchen Bezwingung erproben wollte, die Stärke des Willens, in der sie die eigne Stärke und herrschaftliche Lust wieder erkannten und zu ehren wussten: sie ehrten Etwas an sich, wenn sie den Heiligen ehrten. Es kam hinein solches Ungeheures von Verneinung, von Wider-Natur wird nicht umsonst begehrt worden sein, so sagten und fragten sie sich. Es giebt vielleicht einen Grund dazu, eine ganz grosse Gefahr, über welche der Asket, Dank seinen geheimen Zusprechern und Besuchern, näher unterrichtet sein möchte? Genung, die Mächtigen der Welt lernten vor ihm eine neue Furcht, sie ahnten eine neue Macht, einen fremden, noch unbezwungenen Feind:—der "Wille zur Macht" war es, der sie nöthigte, vor dem Heiligen stehen zu bleiben. Sie mussten ihn fragen. [KGW VI/2, 69]

This aphorism is perplexing if read according to the second, monomorphic interpretation of will to power as being only life affirming. In the above aphorism, the ascetic priest appears to have a very large "dose" of will to power; yet given the second interpretation of will to power, we would think that the ascetic, being the epitome of slave-type, life-denying morality, would exhibit a very small dose of will to power. But if this is so, why would the powerful human beings bow before the ascetic priest? What is Nietzsche presenting here?

This aphorism is crucial to resolving the dilemma in favor of the first interpretation of will to power—that will to power is at least dualistic. The opposing interpretation that will to power is only life affirming would create the contradiction in *Beyond Good and Evil* 51 that the ascetic priest had both a large and small dose of will to power. However, the pluralistic interpretation can deal with this passage fairly easily.

This ascetic represents the extreme of "away from," or reactive, will to power. He is "otherworldly"—renouncing this world in favor of a transcendental afterlife. He embraces Christianity, which Nietzsche considers "slavish"; however, he has complete mastery over his emotions and faculties—hunger, lust, jealousy, and so on are all held in complete check by him. The priest exhibits a tremendous amount of power in relation to himself—all aspects of his person are under his firm control; he is not swayed by his passions. This overt, active, "masterly" control over oneself is attractive to "powerful human beings." They sense a power in the ascetic that rivals their own. They must stop to *ask*. But ultimately this power is rejected by Nietzsche. *Beyond Good and Evil* 51 is an attempt to explain how powerful people, too, can be drawn to Christianity. Christianity is powerful, but on close inspection it reveals that it derives its power reactively; it is slave-type power.

We can look at this in the following way: master and slave morality are not opposites but, rather, counterparts of willing. The ascetic priest becomes the epitome of reactive will to power. As Nietzsche explains in the third essay in *On the Genealogy of Morals*, "Man would rather will *nothingness* than *not* will." In other words, man will will anything, even something unreal or otherworldly (nothing), rather than not will at all. This implies that the opposite of willing is not willing nothingness but, rather, not willing at all. The ascetic priest wills nothingness to the greatest degree—he is the epitome of slave-type willing. And who would represent the epitome of master willing? The answer to that question remains unclear, although I would say that the extreme master will would be exemplified by Nietzsche's *Übermensch*.

So the relationship between the *Übermensch* and the ascetic priest is analogous to the love/hate distinction. Love and hate can be interpreted as the two extremes of emotion one person can have for another, and because they share the common property of intensity of emotion, it can be argued that indifference is the opposite of love. Analogously, human beings will in various degrees, either actively or reactively:

> *There are master and slave morality*—I add immediately that in all higher and more mixed cultures there also appear attempts at mediation between these two moralities, and yet more often the interpenetration and mutual misunderstanding of both, and at times they occur directly alongside each other—even in the same human being, within a *single* soul. (BGE, 260)

> Es giebt *Herren-Moral* und *Sklaven-Moral*;—ich füge sofort hinzu, dass in allen höhren und gemischteren Culturen auch Versuche der Vermittlung beider Moralen zum Vorschein kommen, noch öfter das Durcheinander derselben und gegenseitige Missverstehen, ja bisweilen ihr hartes Nebeneinander—sogar im selben Menschen, innerhalb Einer Seele. [KGW VI/2, 218]

Because morality comes in master and slave types for Nietzsche, and because all morality is an expression of will to power, actions can be explained as some form of master (overt) or slave (covert) will. These types merely *describe* which "state of sensation" the action is—"toward" or "away."

Deciding which actions are "toward" or "away" is no easy task. We cannot simply split all actions into one of these either/or categories, as this example from *Thus Spoke Zarathustra* illustrates:

> You force all things to and into yourself that they may flow back out of your well as the gifts of your love.

Verily, such a gift-giving love must approach all values as a robber; but whole and holy I call this selfishness.

There is also another selfishness, an all-too-poor and hungry one that always wants to steal—the selfishness of the sick: sick selfishness. (TSZ, 187)

Ihr zwingt alle Dinge zu euch und in euch, dass sie aus eurem Borne zurückströmen sollen als die Gaben eurer Liebe.

Warlich, zum Raüber an allen Werthen muss solche schenkende Liebe werden; aber heil und heilig heisse ich diese Selbstsucht.

Eine andre Selbstsucht giebt es, eine allzuarme, eine hungernde, die immer stehlen will, jene Selbstsucht der Kranken, die kranke Selbstsucht. [KGW VI/1, 94]

We cannot simply say that "selfishness" is a master-type trait or a slave-type trait. When selfishness is a case of taking things into oneself so that they may flow out from one again, Nietzsche applauds it. When "selfishness" is simply taking things into oneself to keep to oneself, he calls it "sick selfishness." Even pity, which seems to be the one emotion indicative of slave morality (it is the last temptation Zarathustra must overcome), can be an expression of the master type. In *Beyond Good and Evil* Nietzsche writes,

A man who is by nature a *master*—when such a man has pity, well, *this* pity has value. But what good is the pity of those who suffer. Or those who, worse, *preach* pity. (BGE, 293)

Ein Mann, der von Natur *Herr* ist,—wenn ein solcher Mann Mitleiden hat, nun! *dies* Mitleiden hat Werth! Aber was leigt am Mitleiden Derer, welchen leiden! Oder Derer, welche gar Mitleiden predigen! [KGW VI/2, 246]

As this passage suggests, the actions or emotions do not determine master from slave types, the type of person determines whether the action or emotion is "masterly" or "slavish." Pity from people filled with *ressentiment* is different from pity from Zarathustra. We cannot always label pity "slavish" and automatically assign it into the category of slave-type morality. Nietzsche is far too subtle a thinker to be given to black-and-white distinctions, whatever his writings might suggest at first glance. Descriptive typologies, such as "master and slave," are only starting points for discussing the complex state of nineteenth-century morality—how it arrived where it was and, for Nietzsche, how to go beyond it.

I have argued that the differences between master-type and slave-type moralities are explained by the two different aspects of will to power—active and reactive. These aspects are differentiated by the means and superficial ends by which will to power is expressed. Active will to power seeks its own independent goals and uses direct and overt means to achieve those goals. Reactive will to power adopts its immediate goals based on reactions to others' goals and uses indirect, covert methods born from resentment to attain its goals. However, overtly or covertly, the ultimate end or goal for both healthy and sick forms of will to power is superiority or more power.

But what are we to make of those passages that imply that will to power is only of the life-affirming, active kind? Was Nietzsche simply confused or trying to be purposefully misleading? *Will to power* is a simple-sounding phrase, but it signifies a deceptively complex notion. In most of the passages in the published texts it seems clear that Nietzsche uses *will to power* to mean very generally any striving for superiority, active or reactive. It is only in a few places that Nietzsche seems to use a narrower sense of the term to denote only the active, overt aspect of will to power. I favor the pluralistic interpretation because it can make sense of all the passages in which *will to power* is used, while the more narrow, monomorphic interpretation can only make sense of a few passages.

If we remove the stipulation that the narrower sense imposes—that the striving for superiority must be life affirming—and at this point merely take *will to power* to mean the more general "striving for superiority" in either active (healthy, master-type) or reactive (sick, slave-type) sense, this allows the ascetic priest to express will to power but not necessarily in any life-affirming manner. This more general sense of the phrase also has the advantage of not eliminating the possibility of degrees (or doses) of will to power; there are differing degrees of master-type and slave-type will to power within cultures and individuals. The only interpretation that seems unwarranted is the reading that slave-type individuals evince no or only a small amount of will to power. As we have seen in aphorism 51 of *Beyond Good and Evil,* Nietzsche describes ascetic priests as people who have a high degree of will to power.

Even though the majority of aphorisms containing *will to power* in the works Nietzsche authorized for publication does center around specifically human behavior, Nietzsche does not limit his discussions of will to power to only humans and morality. Nietzsche extends his notion of will to power to life in both *Thus Spoke Zarathustra* and *Beyond Good and Evil*:

> Where I found the living, there I found will to power . . . where there is perishing, a falling of leaves, behold, there life sacrifices itself—for power! . . . Only where there is life is there also will: not will to life but—thus I teach you—will to power! (TSZ, 226–27)

> Wo ich Lebendiges fand, da fand ich Willen zur Macht; . . . wo es Untergang giebt und Blätterfallen, siehe, da opfert sich Leben—um Macht! . . . Nur, wo Leben ist, da ist auch Wille: aber nicht Wille zum Leben, sondern—so lehre ich's dich—Wille zur Macht! [KGW VI/1, 143–45]

> Physiologists should think twice before putting down the instinct of self-preservation as the cardinal instinct of an organic being. A living thing seeks above all to *discharge* its strength—life itself is *will to power*; self-preservation is only one of the indirect and most frequent *results.* (BGE, 13)

> Die Physiologen sollten sich besinnen, den Selbsterhaltungstrieb als kardinalen Trieb eines organischen Wesens anzusetzen. Vor Allem will etwas Lebendiges seine Kraft *auslassen*—Leben selbst ist Wille zur Macht—: die Selbsterhaltung ist nur eine der indirekten und häufigsten *Folgen* davon. [KGW VI/2, 21]

"Exploitation" does not belong to a corrupt or imperfect and primitive society; it belongs to the *essence* of what lives, as a basic organic function; it is a consequence of the will to power, which is after all the will to life. (BGE, 259)

Die "Ausbeutung" gehört nicht einer verderbten oder unvollkommnen und primitiven Gesellschaft an: sie gehört in's *Wesen* des Lebendigen, als organische Grundfunktion, sie ist eine Folge des eigentlichen Willens zur Macht, der eben der Wille zur Lebens ist. [KGW VI/2, 218]

Thus the essence of life, its *will to power,* is ignored; one overlooks the essential priority of the spontaneous, aggressive, expansive, form-giving forces that give new interpretations and directions, although "adoption" follows only after this; the dominant role of the highest functionaries within the organism itself in which the will to life appears active and form-giving is denied. (GM II, 12)

Damit ist aber das Wesen des Lebens verkannt, sein *Wille zur Macht*; damit ist der principielle Vorrang übersehn, den die spontanen, angreifenden, über greifenden, neu-auslegenden, neu-richtenden und gestaltenden Kräfte haben, auf deren Wirkung erst die "Anpassung" folgt; damit ist im Organismus selbst die hereschlaftliche Rolle der höchsten Funktionäre abgeleugnet, in denen der Lebenwille aktiv und formgebend erscheint. [KGW VI/2, 332]

In these passages the references to "organism," "organic function," and "life" suggest not merely human life but all kinds of organisms from single-celled viruses to complex plants and animals. It is evident that Nietzsche extends the notion of will to power beyond only humans.

But how does will to power figure in the organic realm? If we are to believe Nietzsche, will to power is the explanation for any organism's actions or behavior. In *Beyond Good and Evil* 13 Nietzsche states that self-preservation is an indirect result of will to power rather than the cardinal instinct of an organism. For Nietzsche, self-preservation is an inadequate explanation for organic actions because it cannot explain certain kinds of organic behavior. For instance, it cannot adequately explain why organisms do much more than is necessary merely for their own survival. An organism's growth is more than self-preservation, for it could preserve itself in its present state rather than taking in more nourishment or sunlight that it would require for its growth. But plants and other nonhuman organisms grow, and Nietzsche believes self-preservation has difficulty explaining this growth. Instead, Nietzsche believes will to power can explain both self-preservation and growth. As a result of an organism striving to grow, trying to gain superiority over its environment, the organism is more likely to survive—preserve itself. Nietzsche's explanation can explain more organic behavior than the explanation of self-preservation, and so Nietzsche considers will to power to be a better explanation for an organism's behavior than self-preservation.

Nietzsche also sees will to power as a better explanation than scientific explanations. In *On the Genealogy of Morals* Nietzsche touts the value of historical method over scientific, or "mechanistic," method:

I emphasize this major point of historical method all the more because it is in fundamental opposition to the now prevalent instinct and taste which would rather be reconciled even to the absolute fortuitousness, even the mechanistic senselessness of all events than to the theory that in all events a *will to power* is operating. The democratic idiosyncracy which opposes everything that dominates and wants to dominate, the modern *misarchism* (to coin an ugly word for an ugly thing) has permeated the realm of the spirit and disguised itself in the most spiritual forms to such a degree that today it has forced its way, has acquired the *right* to force its way into the strictest, apparently most objective sciences; indeed, it seems to me to have already taken charge of all physiology and theory of life—to the detriment of life, as goes without saying, since it has robbed it of a fundamental concept, that of *activity*. Under the influence of the above-mentioned idiosyncracy, one places instead "adaptation" in the foreground, that is to say, an activity of the second rank, a mere reactivity; indeed, life has been defined as a more and more efficient inner adaptation to external conditions (Herbert Spencer). Thus the essence of life, its *will to power,* is ignored; one overlooks the essential priority of the spontaneous, aggressive, expansive, form-giving forces that give new interpretations and directions, although "adaptation" follows only after this; the dominant role of the highest functionaries within the organism itself in which the will to life appears active and form-giving is denied. (GM II, 12)

Ich hebe diesen Haupt-Gesichtspunkt der historischen Methodik hervor, um so mehr als er im Grunde dem gerade herrschenden Instinkte und Zeitgeschmack entgegen geht, welcher lieber sich noch mit der absoluten Zufälligkeit, ja mechanistischen Unsinnigkeit alles Geschehens vertragen würde, als mit der Theorie eines in allem Geschehn sich abspielenden *Macht-Willens.* Die demokratische Idiosynkrasie gegen Alles, was herrscht und herrschen will, der moderne *Misarchismus* (um ein schlechtes Wort für eine schlechte Sache zu bilden) hat sich allmählich dermaassen in's Geistigste, Geistigste umgesetzt und verkleidet, dass er heute Schritt für Schritt bereits in die strengsten, anscheinend objektivsten Wissenschaften eindringt, eindringen *darf;* ja er scheint mir schon über die ganze Physiologie und Lehre vom Leben Herr geworden zu sein, zu ihrem Schaden, wie sich von selbst versteht, indem er ihr einen Grundbegriff, den der eigentlichen *Aktivität,* eskamotirt hat. Man stellt dagegen unter dem Druck jener Idiosynkrasie die "Anpassung" in den Vordergrund, das heisst eine Aktivität zweiten Ranges, eine blosse Reaktivität, ja man hat das Leben selbst als eine immer zweckmässigere innere Anpassung an äussere Umstände definirt (Herbert Spencer). Damit ist aber das Wesen des Lebens verkannt, sein *Wille zur Macht*; damit ist der principielle Vorrang übersehn, den die spontanen, angreifenden, übergreifenden, neu-auslegenden, neu-richtenden und gestaltenden Kräfte haben, auf deren Wirkung erst die "anspangung" folgt; damit ist im Organismus selbst die herrschaftliche Rolle der höchsten Funktionäre abgeleugnet, in denen der Lebenswille aktiv und formgebend erscheint. [KGW VI/2, 331–32]

This passage indicates that mechanistic theories are inadequate as the basic explanation of organic behavior for Nietzsche because he thought they could not account for organic activity except as reactions to the environment. Therefore, will to power would be considered a better explanation because it allows for the organism to act as well as react to its surroundings. The organism is not merely adapting to its environment—reacting to it—it is also actively affecting the environment. Will to power allows the organism to initiate at least some action rather than be solely a consequence of determined causes. Nietzsche rejects mechanistic explanations because they cannot explain *why* any action occurs in the first place; they can only explain *how* an action could occur. According to Nietzsche, mechanistic explanations are not all encompassing. For instance, they lack any teleological aspect a full explanation may warrant because there may be some cases of organic (and certainly human) behavior in which the consequences of that behavior figure into the explanation of the action. Nietzsche believes will to power can account for both teleological and mechanistic behavior, so it is a better explanation than mechanistic explanations alone.

We now must ask whether Nietzsche's extension of will to power as an explanation of organic behavior alters our provisional meaning of *will to power* as a "striving for superiority." At first glance the extension into the entire organic realm seems to have little effect on our provisional meaning. Instead of the claim that only humans strive for superiority, Nietzsche contends that all living beings strive for superiority, and this shift seems unproblematic. Even the two different kinds of striving, the active, life-affirming kind and the reactive, life-denying kind, can be observed in nonhuman life. The predatory animals might be good examples of aggressive, exploitive will to power. On the other hand, those animals that survive because of camouflage, for example, salamanders and chameleons, might be examples of reactive will to power. Spiders do not actively conquer flies; they catch them indirectly in webs that hold the flies until the spider is ready to feed on them.[12] Spiders and chameleons survive and grow just as well as and sometimes better than lions and cheetahs; only the method of survival is different.

On closer inspection, however, extending will to power as an explanation for all organic behavior seems to raise some complications for interpreting will to power as a striving for superiority. The examples I just used are highly selective and are concentrated on the higher forms of nonhuman life. In the case of lionesses hunting their prey, the use of *strive* may make some sense to us. But perhaps we are being too anthropomorphic in our application of *strive*. Does "striving for superiority" imply an awareness of the striving? If so, we could not substitute *striving for superiority* for *will to power,* for there are many forms of life that we do not consider conscious or aware, and yet they must express will to power if life is will to power.

Strive does not necessarily involve consciousness. It can simply mean to engage or be engaged in some sort of struggle. Being engaged in a struggle does not necessarily involve awareness of the contention; it is sufficient that there is a struggle. Nonconscious organisms, such as bacteria, strive against each other and their environments, not just for survival but for dominance. For Nietzsche, the growth of an organism is evidence of that organism's superiority over the forces around it, evidence of the organism's increased power—its will to power.

But if Nietzsche believes that will to power is an explanation for all organic behavior at all levels of life from the microscopic to the most complex, there are some organic actions that seem quite mundane. These organic actions seem better explained by scientific, or mechanistic, explanation than by will to power. For example, one of the acts that an acorn does is become an oak tree. If all organic activity is explainable by will to power, then an acorn becoming an oak must be explained by the acorn's striving for superiority. It seems strange to say that an acorn becomes an oak because of will to power. We are more inclined to explain the acorn's actions by a mechanistic explanation. To the scientist, an acorn becomes an oak because that is what an acorn *is,* the seed of the oak, and the genetic information the acorn carries, along with favorable environmental factors, allows the acorn to germinate. In what way does the acorn "strive for superiority," in this case, the superiority of being a sturdy oak?

If Nietzsche is right and all life is will to power, then there are trillions of struggles going on at every moment. At the cellular level, the genetic material is struggling to relay its information to the cells; it struggles to stay free from viruses or cancer-like mutations. At another level, the acorn struggles with the natural elements. If it lands on somewhat sandy soil, it will have a tougher struggle than if it lands in topsoil rich in nitrogen. It must also struggle with higher life forms. People and other animals possess so much more power than acorns that the struggle is over very quickly, if, say, an animal decides to eat it. Thus, if an acorn does take root and eventually grow into an oak, we can better understand how Nietzsche might consider this as evidence of will to power—the acorn has striven for superiority over the elements as well as other forces and has grown into an oak.

So the provisional interpretation of will to power as a striving for superiority remains understandable even when applied to nonconscious, nonhuman, organic life. But is this the extent to which will to power pertains? Some writers on Nietzsche claim that will to power is Nietzsche's explanation for everything, that will to power is a metaphysical or cosmological principle for Nietzsche. In order for will to power to be an explanation for the entire cosmos, both the inorganic and organic realms would have to be included.

What textual evidence do these writers have for thinking Nietzsche applies will to power to inorganic things? In the works Nietzsche authorized for publication, there are only two aphorisms that suggest that Nietzsche extends will to power beyond the organic domain—one in *On the Genealogy of Morals* and one in *Beyond Good and Evil.*

The passage from *On the Genealogy of Morals* (II, 12) is typically vague: Nietzsche says fleetingly that "in all events a will to power is operating" within the context of a criticism of preferring scientific method to a genealogical one. This aphorism mentions will to power two other times: one time in connection with a striving for superiority and the other equating will to power with life. *Events* is just too ambiguous a word here to assert with any confidence that Nietzsche means to take will to power into the inorganic realm. Thus, I shall turn to the more detailed discussion of will to power and "the world" that occurs in *Beyond Good and Evil.*

Only aphorism 36 in *Beyond Good and Evil* is an explicit, extended discussion of the *world* being will to power in the works Nietzsche authorized for publication before his collapse. It is so philosophically dense and important that I will ask the reader's patience and reproduce it entirely:

> Suppose nothing else were "given" as real except our world of desires and passions, and we could not get down, or up, to any other "reality" besides the reality of our drives—for thinking is merely a relation of these drives to each other: is it not permitted to make the experiment and to ask the question whether this "given" would not be *sufficient* for also understanding on the basis of this kind of thing the so-called mechanistic (or "material") world? I mean, not as a deception, as "mere appearance," an "idea" (in the sense of Berkeley and Schopenhauer) but as holding the same rank of reality as our affect—as a more primitive form of the world of affects in which everything still lies contained in a powerful unity before it undergoes ramifications and developments in the organic process (and, as is only fair, also becomes tenderer and weaker)—as a kind of instinctive life in which all organic functions are still synthetically intertwined along with self-regulation, assimilation, nourishment, excretion, and metabolism—as a *pre-form* of life. In the end not only is it permitted to make this experiment; the conscience of *method* demands it. Not to assume several kinds of causality until the experiment of making do with a single one has been pushed to its utmost limit (to the point of nonsense, if I may say so)—that is a moral of method which one may not shirk today—it follows "from its definition," as a mathematician would say. The question is in the end whether we really recognize the will as *efficient,* whether we believe in the causality of the will: if we do—and at bottom our faith in this is nothing less than our faith in causality itself—then we have to make the experiment of positing the causality of the will hypothetically as the only one. "Will," of course, can affect only "will"—and not "matter" (not "nerves," for example). In short, one has to risk the hypothesis whether will does not affect will wherever "effects" are recognized—and whether all mechanical occurrences are not, insofar as a force is active in them, will force, effects of will. Suppose, finally, we succeeded in explaining our entire instinctive life as the development and ramification of *one* basic form of the will—namely, of the will to power, as *my* proposition has it; suppose all organic functions could be traced back to this will to power and one could also find in it the solution of the problem of procreation and nourishment—it is *one* problem—then one would have gained the right to determine *all* efficient force univocally as—*will to power.* The world viewed from the inside, the world defined and determined according to its "intelligible character"—it would be "will to power" and nothing else. (BGE, 36)

> Gesetzt, dass nichts Anderes als real "gegeben" ist als unsere Welt der Begirden und Leidenschaften, dass wir zu keiner anderen "Realität" hinab oder hinauf können als gerade zur Realität unsere Triebe—denn Denken ist nur ein Verhalten dieser Triebe zu einander—: ist es nicht erlaubt, den Versuch zu machen und die Frage zu fragen, ob dies Gegeben nicht *ausreicht,* um aus Seines-Gleichen auch die sogenannte mechanistische (oder "Materielle") Welt zu verstehen? Ich meine nicht als eine Täuschung, einen "schein," eine "Vorstellung" (im Berkeley'schen und Schopenhauerischen Sinne) sondern als vom gleichen Realitäts-Range, welchen unser Affect selbst hat,—als eine primitivere Form der Welt der Affecte, in der noch

Alles in mächtiger Einheit beschlossen liegt, was sich dann im organischen Prozesse abzweigt und ausgestalt (auch wie billig, verzärtelt und abschwächt—), als eine Art von Triebleben, in dcm noch sämmtliche organische Funktionen, mit Selbst-Regulirung, Assimilation, Ernährung, Ausscheidung, Stoffwechsel, synthetisch gebunden in einander sind,—als eine *Vorform* des Lebens?—Zuletzt ist es nicht nur erlaubt, diesen Versuch zu machen: es ist, vom Gewissen der *Methode* aus, geboten. Nicht mehrere Arten von Causalität annehmen, so lange nicht der Versuch, mit einer einzigen auszureichen, bis an seine äusserste Grenze getrieben ist (—bis zum Unsinn, mit Verlaub zu sagen): das ist eine Moral der Methode, der man sich heute nicht entziehen darf;—es folgt "aus ihrer Definition," wie ein Mathematiker sagen würde. Die Frage ist zuletzt, ob wir den Willen wirklich als *wirkend* anerkennen, ob wir an die Causalität des Willens glauben: thun wir das—und im Grunde ist der Glaube *daran* eben unser Glaube an Causalität selbst—, so *müssen* wir den Versuch machen, die Willens-Causalität hypothetisch als die einzige zu setzen. "Wille" kann natürlich nur auf "Wille" wirken—und nicht auf "Stoffe" (nicht auf "Nerven" zum Beispiel—): genung, man muss die Hypothese wagen, ob nicht überall, wo "Wirkungen" anerkannt werden, Wille auf Wille wirkt—und ob nicht alles mechanische Geschehen, insofern eine Kraft darin thätig wird, eben Willens-kraft, Willens-Wirkung ist.—Gesetzt endlich, dass es gelänge, unser gesammtes Triebleben als die Ausgestaltung und Verzweigung Einer Grundform des Willens zu ereklä“ren—nämlich des Willens zur Macht, wie es *mein* Satz ist.—gesetzt, dass man alle organischen Funktionen auf diesen Willen zur Macht zurückführen könnte und in ihm auch die Lösung des Problems der Zeugung und Ernährung—es ist Ein Problem—fände, so hätte man damit sich das Recht verschafft, alle wirkende Kraft eindeutig zu bestimmen als: *Wille zur Macht*. Die Welt von innen gesehen, die Welt auf ihren "intelligiblen Charakter" hin bestimmt und bezeichnet—sie wäre eben "Wille zur Macht" und nichts ausserdem. [KGW VI/2, 50–51]

So many things are going on in this aphorism that one hardly knows where or how to begin. Obviously, saying that the "world . . . according to its intelligible character . . . would be 'will to power' and nothing else" would lead us to believe that Nietzsche intends to expand will to power beyond the human and organic into the inorganic realm. Will to power would be the explanation of not only why organisms, including people, act the way they do but also why the world is the way it is at any given moment. But in what way can will to power be said to be an explanation of the world and, more specifically, inanimate objects?

Earlier in the aphorism Nietzsche claims that will can affect only will and not matter. This implies that Nietzsche believes what we normally call matter or physical substance is actually "will" or force. Thus, the usual distinction we make between matter and will is illusory. There is no division between the corporeal and noncorporeal. The inorganic is merely a "pre-form" of the organic, and while we can distinguish between them, they are not metaphysically distinct. Thus, mechanistic explanations are inadequate and ultimately fictitious because they presuppose material things acting on material things. But this aphorism states that there is no "matter," only will. Therefore, scientific explanations, which rely on causal language, are only one way, and not the objectively "True" way, to explain events. Nietzsche suggests that there is only chaotic will. How could one explain events in terms of will, as this aphorism suggests?

Let us look at a classic example of "mechanistic" explanations (cause and effect): the cue ball hitting the eight ball in a game of pool. A mechanistic explanation of the effect the cue ball has on the eight ball would involve physics. The moving cue ball impacts the eight ball, and motion is transferred to the extent that some of the motion of the cue ball transfers to the stationary eight ball, which absorbs some of the motion, repels the cue ball, and moves in the opposite direction, at a lesser velocity, of its being hit.

How would Nietzsche's will to power explanation handle the same event? The moving cue ball would be a will struggling with other wills—the air and the felt of the pool table. The will-felt is slowing the will-cue-ball down a bit, but the force of the air-will is almost negligible. As the will-cue-ball encounters the will-eight-ball, a more difficult struggle ensues. The will-cue-ball may continue to move but slower and on a different trajectory. If the will-cue-ball is moving fast enough, it will have sufficient efficient force to make the stationary will-eight-ball move as well. So in the strivings, or struggles, or battles of differing wills, some struggles are easily overcome, and others are not. Although the will-eight-ball "loses" its ability to remain at rest, it succeeds at remaining a will-eight-ball: the impact of the will-cue-ball is not so strong as to shatter the will-eight-ball, so in the struggle to remain a will-eight-ball, it has "won." A Nietzschean way of explaining pool may not be obviously superior to Newtonian mechanics at this point, but it is an alternative explanation.

Finally, Nietzsche says that if all organic functions could be traced to will to power, then all efficient force is will to power. But we have just seen that Nietzsche *does* think that all organic functions are will to power. The antecedent to the hypothetical is met, so we can logically conclude that Nietzsche thinks that all efficient force is will to power. Thus, Nietzsche has expanded the notion of will to power to account for everything, whether organic or inorganic, because the delineation between the two is already removed earlier in the aphorism. We should not even distinguish between the two because the inorganic is only a pre-form of the organic. It simply has not undergone certain ramifications and developments that organic will has. If there is only one kind of "stuff" (will) and Nietzsche believes all will is reducible to one basic form (will to power), it seems clear that will to power is akin to a metaphysical principle for Nietzsche. Will to power is the fundamental explanation (or principle) of the entire world.

There are, however, some problems with this interpretation of the aphorism. The aphorism begins with the word *suppose*. According to some interpreters, this renders the entire aphorism hypothetical and immediately problematic.[13] The contention is that Nietzsche is simply being ironic with the ideas that follow this opening. Additionally, halfway through the aphorism Nietzsche explicitly asks whether or not it is permissible to make an experiment. This would imply that something new is being tested, and we must try to determine whether Nietzsche comes to any conclusions to his experiment by the end of the aphorism. The experiment Nietzsche wants to conduct is to see whether our "world" (our inner world) of passions and desires would be a sufficient explanation for everything, including the material (outer) world. He then decides not just that the experiment is permissible but that methodologically it is morally imperative.

It is at this point that Nietzsche talks about a "conscience of method." He says that one ought to try to do as much as one can with one explanation before trying to explain events with more than one explanation. However, he also says that a conscientious philosopher must push this one explanation "to the point of nonsense." Is this what he does with will to power? My explanation of the pool balls is very unusual. Does it push Nietzsche's notion of will to power to the point of nonsense?

This part of the aphorism concerning methodology sounds very tongue in cheek about how Nietzsche sees methodology in the nineteenth century. First, the initial *method* is italicized, giving it greater weight, as if one has no choice but to relinquish oneself to methodology. Second, there are the two phrases "conscience of *method*" and "a moral of method," which imply that to do otherwise than to pursue one causal explanation to its limit is an unconscionable breach of methodology to the point of being immoral. But surely there is nothing intrinsically immoral about abandoning some strange form of Ockham's Razor. That the simplest explanation is the right one (and one explanation for all phenomena is simpler than two or more) is simply an assumption science makes—an assumption that Nietzsche challenges in many other passages, most notably in *Beyond Good and Evil* 19, where he criticizes the notion that "will" is somehow immediate, self-evident, and singular. Surely, Nietzsche has not forgotten what he just placed fifteen aphorisms earlier. It is implausible that he has done a complete about-face on the subject. Earlier in *Beyond Good and Evil* he criticizes even language on just this point—that words mask subtle and perhaps important differences and so are simplifications of complexities.[14] Any simplification is inherently suspicious to Nietzsche. Why, then, would he feel compelled to pursue a notion simply because a definition or method demands it? This could be an ironic criticism of philosophical (particularly metaphysical) and perhaps philological and scientific methodology. Perhaps Nietzsche is saying, "Method demands an economy of principle, but, of course, there is no justification for this—it is only a convention, which in the end has no hold on us, but for the moment I will play along."

Next Nietzsche asks whether humans believe that our wills are causal. All of us would say that we believe our wills can effect change. If we do not think our wills are efficient, then the whole meaning of efficient causation is at risk. This seems straightforward enough, but Nietzsche again complicates matters by saying that the belief in our causal wills is a *faith,* implying that we believe in efficient causation even when there is no empirical proof of it. This is not a particularly surprising or original argument; David Hume said very much the same thing a century earlier.[15] Then Nietzsche reiterates that he must continue with the *experiment.*

The ensuing sentences in *Beyond Good and Evil* 36 repeat that matter does not exist. This is to reemphasize the beginning of the aphorism, where Nietzsche suggests that there is only "reality" or "given" and that it is akin to our world of passions rather than "the so-called mechanistic (or 'material') world." This claim is consistent with many other places in the published works where Nietzsche denies the traditional philosophical divisions, that is, corporeal/noncorporeal, phenomena/noumena, and body/soul. So in this experiment, there are not two different worlds—our "inner" experience of drives and desires and our "outer" experience of material objects. Nietzsche invites us to make the experiment that the "outer" world is actually like our "inner" one—composed of drives and desires rather than matter.

Finally, Nietzsche suggests that his proposition of will to power can handle just such an assignment—to explain not only the inner world and all organic functions but also the "outer," material world. Thus, Nietzsche concludes that if we view the outside world "from inside," that is, if we view the outer world as being metaphysically the "same" (at least a "pre-form" of it) as our inner world, it would be will to power, for will to power is his explanation of the inner world.

However, Nietzsche again prefaces his final remarks with the speculative word *suppose*. He also italicizes *my* in "*my* proposition." This suggests to some Nietzsche interpreters that Nietzsche may recognize that there might be other explanations besides will to power that are just as good at explaining the world.[16] If this is so, we could then conclude that Nietzsche is not seriously advancing the idea that will to power is the fundamental metaphysical principle from which everything can be explained, only that *he* explains or interprets the world in this way.[17]

This leaves us with two interpretations of *Beyond Good and Evil* 36, both of which seem to have textual support. Both interpretations acknowledge that Nietzsche is conducting an experiment. The first interpretation finds that although Nietzsche begins with a hypothesis, he comes to a conclusion about the experiment, namely, that everything is will to power. The second interpretation finds that Nietzsche is conducting a playful, ironic thought experiment that stays experimental throughout and that Nietzsche does not come to any conclusion he is willing to defend. Although many of Nietzsche's aphorisms are philosophically dense and open to several interpretations, *Beyond Good and Evil* 36 is particularly enigmatic because it is so explicitly hypothetical. This one aphorism is too problematic to determine definitively whether Nietzsche extends will to power beyond "life" into the inorganic realm or into the realm of metaphysics.

We have, then, almost no textual evidence from the writings Nietzsche authorized for publication that he extends will to power as an explanation for the inorganic realm as well as the organic one. Nevertheless, quite a few Nietzsche scholars have concluded that will to power is Nietzsche's metaphysics, cosmology, or ontology. However, their textual support for these claims is almost exclusively material taken from Nietzsche's unpublished writings. In the following chapter we will examine the unpublished writings on will to power and discuss the problems inherited with them.

FURTHER READING

For Nietzsche's views on morality, see the following:

Deleuze, Gilles. *Nietzsche and Philosophy.* Trans. Hugh Tomlinson. New York: Columbia University Press, 1983; chapters 3–4.

Hunt, Lester. *Nietzsche and the Origin of Virtue.* New York: Routledge, 1991.

Nehamas, Alexander. *Nietzsche: Life as Literature.* Cambridge, Mass.: Harvard University Press, 1985; chapter 7.

Schacht, Richard. *Nietzsche.* Boston: Routledge and Kegan Paul, 1983; chapters 6–7.

———, ed. *Nietzsche, Genealogy, Morality.* Berkeley: University of California Press, 1994.

3

Will to Power in the Unpublished Works

Scholars who think that will to power is Nietzsche's metaphysics or cosmology appeal almost exclusively to textual support from the writings that were never authorized for publication by Nietzsche. The *Nachlass* note most often cited as evidence that will to power is metaphysical is the following:

> And do you know what "the world" is to me? Shall I show it to you in my mirror? This world: a monster of energy, without beginning, without end; a firm iron magnitude of force that does not grow bigger or smaller, that does not expend itself but only transforms itself; as a whole, of unalterable size, a household without expenses or losses, but likewise without increase or income; enclosed by "nothingness" as by a boundary; not something blurry or wasted, not something endlessly extended, but set in definite space as a definite force, and not a space that might be "empty" here or there, but rather as a force throughout, as a play of forces and waves of forces, at the same time one and many, increasing here and at the same time decreasing there; a sea of forces flowing and rushing together, eternally changing, eternally flooding back, with tremendous years of recurrence, with an ebb and a flood of its forms; out of the most complex, out of the stillest, most rigid, coldest forms striving toward the hottest, most turbulent, most self-contradictory, and then again returning home to the simple out of this abundance, out of the play of contradictions back to the joy of concord, still affirming itself in this uniformity of its courses and its years, blessing itself as that which must return eternally, as a becoming that knows no satiety, no disgust, no weariness: this is my *Dionysian* world of the eternally self-creating, the eternally self-destroying, this mystery world of the twofold voluptuous delight, my "beyond good and evil," without goal, unless the joy of the circle is itself a goal; without will, unless a ring feels good will toward itself—do you want a *name* for this world? A *solution* for all its riddles? A *light* for you, too, you best-concealed, strongest, most intrepid, most midnightly men?— *This world is the will to power—and nothing besides!* And you yourselves are also this will to power—and nothing besides! (WP, 1067)

Und wisst ihr auch, was mir "die Welt" ist? Soll ich sie euch in meinem Spiegel zeigen? Diese Welt: ein Ungeheuer von Kraft, ohne Anfang, ohne Ende, eine feste, eherne Grosse von Kraft, welche nicht grosser, nicht kleiner wird, die sich nicht verbraucht sondern nur verwandelt, als Ganzes unveranderlich gross, ein Haushalt ohne Ausgaben und Einbussen, aber ebenso ohne Zuwachs, ohne Einnahmen, vom "Nichts" umschlossen als von seiner Granze, nichts Verschwimmendes, Verschwendetes, nichts Unendlich-Ausgedehntes, sondern als bestimme Kraft einem bestimmte Raum eingelegt, und nicht einem Raume, der irgend—wo "leer" ware, vielmehr als Kraft überall, als Spiel von Kraften und Kraftwellen zugleich Eins und "Vieles," hier sich haufend und zugleich dort sich fluthender Krafte, ewig sich wandelnd, ewig zurucklaufend, mit ungeheueren Jahren der Wiederkehr, mit einer Ebbe und Fluth seiner Gestalten, aus den einfachsten in die vielfaltigsten hinaustriebend, aus dem Stillsten, Starrsten, Kaltesten hinaus in das Gluhendste, Wildeste, Sich-selber-wider-sprechendste, und dann wieder aus der Fulle heimkehrend zum Einfachen, aus dem Spiel der Widerspruche zuruck bis zur Lust des Einklangs, sich selber bejahend noch in dieser Gleichheit seiner Bahnen und Jahre, sich selber segnend als das, was ewig wiederkommen muss, als ein Werden, das kein Sattwerden, keinen Überdruss, keine Mudigkeit—: diese Meine *dionysische* Welt des Ewig-sich-selber-Schaffens, des Ewig-sich-selber-Zerstorens, diese Geheimniss-Welt der doppelten Wolluste, diess mein Jenseits von Gut und Böse, ohne Ziel, wenn nicht im Gluck des Kreises ein Ziel liegt, ohne Willen, wenn nicht ein Ring zu sich selber guten Willen hat,—wollt ihr einem *Namen* fur diese Welt? Eine *Losung* für alle ihre Rathsel? Ein *Licht* auch fur euch, ihr Verborgensten, Stärksten, Unerschrockensten, Mitternächtlichsten?—*Diese Welt ist der Wille zur Macht—und nichts ausserdem!* Und auch ihr selber seid dieser Wille zur Macht— und nichts ausserdem! [KGW VII/3, 38(12), 338–39]

This appears to be an extremely strong statement about the nature of the world or what the world "really is." The addition of "and nothing besides!" implies that will to power is the ultimate nature of the world and that nothing else is just as or more fundamental than will to power. Finally, will to power is not something that we "have" or "do"—it is what we *are*. Not only our behavior is explained by will to power, but our very *being* is will to power, and so is the being of everything, animate or inanimate. If we take a metaphysical principle to be what everything is ultimately reduced to, then will to power seems to be a metaphysical principle. Let us try to make sense of will to power as Nietzsche's metaphysics.

Although the above aphorism is steeped in metaphor, it nevertheless informs us of how Nietzsche views the world. First, Nietzsche considers the world to be composed only of force *(Kraft)*. While there are many configurations possible within this world of forces, the entire amount of force does not grow larger or shrink smaller. This world of forces, however, is spatially finite; "nothingness" surrounds it. There are no spatial "holes" of nothingness in this world; rather, force fills the entire space—"and not a space that might be 'empty' here or there, but a force throughout." There is, however, infinite time through which these forces interplay, combining here and disbanding there—"a sea of forces flowing and rushing together, eternally changing, eternally flooding back." This depiction by Nietzsche has always put me in mind of the infamous "lava lamps" popular in the 1960s. When turned on, the heated globules drift through the thinner gunk, bulging out in some areas, separating in others, but as long as the lamp is on and the globules moving, there is a constant shifting and changing. However unromantic my analogy may be, I think it captures some essential aspects of Nietzsche's aphorism. We might be tempted to call the thicker globules "things," although for Nietzsche they would not be fundamentally different from the thinner gunk. Analogously, we are tempted to separate liquids from solids, yet materialists would agree that both are composed of molecules. So for Nietzsche, rather than talk about molecules, atoms, or quarks, he talks about forces. Some of these forces combine to create "things" like rocks, some combine to create "things" like worms, and some combine to create "things" like human beings. And if you think it is difficult for Nietzsche to explain how "force" can create such diverse things as animate and inanimate things and conscious from nonconscious life, materialists have the same problem. Even more, materialists have a harder time explaining motion than force theorists, so it would seem that Nietzsche's explanation has at least one advantage over classical materialist theories.

Nietzsche has a relatively long history of being against materialism, which had been shaped by some of the scientific and philosophical theories advanced in the mid–nineteenth century and earlier. Nietzsche first encountered the work of Friedrich Lange in 1866, six years before *The Birth of Tragedy out of the Spirit of Music* was published. Lange was one of numerous theoretical scientists who were investigating the possibility that the world was the result of forces acting on each other at the molecular level. More importantly, these forces were not divinely directed. The forces were simply "dynamic" in themselves. There was no telos, no aim or goal, to their dynamics; the motions of the forces were described in terms of attraction and repellence. That Nietzsche was aware of these scientific theories has been well demonstrated.[1] What we need to see at this point is how they are incorporated into Nietzsche's own writings.

Nietzsche wrote in a letter to a friend that he read Lange's *History of Materialism* and was impressed with it. Through it, Nietzsche became acquainted with numerous thinkers on dynamic theory, from Ruggiero Boscovich to Ernst Mach. What these theorists held in common, along with Lange, who was undoubtedly promoting their thoughts, was that there is no such thing as substance. The debate on whether the universe is composed of molecules or something smaller was entirely moot to these thinkers; molecules, atoms, or anything purporting to be the substantial building blocks of physical substances were the stuff of fantasy. According to these thinkers, there is no substance, there is only force.

We have seen that Nietzsche equates the world with a "sea of forces" and "will to power." Is will to power simply identical to this flux of forces? Unfortunately, the answer to this question is both yes and no. The "yes" side occurs because for both "forces" and "will to power" there is motion going on, so in this sense they are the same.

The "no" answer to the question occurs for two reasons. First, according to Nietzsche, we cannot *explain* will to power by equating it with "forces" because the idea of "forces" is no clearer or more informative than will to power. For Nietzsche, "force" cannot be demonstrated:

> Has a *force* ever been demonstrated? No, only *effects* translated into a completely foreign language. We are so used, however, to regularity in succession that its oddity no longer seems odd to us. (WP, 620)

> Ist jemals schon eine Kraft constatirt? Nein, sondern Wirkungen, ubersetzt in eine vollig fremde Sprache. Das Regelmassige im Hintereinander hat uns aber so verwohnt, dass wir uns *über das Wunderliche daran nicht wundern.* [KGW VIII/1 2(59), 141]

We cannot perceive "pure" force. All we can perceive are the effects, the results, of forces. Similarly, there is no "pure" will to power; will to power is nothing other than these effects. There is no "pure," "raw," or "naked" will to power to which the phrase refers. There are just the effects, as the following passage from *On the Genealogy of Morals* demonstrates:

> A quantum of force is equivalent to a quantum of drive, will, effect—more, it is nothing other than precisely this very driving, willing, effecting, and only owing to the seduction of language (and of the fundamental errors of reason that are petrified in it) which conceives and misconceives all effects as conditioned by something that causes effects, by a "subject," can it appear otherwise. . . . [T]he popular mind separates lightning from its flash and takes the latter for an *action,* for the operation of a subject called lightning. . . . But there is no such substratum; there is no "being" behind doing, effecting, becoming; "the doer" is merely a fiction added to the deed—the deed is everything. (GM I, 13)

> Ein Quantum Kraft ist ein eben solches Quantum Trieb, Wille, Wirken—vielmehr, es ist gar nichts anderes als eben dieses Treiben, Wollen, Wirken selbst, und nur unter der Verführung der Sprache (und der in ihr versteinerten Grundirrthümer der Vernunft), welche alles Wirken als bedingt durch ein Wirkendes, durch ein "Subjekt" versteht und missversteht, kann es anders erscheinen. . . . [D]as Volk den Blitz von seinem Leuchten trennt und letzteres als *Thun,* als Wirkung eines Subjekts nimmt, das Blitz heisst. . . . Aber es giebt kein solches Substrat; es giebt kein "Sein" hinter dem Thun, Wirken, Werden; "der Thäter" ist zum Thun bloss hinzugedichtet,—das Thun ist Alles. [KGW VI/2, 293]

This passage shows that the quantum of power is not only recognizable by "its effect," it is nothing other than "its effect." The lightning is nothing other than "its" flash. In fact, to even speak of the flash as an effect caused by the lightning is erroneous (hence my scare quote marks), for to speak of something as an effect is to immediately imply a cause. But, remember, Nietzsche denies the existence of causes or effects:

> Cause and effect: such a duality probably never exists; in truth we are confronted by a continuum out of which we isolate a couple of pieces, just as we perceive

motion only as isolated points and then infer it without ever actually seeing it. The suddenness with which many effects stand out misleads us; actually, it is sudden only for us. In this moment of suddenness there is an infinite number of processes that elude us. An intellect that could see cause and effect as a continuum and a flux and not, as we do, in terms of an arbitrary division and dismemberment, would repudiate the concept of cause and effect and deny all conditionality. (GS, 112)

Ursache und Wirkung: eine solche Zweiheit giebt es wahrscheinlich nie,—in Wahrheit steht ein continuum vor uns, von dem wir ein paar Stücke isoliren; so wie wir eine Bewegung immer nur als isolirte Puncte wahrnehemen, also eigentlich nicht sehen, sondern erschlissen. Die Plötzlichkeit, mit der sich viele Wirkungen abheben, führt uns irre; es ist aber nur eine Plötzlichkeit für uns. Es giebt eine unendliche Menge von Vorgängen in dieser Secunde der Plötzlichkeit, die uns entgehen. Ein Intellect, der Ursache und Wirkung als continuum, nicht nach unserer Art als willkürliches Zertheilt—und Zerstücktsein, sähe, der den Fluss des Geschehens sähe,—würde den Begriff Ursache und Wirkung verwerfen und all Bedingtheit leugnen. [KGW V/2, 151]

According to Nietzsche, we artificially carve or bracket out sections of the continuous flux of becoming and set these sections in another contrived or artificial relationship, either as a cause or an effect. But cause and effect are orders imposed on becoming by the human mind; they do not exist in the world. So Nietzsche talks about *a*ffects of will to power to differentiate his conception of the world as becoming from the conventional scientific conception of the world as conforming to causal laws.

Will to power, then, does not lurk behind affects, causing affects. Will to power consists of the affects themselves. It is the event by which becoming and affects are recognizable. The relationship between will to power and affects—actions and relationships among actions—is one of identity. So to say will to power causes affects or is the force behind affects is to be seduced by the preposition *of* in "affects of will to power." Yet our language leaves us little alternative for expressing Nietzsche's position other than "affects of will to power." The *of* is not possessive, for example, the daughter of George, but, rather, constitutive, for example, the army of men, where the army simply *consists in* men. Take away the men, and there is no pure "army" left over. Will to power is analogous to an onion, where the whole onion is the world of becoming at any given moment. The layers of the onion correspond to specific events—affects of will to power. By stripping away the layers of the onion, we hope to arrive at its core, its essence. But, of course, there is no core; the onion simply consists in its layers. Analogously, we cannot strip away the affects of will to power hoping to discover "pure" will to power devoid of "its" affects; will to power is nothing other than affects, and the world is nothing other than the totality of affects at any given moment. Looking for will to power "underneath" or "behind" things or events is like looking for lightning underneath its flash. Because lightning *is* the flash, there is nothing underneath it, behind it, or supporting it.

The second reason that "forces" cannot simply be equated with "will to power" stems from Nietzsche's belief that "forces" cannot be random. Both Lange and

Schopenhauer conceive of "force" as being completely chaotic. According to Nietzsche, this conception is senseless:

> The victorious concept "force" by means of which our physicists have created God and the world, still needs to be completed: an inner will be ascribed to it, which I designate as "will to power," i.e., as an insatiable desire to manifest power; or as the employment and exercise of power, as a creative drive, etc. Physicists cannot eradicate "action at a distance" from their principles; nor can they eradicate a repellent force (or an attracting one). There is nothing for it: one is obliged to understand all motion, all "appearances," all "laws," only as symptoms of an inner event and to employ man as an analogy to this end. In the case of an animal, it is possible to trace all its drives to the will to power; likewise all functions of organic life to this one source. (WP, 619)

> Der siegreiche Begriff "Kraft," mit dem unsere Physiker Gott und die Welt geschaffen haben, bedarf noch einer Ergänzung: es muss ihm eine innere Welt zugesprochen werden, welche ich bezeichne als "Willen zur Macht," d.h. als unersättliches Verlangen nach Bezeigung der Macht; oder Verwendung, Ausübung der Macht, als schöpferischen Trieb usw. Die Physiker werden die "Wirkung in die Ferne" aus ihren Principien nicht los: ebensowenig eine abstossende Kraft (oder anziehende). Es hilft nichts: man muss alle Bewegungen, alle "Erscheinungen," alle "Gesetze" nur als Symptome eines innerlichen Gesechehens fassen und sich der Analogie des Menschen zu Ende bedienen. Am Thier ist es möglich, aus dem Willen zur Macht alle seine Triebe abzuleiten: ebenso alle Funktionen des organischen Lebens aus dieser Einen Quelle. [KGW VII/3, 36(31), 287]

Here Nietzsche indicates that mere force is not enough to account for life as he sees it. He claims that even physicists—"mechanistic scientists"—must attribute some directional impetus to their concept of force. Contrary to Schopenhauer, Nietzsche's "will" is not blind or random. Nietzsche believes there must be an explanation why force goes one way rather than another. Force needs a *conatus* or an inherent directional impulse. Physicists may attempt to explain such impetus as "attraction" or "repulsion," but Nietzsche accuses these terms of being too anthropomorphic:

> "Attraction" and "repulsion" in a purely mechanistic sense are complete fictions: a word. We cannot think of an attraction divorced from an intention.—The will to take possession of a thing or to defend oneself against it and repel it—*that* "we understand": that would be an interpretation of which we could make use. (WP, 627)

> "Anziehen" und "Abstossen" in rein mechanischem Sinne ist ein vollständige Fiktion: ein Wort. Wir können uns ohne eine Absicht ein Anziehen nicht denken.— Den Willen sich einer Sache zu bemächtigen oder gegen ihre Macht sich zu wehren und sie zurück-zustossen—*das* "verstehen wir": das wäre eine Interpretation, die wir brauchen könnten. [KGW VIII/1, 2(83), 100–01]

We humans ascribe an "inner event" for our own motions—the will. Thus, the motions of other objects must have inner events as well, if we are to make sense of these nonhuman motions. Scientists call these inner events "attraction," "repulsion," "cause," and so on, but, to Nietzsche, these words are anthropomorphic terms humans impose on the world. Does will to power avoid Nietzsche's criticism of anthropomorphism? It does not appear to; in fact, it seems to emphasize anthropomorphism. The phrase contains the word *will*. That word, too, seems highly anthropomorphic and subject to Nietzsche's own criticism of it as we have seen in *Beyond Good and Evil* 19 in the last chapter. In addition, as discussed in *Beyond Good and Evil* 36, Nietzsche purposely (whether in irony or not) thrusts this "inner world" onto the material world.[2] Nietzsche believes some impetus to this force is required, or else why does force move in the direction that it does? Because humans believe that their "will" propels their movements, "will" is the origin of all movement. And the teleological end that propels force to go in a certain direction rather than another, according to Nietzsche, is power. Hence Nietzsche calls his idea "will to power." The question now becomes whether Nietzsche can explain the entire world as will to power.

It is apparent that Nietzsche's thinking mirrors Lange's endorsement of Boscovich and others' antimaterialist theories. What we call "things" are force groupings and not material "stuff":

> "Things" do not behave regularly, according to a *rule*: there are no things (—they are fictions). (WP, 634)

> "Die Dinge" betragen sich nicht regelmassig, nicht nach einer *Regel*: es giebt keine Dinge (—das ist unsere Fiktion). [KGW VIII/3, 14(79), 49]

> No things remain but only dynamic quanta, in a relation of tension to all other dynamic quanta; their essence lies in their relation to all other quanta, in their "effect" upon the same. (WP, 635)

> [S]o bleiben keine Dinge übrig, sondern dynamische Quanta, in einem Spannungverhältniss zu allen anderen dynamischen Quanten: deren Wesen in ihrem Verhaltniss zu allen anderen Quanten besteht, in ihrem "Wirken" auf dieselben. [KGW VIII/3, 14(79), 51]

> Linguistic means of expression are useless for expressing "becoming"; it accords with our inevitable need to preserve ourselves to posit a crude world of stability, of "things," etc. We may venture to speak of atoms and monads in a relative sense; and it is certain that the smallest world is the most durable—There is no will: there are treaty drafts of will that are constantly increasing or losing their power. (WP, 715)

> Die Ausdrucksmittel der Sprache sind unbrauchbar, um das Werden auszudrücken: es gehort zu unserem *unablöslichen Bedurfniss der Erhaltung,* beständig die eine grobere Welt von Bleibend[em], von "Dingen" usw. zu stezen. Relativ, dürfen wir von Atomen und Monaden reden: und gewiss ist, dass die *kleinste Welt an Dauer die dauerhafteste ist* . . . es *giebt keinen Willen*: es giebt Willens-Punktationen, die beständig ihre Macht mehren oder verlieren. [KGW VIII/2, 11(73), 278–79]

These passages indicate at least two things. First, our supposedly common notion of a "thing" as a complete, separate unity distinct from other "things" is mistaken. According to Nietzsche, there are only amounts or quanta of energy that at certain times and in certain areas become more concentrated. These "constellations" or federations of energy—Nietzsche calls them *Willespunktuationen*[3]—are what we designate as "things," but they are not really separate entities. They merely have a certain quantum of energy that may be significantly greater than the surrounding quanta. This concentration of energy is sufficient for us to perceive it, and we designate it as a "thing," but "its" only difference is the quantum of force. There is no *essential* difference between people, daffodils, or pencils.

Second, what we commonly call "things" are in constant flux. What we perceive as stable entities are actually quanta of fluctuating forces. They have no "being" as Nietzsche uses *being*—as a set of fixed or permanent characteristics. Of course, "things" have Being—they *exist* as centers of forces, but Nietzsche is using *being* to contrast with *becoming,* whereby *being* signifies permanence and stability.

It is difficult to imagine things that seem so permanent, for example, the rock of Gibraltar, to be in constant states of flux. What we call "inanimate objects," like keys, just lie on the table where we put them; they continue to unlock the same lock day after day. If keys were in a constant state of flux, wouldn't we expect that the same key would never unlock the same lock more than perhaps every fifty years or so? Also, wouldn't it be impossible to say "same key" or "same lock" because the "things" would be constantly changing?

If we are to make any sense of how "inanimate objects" are will to power, we must wrench our thoughts about them in a radical way. Generally we think of "objects" like books and keys as stable and inactive until something changes them, like fire burning or melting them. We think their natural or usual state is cohesive and fixed, and things only arouse our curiosity when they change. But what if we reverse this? Then we would ponder not how things change but how they manage to stay relatively stable. For Nietzsche, the question may not be "Why do things change?" but "Why do things stay together?"

Nietzsche's answer to this question, of course, would be will to power. Now we are in a position to make sense of this answer. A "thing," being a "power-constellation," is constantly struggling to maintain that constellation in the midst of "its" surrounding forces. This struggle can be viewed in two ways. One way is that the power-constellation struggles to maintain "its" constellation amid the potentially destructive forces around "it"—gravity, sunlight, air pressure, temperature, and so forth. In this view, these other forces (power-constellations) are attempting to destroy the present power-constellation.

The other view is that these same forces are what holds the power-constellation together. The power-constellation is "itself" trying to disband, but the surrounding forces prohibit "it" from doing so. Nietzsche himself never explicitly advances either of these models, but either one is consistent with his remarks about "things" and "substances."

Nietzsche's world is a world of change, of becoming. So if a key remains for the most part intact after the friction of the lock, "it" is evidencing "its" will to power. Again, it is important to remember that it is not the case that this struggle is intentional—the key is not consciously willing itself to stay together. But if the world is a "sea of forces" and is in constant flux, we might expect "inanimate objects" to change much more than we perceive they do. Thus, Nietzsche's will to power would have to explain the apparent stability of these objects. "Thing" will to power, however severely limited when compared with organic and especially human will to power, is enough to hold objects together.

What effect does all this have on the meaning of will to power? At the end of the previous chapter, we had good support for the view that (1) will to power is a teleological explanation for all human and other organic activity, (2) will to power is dualistic in that there are active and reactive ways of gaining power, and (3) mere growth is evidence of power. As many "inanimate objects" exhibit no growth or "behavior," except just sitting there, it would seem that a teleological explanation would have no place in the inorganic realm. But we have discovered that, for Nietzsche, there are no such things as inanimate objects in the sense of separate, nonactive substances. What we call "things" are fluctuating power-constellations and are constantly active; therefore, a teleological explanation may be appropriate, if these teleological explanations for nonhuman actions can be taken as dead metaphors of teleological explanations for human actions.[4] The main feature of teleological explanations for nonhuman actions is just that the consequence of the action somehow plays a part in the action itself, for example, bringing about or initiating the action. For Nietzsche, the consequence that plays a part in initiating an action is power, whether it is the power of remaining a power-constellation or the power of the outside forces keeping the power-constellation intact.

If will to power is Nietzsche's metaphysics, then nonhuman organic life and behavior must also be reducible to will to power. At the end of the last chapter, we believed that Nietzsche meant to explain more than human behavior with his references to "life" being will to power. The *Nachlass* notes, however, provide a much more detailed account of how will to power can explain organic behavior. In fact, these *Nachlass* entries seem to differ stylistically from the more metaphorical and ambiguous passages from the writings Nietzsche authorized for publication. In the works Nietzsche published himself, will to power is mentioned as an explanation for organic behavior, but Nietzsche leaves it to the reader to make sense of it. By contrast, in the *Nachlass* material Nietzsche explicitly details how hunger, happiness, self-preservation, and even mechanistic explanations of nonhuman, organic life can be interpreted as derivations of will to power:

> Let us take the simplest case, that of primitive nourishment: the protoplasm extends
> its pseudopodia in search of something that resists it—not from hunger but from

will to power. Thereupon it attempts to overcome, appropriate, assimilate what it encounters: what one calls "nourishment" is merely a derivative phenomenon, an application of the original will to become *stronger*. (WP, 702)

Nehmen wir den einfachsten Fall, den der primitiven Ernährung: das Protoplasma streckt seine Pseudopodien aus, um nach etwas zu suchen, was ihm widersteht— nicht aus Hunger, sondern aus Willen zur Macht. Darauf macht es den Versuch, daselbe zu überwinden, sich anzueignen, sich einzuverleiben:—das, was man "Ernährung" nennt, ist bloss eine Folge-Erscheinung, eine Nutzanwendung jenes ursprünglichen Willens, *stärker* zu werden. [KGW VIII/3 14(174), 152]

One cannot ascribe the most basic and primeval activities of protoplasm to will to self-preservation, for it takes into itself absurdly more than would be required to preserve it, and, above all, it does not thereby "preserve itself," it falls apart. (WP, 651)

Man kann die unterste und ursprünglichste Thätigkeit im Protoplasma nicht aus einem Willen zur Selbsterhaltung ableiten: den es nimmt auf eine unsinnige Art mehr in sich hinein, als die Erhaltung bedingen würde: und vor allem, es "erhält sich" damit eben *nicht,* sondern *zerfällt.* [KGW VIII/2, 11(121), 299]

A protoplasm divides in two when its power is no longer adequate to control what it has appropriated. (WP, 654)

Die Theilung eines Protoplasma in 2 tritt ein, wenn die Macht nicht mehr ausreicht. [KGW VIII/1, 1(118), 34]

"Man strives after happiness," e.g.—how much of that is true? In order to understand what "life" is, what kind of striving and tension life is, the formula must apply as well to trees and plants as to animals. . . . For what do the trees in a jungle fight each other? For "happiness"?—For *power!* (WP, 704)

"Der Mensch strebt nach Glück" z.B.—was ist daran wahr! Um zu verstehn, was Leben ist, welche Art Streben und Spannung Leben ist, muss die Formel so gut von Baum und Pflanze als vom Thier gelten. . . .Worum kampfen die Baume eines Urwaldes mit einander? Um "Glück"?—Um *Macht.* [KGW VIII/2, 11(111), 294]

These entries echo the textual evidence from the writings Nietzsche authorized for publication that Nietzsche extended his notion of will to power to all organisms and that will to power is meant to contrast with other, competing explanations of organic behavior. These other accounts would explain why an organism acted in a certain way by saying that the organism sought to preserve itself, make itself happy, or feed itself. Nietzsche rejected all these explanations as the basic motivations of organisms. Instead, he saw them all as corollaries of another, presumably more basic motivation—will to power. These other explanations are inadequate because they cannot, by themselves, account for all organic behavior.

For Nietzsche, to say that pleasure is the basic motivation for even human, much less other organisms', behavior is a mistake. He believes that if our choice is to be between pleasure and displeasure, it is "constructive" displeasure that would motivate people. "Pleasure" is, for Nietzsche, an increase in the feeling of power. This is possible only if one has overcome some resistance. Seeking a resistance to overcome (what we usually consider "displeasure" because it is an obstacle to our will), then, is the necessary prerequisite for pleasure:

> Man does *not* seek pleasure and does *not* avoid displeasure. . . . Displeasure, an obstacle to its will to power, is therefore a normal fact, the normal ingredient of every organic event; every victory, every feeling of pleasure, every event, presupposes a resistance overcome. (WP, 702)

> Der Mensch sucht *nicht* die Lust und vermeidet *nicht* die Unlust. . . . Die Unlust, als Hemmung seines Willens zur Macht, ist also ein normales Faktum, das normale Ingredienz jedes organischen Geschehens, der Mensch weicht ihr nicht aus, er hat sie vielmehr fortwährend nöthig: jeder Sieg, jedes Lustgefühl, jedes Geschehen setzt einen überwundenen Widerstand voraus. [KGW VIII/3, 14(174), 152]

Those who equate all displeasure with losing to the obstacle have, according to Nietzsche, "confused displeasure with one *kind* of displeasure." This kind of displeasure can be called "destructive" because it leads to a "profound diminution" in the feeling of power and "exhaustion." However, "constructive" displeasure leads to increased stimulation—somewhat like the rush of energy or the elation one feels when one plays a particularly tough sporting event. The intense competition, win or lose, is invigorating. The mistake is to conflate the two kinds of displeasure and then claim that people are fundamentally motivated to avoid displeasure. As with our examples of selfishness and pity in the previous chapter, displeasure cannot simply be stuck in the "avoid" category. There is "healthy" displeasure as well as "sick" displeasure. Only "destructive" displeasure is avoided, according to Nietzsche, because it does not result in an increase in the feeling of power.

In many cases people purposely pursue painful activities. If seeking pleasure and avoiding displeasure were the fundamental motivations of humans, this principle could not account for these people's behavior. However, pleasure as a derivative of a feeling of an increase in power, in overcoming resistance, could account for their behavior. Thus, pleasure cannot be the most basic motivation for organisms, according to Nietzsche, because it is the result of something more fundamental—striving for an increase in the feeling of power.

Because Nietzsche lumps human behavior within the broader category of organic behavior, any basic motivation must also account for not only human behavior but all organic behavior. Thus, the "happiness" explanation of behavior, which might seem reasonable as an explanation of basic human motivation, seems ludicrous when applied to plants, insects, bacteria, and other organisms we consider to be nonconscious. Thus, will to power can explain more behavior than happiness can.

In Nietzsche's account of protoplasm behavior, self-preservation and hunger also cannot be the explanations of basic organic behavior. This is illustrated by the protoplasm's continual processing of food. Nietzsche believes that the amoeba eats "absurdly" more than it needs to maintain its existence:

> It is not possible to take hunger as the *primum mobile,* any more than self-preservation. To understand hunger as a consequence of undernourishment means: hunger as a consequence of a will to power that no longer achieves mastery. It is by no means a question of replacing a loss—only later, as a result of the division of labor, after the will to power has learned to take other roads to its satisfaction, is an organism's need to appropriate *reduced* to hunger, to the need to replace what has been lost. (WP, 652)

> Es ist nicht möglich, den *Hunger* als primum mobile zu nehmen: ebenso wenig als die Selbsterhaltung: der Hunger als Folge der Unterernährung aufgefasst, heisst: der Hunger als Folge eines *nicht mehr Herr werdenden* Willens zur Macht . . . es handelt sich durchaus nicht um eine Wiederherstellung eines Verlustes,—erst spät, in Folge Arbeitstheilung, nachdem der Wille zur Macht ganz andere Wege zu seiner Befriedigung einschlagen lernt, wird das Aneignungsbedürfniss des Organismus *reduzirt* auf den Hunger, auf das Wiederersatzbedürfniss des Verlorenen. [KGW VIII/3, 14(174), 153]

Hunger becomes a motive (but never a prime motive) only when an organism's will to power has directed the organism toward other areas to such an extent that it needs to take in energy in order to accomplish other tasks. Nourishment only takes place when nourishment becomes the way to increase power.

Self-preservation cannot be the primary explanation for organic behavior, either, because some organisms eat much more than they need to survive. If one of these organisms merely sought to preserve itself, it would stop eating when it had acquired enough food to sustain itself. Instead, it eats much more, and the extra food results in the organism's division—an occurrence that would not happen if the organism only preserved itself: it would preserve itself as a single-celled organism. The amoeba's actions, instead, evince appropriation and exploitation of its environment; it grows, multiplies—it exhibits will to power.

In the botanical kingdom, plants' photokinesis can be interpreted as will to power rather than self-preservation. Turn a plant away from the window, and its leaves will twist around back toward the window. The amount of sunlight in the room may be quite sufficient for the plant to survive, to preserve itself, but it still seeks out the window. The plant is striving for the maximum amount of sunlight for its photosynthesis. Photosynthesis promotes more growth of the plant, and growth is evidence of power over the environment. The plant is not merely surviving (self-preservation) but also growing, which can be better explained by will to power than by an instinct for self-preservation.

Nietzsche also adds that hunger and happiness cannot be sufficient explanations for organic behavior. "Pleasure" cannot account for some beings' search for nonpleasurable activities. "Hunger" cannot account for some beings' overeating. "Self-preservation" cannot account for some beings' active pursuit of dangerous situations. And "mechanics" (scientific explanations) cannot account for spontaneous and aggressive activity, only reactivity. While Nietzsche does not discard these explanations as possible accounts of some organic behavior, he does reject each of them as the sole explanation for all organic behavior. Further, he claims that will to power can account for all four of these supposedly fundamental explanations. Because these four explanations are derivations of will to power, will to power is more fundamental than any of them.

If all accounts of behavior and, indeed, the entire world are not only explained by but *are* will to power, it seems clear that will to power is a metaphysical principle in the sense that everything can be reducible to it. Yet there are some Nietzsche scholars who reject the notion that will to power is Nietzsche's metaphysics. Why is there such a controversy surrounding will to power's metaphysical status? Aside from the fact that philosophers have a difficult time agreeing on what counts as metaphysics to begin with, Nietzsche presents us with two additional problems.

First, Nietzsche has left a long record of criticism against metaphysics. From *Human, All-Too-Human* on, Nietzsche maintains a consistent critique of metaphysics. His criticism is not of the specific metaphysical principles or theories offered; his criticism is of the entire enterprise itself. In several places, he calls himself an "anti-metaphysician."[5] Why would he then turn around and present will to power as his metaphysics? I do not believe Nietzsche is that stupid or forgetful. Second, the source of the aphorisms that put will to power so clearly in the metaphysical arena come from the *Nachlass,* and there are many problems connected with Nietzsche's *Nachlass.* Why does it present such problems for Nietzsche scholarship?

The *Nachlass* can be divided roughly into three different kinds of works. The first kind comprises the works Nietzsche was editing right before his collapse. These works are *Ecce Homo, Nietzsche Contra Wagner,* and *The Antichrist,* and they are so polished that we can safely take them as equal in status to the works that Nietzsche had already published or that were being published at the time of his collapse (e.g., *Twilight of the Idols*).

The second kind are Nietzsche's early, finished pieces that were never published, the so-called *Schriften*—primarily his lectures and writings while he was employed at Basel. These pieces are presumably complete and polished; however, Nietzsche chose not to publish them. These works do not affect our present inquiry, for, again, will to power was a relatively late concept for Nietzsche.

The third kind of work consists of Nietzsche's notes. These notes vary from near essay length and form, to extremely sketchy outlines of various projects, to single sentences or sentence fragments. Nietzsche's notebooks look like anyone's notebook—there are passages lined out, words jotted in the margins, and some overwriting. The famous aphorism where Nietzsche declares that this world is will to power and nothing besides is entirely crossed out. Also, Nietzsche often liked to write back to front in his notebooks. Karl Schlecta was unaware of this tendency, so the third volume of his collection should be read with some care; the order of the *Nachlass* notes is unreliable. Some of the passages in the *Nachlass* can be found with only very minor revisions in the books Nietzsche had published. Surely these notes must be regarded as rough drafts of the published aphorisms, for he painstakingly recopied his books in his neatest handwriting right before he sent them to the publisher.

The notes that did not find their way into publication in any form present the problem. I shall refer to these notes as the "controversial notes." What are we to make of these? Are they rough drafts of some future work that Nietzsche was unable to realize because of his illness? If so, some of these controversial notes would have been waiting for years and would raise the question of why Nietzsche chose not to publish them earlier. Even if we consider them rough drafts of future works, it remains unclear whether we should consider what is written in these notes to be as indicative of what Nietzsche thought as the works he authorized for publication. Sometimes what is written in the unpublished notes on a particular topic is very different from what is written on that topic in the published works.

In his book *Nietzsche's Existential Imperative,* Bernd Magnus examines Nietzsche's notion of eternal recurrence as found in the works Nietzsche authorized for publication and as found in the *Nachlass* notes. The difference in the way eternal recurrence is presented in each case is profound. In the works Nietzsche authorized for publication, eternal recurrence is couched within a hypothetical "what if." This has led some Nietzsche commentators to conclude that eternal recurrence is a normative claim that Nietzsche is advancing. On the other hand, in many of the *Nachlass* notes, eternal recurrence is considered "empirically." This leads some other Nietzsche commentators to believe that eternal recurrence is a cosmological principle. So the difference between the published and unpublished writings on eternal recurrence is startling and leads to two very different and incompatible interpretations. If eternal recurrence is actually the case (the cosmological view), then the normative imperative to act *as if* it were true loses its command. This problem convinces Magnus that neither interpretation is correct, and he devises his own. Magnus notes that even the styles of the published and unpublished material differ: the former has graphic imagery and poetic intensity and immediacy, and the latter tends to be declarative, argumentative, and unpoetic. So in this one case at least, the unpublished material bears a striking difference from the published material. And while the stylistic differences are not as apparent in the case of will to power as they are in that of eternal recurrence, we have seen that the scope of will to power as an explanation is greatly expanded in the *Nachlass*. If the controversial notes on will to power are analogous to those in the eternal recurrence situation, then including them will bias our interpretation of will to power in ways that Nietzsche may have rejected himself.

Perhaps we should not consider any of these controversial *Nachlass* notes to be indicative of Nietzsche's ultimate position on any given topic. These notes could be ideas that Nietzsche wrote down but later decided against publishing and, thus, were never meant to be published. Is there any evidence that Nietzsche was saving them or had no intention of using them?

There is no conclusive evidence one way or another. R. J. Hollingdale, who considers all the controversial notes "reject material,"[6] offers only this story as evidence. When Nietzsche left Sils Maria for the last time in 1888, he told his landlord, Durish, that the pile of loose notes in his room could be burned. Instead, Durish saved them and handed them out to touring Nietzschephiles. When an account of this was written in *Magazine für Literatur* in 1893, Nietzsche's sister, Elisabeth, insisted that the remaining notes be sent to her. At this time Nietzsche was already four years into his illness and was incapable of managing his own affairs. Elisabeth had declared herself "executrix" of his literary estate. She also had delusions of becoming the ultimate authority for all interpretations of Nietzsche's writing, and she was in the process of compiling the notes that would eventually be published under the title *The Will to Power.* Whether any Sils Maria notes were included in *The Will to Power* is impossible to determine with certainty; however, anything written between June and 20 September 1888 would be particularly suspect, for that was the length of Nietzsche's last stay at Sils Maria.

Hollingdale uses this incident as evidence that Nietzsche was not interested in the fate of his unpublished notes, but even this story is not without its problems. As Magnus writes in "The Use and Abuse of *The Will to Power,*" the *Magazine für Literatur* article is about a version of the preface for *Twilight of the Idols* that Nietzsche was editing at the time. However, Magnus and Michael Platt did find a version of Hollingdale's story in Carl Bernoulli's *Franz Overbeck und Friedrich Nietzsche: Ein Freundschaft,* which has a 1908 printing date.

All in all, this one dubious example seems insufficient grounds to reject all the controversial *Nachlass* notes. Remember, Nietzsche was sending *Twilight of the Idols* off to the publisher at this time, and his reportedly "rejected" notes might simply be the less neatly written notes of *Twilight of the Idols.* The article about Nietzsche's notes that *is* in the *Magazine für Literatur* concerns a slightly altered portion of the preface to *Twilight of the Idols.* That would provide support for this latter interpretation. At this point, there is no evidence that all the controversial notes should be rejected.

Another complication with the *Nachlass* notes is the accuracy of the notes themselves. Some of these notes were scribbled down while Nietzsche was on walks or anywhere else he happened to be. The handwriting of many of the notes is difficult to make out. Also, as his illness was progressing and his eyesight was getting worse, Nietzsche's handwriting deteriorated as well. One of Nietzsche's good friends and protégés, Heinrich Köselitz (Peter Gast), was assigned by Elisabeth to decipher these notes, and he did his best to translate them into something legible and understandable—Nietzsche sometimes dropped prepositions or used abbreviations. Karl Schlechta suggests that Köselitz may have made stylistic changes by dropping or adding words or phrases.

Along this same line, Elisabeth has also been charged with tampering with her brother's notes. Erich Podach and Karl Schlechta are particularly suspicious of the accuracy of the *Nachlass* material; Schlechta documents forgeries by Elisabeth.

However, Arthur Danto thinks that any changes were wholly stylistic in nature and that any philosophical content has remained intact. He maintains that Elisabeth was more interested in preserving her honor than in preserving Nietzsche's philosophy. Why would she stoop to forgery?

Elisabeth's husband was Bernhard Förster, an ardent anti-Semite. Nietzsche had been against Elisabeth marrying him, and he had threatened that he would cut off communication with and affection for her if she married Förster. There were a few bitter and nasty letters exchanged between them at this time. Förster went to Paraguay to establish an Aryan-pure colony. From there Förster wrote anti-Semitic articles that were published back in Germany and also solicited funds for maintaining and expanding the colony. When Förster committed suicide, Elisabeth returned to Germany deep in the debts that her husband had incurred. Publishing her brother's writings was a source of some income, for Nietzsche had begun to become a kind of folk hero because of his mysterious illness. Could God be exacting revenge for Nietzsche's anti-Christian remarks? No doubt Elisabeth encouraged this image. At one time tours to the Nietzsche family's home included a glimpse of the famous philosopher himself helplessly propped up in bed. Elisabeth was certainly instrumental in fostering the belief that Nietzsche was anti-Semitic and pro-Reich, mainly by quoting him out of context. Although Nietzsche did make some scathing remarks about Jews in context, these were usually immediately followed by even more scathing remarks about Germans. These latter remarks never seemed to be included in the World War II propaganda.

Despite Schlechta's documentation of forgeries on Elisabeth's part, Walter Kaufmann notes that all of Schlechta's evidence is confined to letters; there is no evidence that Nietzsche's notebook entries were changed significantly philosophically. Still, it does make one pause. Elisabeth was quite conscious of public opinion. As Nietzsche's writings became more popular, she realized what total control over her brother's literary estate could mean to her. Elisabeth somehow got their mother to sign over her rights to the material and profits to her. It was Elisabeth who decided what of Nietzsche's would be published and when. She set herself up as the sole authority in Nietzsche interpretation. Many Nietzsche commentators are convinced that she delayed the publication of *Ecce Homo,* which was entirely complete before Nietzsche's collapse, until 1908, nearly twenty years after he wrote it, so she could establish her authority in interpreting Nietzsche's works rather than let Nietzsche speak for himself.

All of this adds considerable confusion to how to interpret the material amassed under the title *The Will to Power.* This book was published originally with only some 400 or so aphorisms. Five years later, a second, expanded edition appeared with a total of 1,067 aphorisms. This is the book that Kaufmann and Hollingdale translated into English. All Nietzsche commentators agree that the book *The Will to Power* that Elisabeth published is not the book that Nietzsche promises in a footnote in *On the Genealogy of Morals*:

I shall probe these things more thoroughly and severely in another connection (under the title "On the History of European Nihilism," it will be contained in a work in progress: *The Will to Power: Attempt at a Revaluation of All Values*). (GM III, 27)

Jene Dinge sollen von mir in einem andren Zusammenhange gründlicher und härter angefasst werden (unter dem Titel "Zur Geschichte des europaischen Nihilismus"; ich verweise dafür ein werk, das ich vorbereite: *Der wille zur Macht, Versuch einer Umwerthung aller Werthe*). [KGW VI/2, 426–27]

Yet the belief persists today that our present edition of *The Will to Power* contains a good cross section of Nietzsche's notes. There are several problems with this belief.

First, Giorgio Colli and Mazzino Montinari, who spent more than a decade laboriously reconstructing Nietzsche's writings, are convinced that Nietzsche abandoned his project of writing a book entitled *The Will to Power*. But Nietzsche did consider it for some time. He collected and wrote 374 entries under that title in mid-February 1888. According to one of his first provisional drafts, dated 1887, one of the main sections of *The Will to Power* was to be called "Attempt at a Revaluation of All Values." In a later *Nachlass* entry, Nietzsche removes "Attempt at a Revaluation of All Values" from a section heading and uses it as the subtitle of the book itself; this is roughly around the time of the *On the Genealogy of Morals* parenthetical remark. Still later, Nietzsche appears to have abandoned the title *The Will to Power* altogether.

The succession of *Nachlass* notes suggests that Nietzsche decided on a new title for his book—*The Revaluation of All Values*. In the outline for this project, the first part was to be called "The Antichrist."[7] Colli and Montinari believe that Nietzsche started working on *The Revaluation of All Values* in early September 1888. From the middle of September to the end of that month, Nietzsche polished sections 29 to 62 of *The Antichrist*, at that point the first book of *The Revaluation of All Values*. Nietzsche then had plans to write the second book, tentatively entitled "The Free Spirit," but he interrupted them to write *Ecce Homo*. By the end of November, Nietzsche had switched the titles, with the main title of his book being *The Antichrist* and "The Revaluation of All Value" being the subtitle. Finally, at the end of December, or possibly at the very beginning of January, 1889, Nietzsche changed the subtitle of *The Antichrist* to "A Curse on Christianity" and then again changed the subtitle to "Attempt at a Critique of Christianity," which is how the book is reprinted today.

Hollingdale offers two more reasons to support Colli and Montinari's view that Nietzsche had indeed abandoned the project *The Will to Power*. The first is from a letter dated November 1888 to George Brandes, in which Nietzsche writes, "The whole work *(Ecce Homo)* is a prelude to *The Revaluation of All Values* which lies completed before me." At that point in time, the only completed portion of *The Revaluation of All Values* had to be *The Antichrist*.

The second is a prelude from *Ecce Homo,* in which Nietzsche writes,

> I attacked the tremendous task of the *Revaluation* and . . . without permitting my-
> self to be distracted for a moment, I went on with my work: there was only the last
> quarter of the book still to be disposed of. (EH, "Twilight," 3)

> Griff ich die ungeheure Aufgabe der *Umwerthung* an . . . ohne mich einen
> Augenblick abziehn zu lassen, gieng ich wieder an die Arbeit: es war nur das letzt
> Viertel des Werks noch abzuthun. [KGW VI/3, 353–54]

Because Nietzsche was working on *The Antichrist* at the time, Hollingdale concludes that Nietzsche envisioned *The Antichrist* as a book unto itself and not simply the first chapter of a larger work. If Nietzsche had abandoned both *The Will
to Power* and *The Revaluation of All Values,* then, according to Hollingdale, we
need not be concerned that these notes might have been saved for future works.
With *Twilight of the Idols* at the publisher and *Ecce Homo* and *The Antichrist* in
final form, we can infer that Nietzsche was not in the middle of a book when he
collapsed. Thus, notes that had not made their way into *Ecce Homo* or *The Antichrist* were not waiting for Nietzsche to begin *The Will to Power.* This does not
necessarily lead us to Hollingdale's recommendation that the controversial
Nachlass notes be ignored completely, but *The Will to Power* that is in circula-
tion today is to be met with some skepticism.

Another serious problem with *The Will to Power* is that many of the numbered
aphorisms are chopped up versions of longer entries. Sections have been deleted
or moved to totally different headings. One lengthy note has been reedited to
become 634, 635, and 693 in *The Will to Power.* Another starts as 702, then, after the penultimate paragraph, one must go back to 652, then come back to the
ultimate paragraph of 702, and finally tack on 703 to get the original entry. Still
another single notebook entry is broken into eighteen different aphorisms scat-
tered throughout aphorisms 234 and 970 in *The Will to Power.* Some entries that
Nietzsche crossed out have been included.

A third problem is the form of *The Will to Power* itself. Elisabeth and Köselitz
chose one of Nietzsche's sketchiest outlines on which to pattern the book. There
were many more detailed plans—including the list of 374 entry headings—and
several that were penned after the brief one chosen. Bernd Magnus notes that these
later outlines all drop the famous "Will to Power as Nature" heading that Elisabeth
chose to use.[8] Also, of the 374 entry headings that Nietzsche collected in mid-
February 1888, none comes even close to the famous, final entry in *The Will to
Power,* written in June–July 1885, on which so much interpretation of will to
power as Nietzsche's metaphysics rests. So there may be some evidence that
Nietzsche may not have wanted to extend will to power into the inorganic or inanimate realm.

Even if these particular problems of Nietzsche's notebooks could be resolved,
the question as to what to do with *any* writer's notebooks remains. Should we

consider them as guides to the development of the writer's thoughts? Should we ignore them and only consider the published material, or should we focus on the notes and ignore the published material? Perhaps we should make no distinction between the two, as many commentators do. Certainly, at age forty-four, Nietzsche should have had more productive years ahead of him had it not been for his collapse. Although he may not have been in the middle of a writing project in early January 1889, there is no indication that he would have given up writing altogether after the completion of *The Antichrist.* There is still a possibility that some of the notes may have been used or revised for future works. On the other hand, Nietzsche wrote down all sorts of things, from laundry lists, to fragments of sentences, to lengthy, densely philosophical pieces. Part of Colli and Montinari's task of editing Nietzsche's written remains was to decide which pieces were suitable to be included in the *Nachlass.* Which fragments ought to be ignored in a philosophical study, and which ought to be taken seriously?

It comes as no surprise that Nietzsche commentators are divided on this issue. Those who want to use some of the controversial notes to support their interpretations of Nietzsche's philosophy defend using the *Nachlass* notes or simply ignore the *Nachlass* problems altogether. These commentators have been labeled "lumpers."[9] They lump the controversial notes together with the published material and make no distinction between them. By contrast, there are the "splitters." There are two types of splitters: those who separate the *Nachlass* notes and only use the published material and those who separate the *Nachlass* notes and emphasize the controversial notes.

Of the latter type of splitter, Martin Heidegger is the most renowned. Heidegger believes that the works Nietzsche published are too literary, that they were written merely for style and effect:

> But Nietzsche's philosophy proper, the fundamental position on the basis of which he speaks in these and in all the writings he himself published, did not assume a final form and was not itself published in any book, neither in the decade between 1879 and 1889 nor during the years preceding. What Nietzsche himself published was always foreground. . . . His philosophy proper was left behind as posthumous, unpublished work.[10]

The "real" philosophy of Nietzsche, according to Heidegger, is in the *Nachlass,* so he takes the *Nachlass* material more seriously than the published works. Heidegger believes Nietzsche wrote these notes to himself, so they represent Nietzsche's thoughts more accurately than the writings stylized for public consumption. In Heidegger's view, themes such as eternal recurrence and will to power are either watered down or cloaked in hyperbole to cater to the public's diminished capacity for deep thinking. This would account for the discrepancy between the published presentations and those of the *Nachlass* that Magnus finds with eternal recurrence and that we find with will to power. By ignoring the published presentations of eternal recurrence and will to power, Heidegger's interpretation of will to power, not surprisingly, emphasizes solely the metaphysical aspects. As we have seen, will to power is more firmly rooted in the metaphysical realm in the *Nachlass* notes and is offered only as an account for human behavior and morality (with a few couplings with "life") in the published works. This allows Heidegger to advance his claim that Nietzsche is the "last metaphysician" and that his investigation into the question of Being is a radical departure from traditional philosophy and the true focus of philosophy proper. But all this sounds a bit too self-serving, doesn't it? It seems like the real reason Heidegger prefers the *Nachlass* notes to the published writings is that the unpublished notes support his interpretation of Nietzsche as a metaphysician.[11]

Wolfgang Müller-Lauter tries to find some more fuel for Heidegger's position, although Müller-Lauter takes the more modest position that the controversial notes are *at least* as important as the works Nietzsche published.[12] He cites a *Nachlass* fragment from the year 1887 as support:

> I don't respect readers anymore: how could I write for readers? . . . When I write myself, I write for myself. (my translation)
>
> Ich achte die Leser nicht mehr: wie könnte ich für Leser schreiben? . . . Aber ich notire mich, für mich. [KGW VIII/2, 9(188), 114]

Müller-Lauter believes this fragment indicates that what Nietzsche held back from publication is just as philosophically important as the published writings.

But this passage is part of a longer entry that has as its main thrust Nietzsche's disgruntlement at having written his books, especially *Thus Spoke Zarathustra,* in the German language because his books require thinking and Germans don't think anymore: "Die Deutschen von Heute sind keine Denker mehr. . . ." According to Nietzsche, they persist in systematizing everything, even those ideas, like Nietzsche's, that resist being categorized. This "will to systematize" Nietzsche calls a character sickness. It is only after this harangue on the character and intelligence of Germans that he says he writes for himself.

This kind of remark should come as no surprise. There are several places in the published works where Nietzsche makes a similar claim. One example is the subtitle of *Thus Spoke Zarathustra*: "A Book for All and None." This has generally been interpreted to mean that while all who read the book will think they understand it, in fact its deeper messages will be missed entirely and hence not grasped by anyone. Yet, even though Nietzsche had little faith in his then current readership, he published the book nonetheless. Thus we should not interpret "A Book for . . . None" to mean that no one should read it, or else the question would arise as to why Nietzsche had it published in the first place.

Another example of Nietzsche's "writing for himself" is found in the preface of *The Antichrist*:

> This book belongs to the very few. Perhaps none of them is even living yet. Maybe they will be readers who understand my *Zarathustra*: how *could* I mistake myself

for one of those for whom there are ears even now? Only the day after tomorrow belongs to me. Some are born posthumously. (AC, "Forward")

Dies Buch gehört den Wenigsten. Vielleicht lebt selbst noch Keiner von ihnen. Es mögen die sein, welche meinen *Zarathustra* verstehn: wie *dürfte* ich mich mit denen verewechseln, für welche heute schon Ohren waschen?—Erst das Übermorgen gehört mir. Einige werden posthum geboren. [KGW VI/3, 165]

Even though Nietzsche did not consider any of his contemporaries able to understand him, he obviously hoped some person(s) in future generations might be able to comprehend and enjoy his ideas. In light of these examples, we could reinterpret Müller-Lauter's citation to be saying that Nietzsche did not write for the then present European, and particularly German, community.

The consequence of adopting Müller-Lauter's interpretation and seriously thinking that Nietzsche wrote only for himself is confusion. Why did Nietzsche publish his work? Why didn't he just keep all his notes for his eyes only? Publishing his work would be irrational if he truly wrote for just himself. It would also contradict his letters, in which he expresses his dissatisfaction with the way his books were selling. He was upset that more people were not reading and discussing his work and wanted his editor to advertise them better. The *Nachlass* passage that Müller-Lauter cites is too fragile to support the entire weight of Heidegger's or his own position.

The other kind of splitter, the one that completely ignores the *Nachlass* material, is exemplified by Harold Alderman and R. J. Hollingdale. As we have already seen, Hollingdale rejects the controversial notes because Nietzsche was not in the middle of writing *The Will to Power.* Alderman argues that the vast majority of the controversial notes was written between 1882 and 1888, the very peak of Nietzsche's productivity. *The Case of Wagner, The Gay Science, Thus Spoke Zarathustra, Beyond Good and Evil,* and *On the Genealogy of Morals* were published; *Twilight of the Idols* was at the publisher's; and *Ecce Homo* and *Nietzsche Contra Wagner* were complete but not publisher ready. Alderman argues that because Nietzsche decided not to publish these notes, we should defer to Nietzsche's judgment and disregard them as well. But even if Nietzsche did reject these notes, must we ignore them totally?

Lumpers generally do not argue for their position; they just cite unpublished material along with published material indiscriminately. However, they could argue that the fact that Nietzsche wrote these ideas down demonstrates that he was seriously considering them and that any idea that Nietzsche had in his life is open to philosophical scrutiny. The problem with the *Nachlass* notes arises when lumpers try to make the case that the controversial notes represent Nietzsche's "real" or final position on philosophical topics. Richard Schacht's otherwise excellent book, *Nietzsche,* is one of the most notable examples of this. I believe that to equate the *Nachlass* notes with the material Nietzsche authorized for publication is to invite confusion for the reader and trouble in interpretation from all the problems inherent in using them. I hope this chapter has demonstrated how differently will to power is presented in the *Nachlass* material from the way Nietzsche uses the idea in the works he himself published or authorized for publication.

Not surprisingly, there is a one-to-one correlation between commentators' positions on the *Nachlass* notes and their positions on whether will to power is metaphysical. Those who reject the *Nachlass* material, for example, Hollingdale and Alderman, either argue that will to power is not a metaphysical principle or do not even discuss the possibility at all. Heidegger, who regards the *Nachlass* material as more valid than the published works, zeroes in on just the metaphysical aspects of will to power—as a metaphysical principle that does away with metaphysics altogether. Lumper commentators, too numerous to mention all by name, either are ignorant of the whole distinction between published and *Nachlass* material or casually brush aside any concerns. Not surprisingly, their positions also suggest that will to power is in some sense metaphysical.

The prudent position would be a cautious and sensitive approach to these controversial notes. Happily, this seems to be the approach most often taken in current Nietzsche scholarship, although vigilance against lumpers is still required. It is too harsh to ignore the vast richness of the *Nachlass*. Even if these notes are "thought experiments," as Walter Kaufmann suggests, that Nietzsche ultimately rejected, it is by no means clear that *we* should disregard them completely. It may still be philosophically valuable to reconstruct and investigate them. It was a challenge to me to explain how inorganic "things" could be will to power. But we must be sure that any reconstructions we undertake are clearly noted to be *our* interpretations of the material and not said to be Nietzsche's final position without providing ample support from the material Nietzsche authorized for publication. It may be more profitable to note the differences between how something is presented in the published writing and how it is portrayed in the *Nachlass* entries. This approach has been quite informative, particularly with Nietzsche's notions of eternal recurrence, as Magnus has documented, and will to power, as I have documented. In the case of will to power, there is *very* dubious evidence in the published material that will to power is extended beyond the organic realm. And even if Nietzsche gives us evidence that will to power is an explanation for organic behavior, it is only in the *Nachlass* material that he talks about every other explanation being a derivation of will to power. In the works Nietzsche authorized for publication, Nietzsche does not give will to power such a foundational role. Instead, it is given the role of an alternative explanation to the ones current in the nineteenth century, not the more foundational metaphysical-sounding role apparent in the *Nachlass*. Further, there is evidence that Nietzsche did not want will to power to be considered metaphysical.

As we have noted, Nietzsche calls himself an "anti-metaphysician" in several places. The entire first chapter of *Human, All-Too-Human* is a scathing indictment of metaphysics, which is excoriated—mocked!—throughout the succeeding published books. There are also plenty of passages in the *Nachlass* against metaphysics as well: "metaphysics, morality, religion, science—in this book these things merit consideration only as various forms of lies. . . ." With over ten years of constant criticism against metaphysics, it is hardly likely that Nietzsche simply "forgot" about his position. Nietzsche's various criticisms against metaphysics were about the entire enterprise of metaphysics and not just the various candidates for supreme metaphysical principle. Thus, his judgments against the Christian God are not that Christianity has the wrong metaphysical underpinning. Nietzsche is not saying that Christians should be worshiping will to power instead of God; he is arguing against the notion of metaphysical underpinnings in the first place, whether those underpinnings take the form of transcendental deities or scientific atoms. So, too, it would seem, the arguments would be apropos of "forces" in the form of will to power. It is not that the previous philosophers simply had the wrong metaphysical principle; it is that metaphysical principles themselves are erroneous. To then present will to power as a metaphysical principle would be the height of self-contradiction. Nietzsche seems too philosophically astute to make this kind of self-referential blunder; yet what are we to make of his assertions that "the innermost essence of Being is will to power"?[13]

This rather obvious self-reflective problem is the reason why some Nietzsche commentators have explicitly separated their interpretations of will to power from metaphysics, linking it to ontology or cosmology. Considering Nietzsche calls himself an "anti-metaphysician," his theory of will to power must be something else. We could differentiate between metaphysics and cosmology by saying that metaphysics is concerned with transcendental ("otherworldly") or a priori principles. To say that will to power is a cosmology allows it to be the product of empirical observation in a way that transcendental metaphysical musings cannot be. But unlike God, who is not of this world, will to power is very much a part of this world—it is the world. This differentiation depends, of course, on a very narrow interpretation of metaphysics, though not an unduly uncharitable one in Nietzsche scholarship, for it was one that Nietzsche himself liked to espouse, especially in *Human, All-Too-Human* and *Daybreak*.

In the writings of Nietzsche's middle period, metaphysics is contrasted with science, and, in this "positivistic" period, science is preferred by Nietzsche. While science examines the world as it is, metaphysics concerns itself with questions and issues that cannot be answered by empirical observation:

> *Metaphysical world.*—It is true, there could be a metaphysical world; . . .but one can do absolutely nothing with it, not to speak of letting happiness, salvation, and life depend on the gossamer of such a possibility.—For one could assert nothing at all of the metaphysical world except that it was a being-other; it would be a thing with negative qualities.—Even if the existence of such a world were never so well demonstrated, it is certain that knowledge of it would be the most useless of all knowledge: more useless even than knowledge of the chemical composition of water must be to the sailor in danger of shipwreck. (HAH I, 9)

Metaphysische Welt.—Es ist wahr, es könnte eine metaphysische Welt geben; . . . aber mit ihr kann man gar Nichts anfangen, geschweige denn, dass man Glück, Heil and Leben von den Spinnenfäden einer solchen Möglichkeit abhängen lassen dürfte.—Denn man könnte von der metaphysischen Welt gar Nichts aussagen, als ein Anderssein, ein uns unzugängliches, unbegreifliches Anderssein; es wäre ein ing mit negativen Eigenschaften.—Wäre die Existenz einer solchen Welt noch so gut bewiesen, so stünde doch fest, dass die gleichgültigste aller Erkenntniss eben ihre Erkenntniss wäre: noch gleichgültiger als dem Schiffer in Sturmesgefahr die Erkenntniss von der chemischen Analysis des Wassers sein muss. [KGW IV/2, 25–26]

For the metaphysical outlook bestows the belief that it offers the last, ultimate foundation upon which the whole future of mankind is then invited to establish and construct itself. (HAH I, 22)

Denn metaphysische Ansichten geben den Glauben, dass in ihnen das letzte endgültige Fundament gegeben sei, auf welchem sich nunmehr alle Zukunft der Menschheit niederzulassen und anzubauen genöthigt sei. [KGW IV/2, 39]

It is the empirical aspect of will to power that commentators, especially Walter Kaufmann, like to emphasize. It is Kaufmann's contention that will to power began as an empirical observation about human conduct. It was next extended to psychological motivation, then to all organic behavior, and finally to the inorganic realm. This progression is crucial for Kaufmann, for it is meant to persuade us that at all times Nietzsche was consistently basing his conclusions on empirical observations and avoiding metaphysical thinking and, therefore, never contradicting himself. Instead, as with any empirical, scientific theory, he was merely extending an explanation to see how far it could be taken (before it becomes nonsense, as Nietzsche suggests in BGE 36?). This experiment with will to power was extended to the entire world, but Kaufmann maintains that Nietzsche was never entirely comfortable or persuaded by his writings about will to power in the inorganic realm. That is why those aphorisms remain solely in the *Nachlass* and do not appear in the works Nietzsche authorized for publication. This may be a plausible reconstruction of Nietzsche's method and intentions, but perhaps Nietzsche avoided making it an empirically based explanation for the world because he did not want it to be considered a "science." In his writings on metaphysics in the later works, beginning with *The Gay Science,* Nietzsche criticizes science along the same lines as his criticisms against transcendental deities:

But you will have gathered what I am driving at, namely, that it is still a *metaphysical faith* upon which our faith in science rests—that even we seekers after knowledge today, we godless anti-metaphysicians still take our fire, too, from the flame lit by a faith that is thousands of years old, that Christian faith which was also the faith of Plato, that God is the truth, that truth is divine.—But what if this should become more and more incredible, if nothing should prove to be divine any more unless it were error, blindness, the lie—if God himself should prove to be our most enduring lie? (GS, 344)

Doch man wird es begriffen haben, worauf ich hinaus will, nämlich dass es immer noch ein *metaphysischer Glaube* ist, auf dem unser Glaube an die wissenschaft ruht,—dass auch wir Erkennenden von heute, wir Gottlosen und Antimetaphysiker, auch *unser* Feuer noch entzündet hat, jener Christen-Glaube, der auch der Glaube Plato's war, dass Gott die Wahrheit ist, dass die Wahrheit göttlich ist—Aber wie, wenn dies gerade immer mehr unglaubwürdig wird, wenn Nichts sich mehr als göttlich erweist, es sei denn der Irrthum, die Blindheit, die Lüge,—wenn Gott selbst sich als unser längste lüge erweist? [KGW V/2, 259]

Metaphysics is still needed by some; but so is that impetuous *demand for certainty* that today discharges itself among large numbers of people in a scientific-positivistic form. The demand that one *wants* by all means that something should be firm (while on account of the ardor of this demand one is easier and more negligent about the demonstration of this certainty)—this, too, is still the demand for a support, a prop, in short, that *instinct of weakness* which, to be sure, does not create religious, metaphysical systems, and convictions of all kinds but—conserves them. (GS, 347)

Metaphysik haben Einige noch nöthig; aber auch jenes ungestüme *Verlangen nach Gewissheit,* welches sich heute in breiten Massen wissenschaftlich-positivistisch entladet, das Verlangen, durchaus etwas fest haben zu *wollen* (während man es wegen der Hitze diese Verlangens mit der Begründung der Sicherheit leichter und lässlicher nimmt): auch das ist noch das Verlangen nach Halt, Stütze, kurz, jener *Instinkt der Schwäche,* welcher Religionen, Metaphysiken, Ueberzeugungen aller Art zwar nicht schafft, aber—conservirt. [KGW V/2, 263–64]

Thus, science can no more be the foundation for anything than God; there is no foundation, period. The consequences of this for Nietzsche will be more fully discussed in chapter 4. At this point, it seems clear that Nietzsche's criticism of metaphysics extends to anything that tries to establish a foundation in what he sees as a sea of becoming. If will to power were the foundational explanation for everything, it would be subject to the same criticisms Nietzsche levels against setting up God and science as foundations.

To reduce everything to will to power, then, would seem to come under the same attack leveled at religion and science. Also, it would seem that emphasizing will to power as an empirical observation is not going to let will to power escape this criticism, for science is also empirical in method. Perhaps Nietzsche realized that reducing everything to will to power would rob will to power of its explanatory effectiveness. Maudemarie Clark states that "the enlightening character of explanations of behavior in terms of the desire for power is dependent on an implicit contrast with other motives, and it is therefore lost as soon as all other motives are expressions of the will to power."[14] In Clark's example, to explain rape as an act of power has explanatory power only when contrasted with the explanation that rape is an act of repressed sexual desire. But if sexual desire is itself an act of power, then the explanation loses its revelatory and explanatory punch. Thus, making will to power a cosmological principle rather than a metaphysical principle does not extricate it from being problematic for Nietzsche.

The other distinction is made between metaphysics and ontology. Ontology fares better because it is concerned with how beings experience the world and not with the ultimate foundation of the world. Thus, Nietzsche can say without apparent contradiction that there is no ultimate foundation of the world and that all beings' experience in the world is one of power, for will to power would be more a way of being in the world than the ultimate constitution of it. Again, the pluses of this distinction are that ontology does not preclude empirical observation and that ontology is concerned less about the ultimate constitution of the world and more about the kind of existence experienced in the world. That is why many current commentators call will to power Nietzsche's ontology rather than his cosmology or metaphysics. However, in today's philosophical climate, many times ontology is included under the broad heading of metaphysics.

The question of will to power being Nietzsche's metaphysics centers around how narrowly one construes *metaphysics*. Nietzsche's criticisms are against a fairly narrow interpretation of "metaphysics" as concerned with a priori concepts or transcendent, otherworldly matters, specifically God. Will to power is neither a priori nor transcendent. On the other hand, there is W. V. O. Quine's more sweeping interpretation of metaphysics: that it is any answer to the question "What is there?" Surely we would be tempted to say that "will to power" is Nietzsche's answer to Quine's question. So will to power is not metaphysical in Nietzsche's interpretation of metaphysics, which does not include the more contemporary idea of ontology, but it may be considered metaphysical in the broadest interpretation of metaphysics, such as Quine's. If this move of distinguishing between a narrow and a broad definition of metaphysics is made, then Nietzsche avoids the self-referential problem by arguing against metaphysics in the narrow sense and then positing will to power as the answer to Quine's question of metaphysics in the broad sense.

But even this move can be hazardous. When *will to power* appears in the writings Nietzsche authorized for publication, the contexts are almost exclusively about organic, and primarily human, behavior. The most metaphysical-sounding passages on will to power occur in the controversial unpublished notes. Thus, we cannot be totally confident that "will to power" is Nietzsche's answer to Quine's question. At best, all we can say is that the published aphorisms that contain *will to power* imply that will to power might be Nietzsche's answer to Quine's question.

The question of whether Nietzsche's remarks on will to power are contradictory to his criticism of metaphysics may be a twentieth-century dilemma. One of the main reasons we can talk about a narrow or broad interpretation of metaphysics or about will to power being ontological is because of Nietzsche's influence on later philosophers. His criticisms against metaphysics were instrumental in getting some subsequent philosophers to expand on or abandon altogether the notion of metaphysics. With the ensuing broadening of the term to encompass cosmology and ontology, late-twentieth-century philosophers can talk about different positions within metaphysics. But Nietzsche was in no such position.

For him, there were not several subsets of metaphysics from which to choose. Being steeped in the classics, he interpreted "metaphysics" as the ancient Greeks did—as "beyond nature." Will to power is not *beyond* nature, it *is* nature, so perhaps no self-referential problem arose in Nietzsche's thinking.

I hope I have shown that the entries about will to power in the *Nachlass* are not only distinctly broader in scope than those passages Nietzsche chose to publish but also, in the case of extending will to power to explain the nonorganic realm, distinctly different. While the *Nachlass* entries about human and organic behavior broaden the views presented in the published works, they at least have some counterparts in the writings that Nietzsche authorized for publication. However, the difference is striking and significant in the case of Nietzsche's remarks about will to power in the inorganic realm. I have already discussed the problems with interpreting *Beyond Good and Evil* 36 in any definitive way. The *Nachlass* entries on will to power as force share the same writing style Magnus describes for Nietzsche's *Nachlass* entries on eternal recurrence: they are unimaginative, argumentative, straightforward, and "scientific" sounding. The notable exception to this style is, of course, the marvelously metaphorical entry I quote at the beginning of this chapter. Its poetical and imaginative style is almost unsurpassed in the published writings. But this entry was written in 1885, just after Nietzsche wrote *Thus Spoke Zarathustra*. The fact that Nietzsche wrote eight books after this time and never chose to publish that entry seems to me to be a strong indication that Nietzsche was somehow dissatisfied with it. Colli and Montinari comment that Nietzsche's entries about will to power in this time period reflect his positivistic and pro-scientific period.[15] Given these considerations, I interpret will to power nonmetaphysically, noncosmologically, and nonontologically. But then how do I interpret it?

In order to answer that question, we need to examine Nietzsche's discussion of will to power's connection with will to truth. I propose we shift the focus of the problem away from the question of metaphysics and toward the question of truth. In my discussion of will to power, I have presented Nietzsche's views as if his texts faithfully reveal Nietzsche's thoughts, as if there were a "true picture" of Nietzsche's thoughts on will to power. But what if a "true picture" of will to power is not possible? Indeed, Nietzsche suggests that it isn't even desirable. Given these complications, what are we to make of will to power? The following chapter discusses Nietzsche's remarks on will to power in connection with his remarks on the nature of truth.

FURTHER READING

Heidegger, Martin. *Nietzsche*, 4 vols. Trans. David Krell. New York: Harper and Row, 1979; see especially vol. 3.

Magnus, Bernd. "The Use and Abuse of *The Will to Power*." In *Reading Nietzsche*, ed. Robert Solomon and Kathleen M. Higgins. New York: Oxford University Press, 1988.

Poellner, Peter. *Nietzsche and Metaphysics.* Oxford: Clarendon Press, 1995.
Schacht, Richard. *Making Sense of Nietzsche.* Urbana: University of Illinois Press, 1995; see especially part 1, chapter 6.
Stack, George. *Man, Knowledge, and Will to Power.* Durango, Colo.: Hollowbrook Press, 1994.
———. *Lange and Nietzsche.* New York: Walter de Gruyter and Co., 1983.

4

Will to Power and Truth

It would be impossible to write on will to power without discussing Nietzsche's views on truth. Nietzsche's criticisms against foundational views of metaphysics interweave with his epistemological views. His critique against the notion of any objective or perspective-neutral foundation for truth has been more thoroughly and eloquently discussed elsewhere,[1] so I will offer only a brief summary and then go on to a discussion of how Nietzsche's criticisms against truth affect his notion of will to power. Nietzsche's epistemological critique evolved over the course of his writings, but his antifoundational stance remained the same. Nietzsche's earliest attacks on truth center on a critique of language.

In an unpublished piece entitled "On Truth and Lies in the Nonmoral Sense," written in 1873, Nietzsche argues that language is a convention, wholly nonnatural, which stresses similarities over differences in its invention of words, nouns especially. Because language ignores individual differences and concentrates on gross similarities, words other than proper nouns operate as a kind of shorthand, or economy, for human experience. For Nietzsche, the conventional model of language holds a one-to-one correspondence to nature, for example, the word *tree* designates a natural thing—an actual tree. This model has language as a nondistorting mirror of reality. Because truth and falsehood apply to statements about the world rather than to the world itself, we can determine the truth of the statement "grass is green" supposedly by looking at grass in the world and observing whether it is indeed green.[2] In "On Truth and Lies in the Nonmoral Sense" Nietzsche claims that words themselves, such as simple nouns like *leaf,* are already distortions, "lies," in the sense that they are economies for what humans experience. Any attempt to capture human experience in language necessarily alters and, according to Nietzsche, deadens it. At best, the word *leaf* is a metaphor; at worse it is a lie:

> The creator (of language) only designates the relations of things to men, and for
> expressing these relations he lays hold of the boldest metaphors. To begin with, a

nerve stimulus is transferred into an image: first metaphor. The image, in turn, is imitated in a sound: second metaphor. And each time there is a complete overleap-ing of one sphere right into the middle of an entirely new and different one. . . . It is this way with all of us concerning language: we believe that we know something about the things themselves when we speak of trees, colors, snow, and flowers; and yet we possess nothing but metaphors for things—metaphors which correspond in no way to the original entities. (Breazeale, 82–83)

Er bezeichnet nur die Relationen der Dinge zu den Menschen und nimmt zu deren Ausdrucke die kühnein Methaphern zu Hülfe. Ein Nervenreiz zuerst übertragen in ein Bild! Erste Metapher. Das Bild wieder nachgeformt in einem Laut! Zweite Metapher. Und jedesmal vollständiges Ueberspringen der Sphäre, mitten hinein in eine ganz andere und neue . . . so geht es uns allen mit der Sprache. Wir glauben etwas von den Dingen selbst zu wissen, wenn wir von Bäumen, Farben, Schnee, und Blumen reden und besitzen doch nichts als Metaphern der Dinge, die den ursprünglichen Wesenheiten ganz und gar nicht entsprechen. [KGW III/2, 373]

As the above quote indicates, Nietzsche's more radical contention is that words themselves are "lies." If I say the word *leaf* to you, the sound of the word in no way bears a resemblance to an actual leaf. The image in your mind of a green substance with veins is only a pale resemblance to a living leaf. The written word fares no better. The individual letters do not resemble the object in any way, and again, any mental image that they may engender in the reader's mind is only a pale reflection of an actual leaf:

Every concept arises from the equation of unequal things. Just as it is certain that one leaf is never totally the same as another, so it is certain that the concept "leaf" is formed by arbitrarily discarding these individual differences and by forgetting the distinguishing aspects. This awakens the idea that, in addition to the leaves, there exists in Nature the "leaf": the original model according to which all leaves were perhaps woven, sketched, measured, colored, curled, and painted—but by incom-petent hands, so that no specimen has turned out to be a correct, trustworthy and faithful likeness of the original model. (Breazeale, 83)

Jeder Begriff entsteht durch Gleichsetzen des Nicht-Gleichen. So gewiss nie ein Blatt einem anderen ganz gleich ist, so gewiss ist der Begriff Blatt durch beliebiges Fallenlassen dieser individuellen Verscheidenheiten, durch ein Vergessen des Unterscheidenden gebildet und erweckt nun die Vorstellung, als ob es in der Natur ausser den Blättern etwas gäbe, das "Blatt" wäre, etwa eine Urform, nach der alle Blätter gewebt, gezeichnet, abgezirkelt, gefärbt, gekräuselt, bemalt wären, aber von ungleeschickten Händen, so dass kein Exemplar correckt und zuverlässig als treues Abbild der Urform ausgefallen wäre. [KGW III/2, 374]

Common nouns are "false" in the sense that a common noun, such as *leaf*, must overlook many differences among the individual leaves of a maple tree, not to mention differences among leaves from maple, oak, and elm trees and so forth. To call all of these individual botanical growths "leaves" is to focus too much on their similarities rather than on their differences. This focus on similarities is a great economy, a linguistic shortcut, that conveniently lumps experience into manageable groups. It would be difficult to imagine communication with others if everything had its own proper name. By necessity language has to include classes and common nouns, but this process inherently falsifies lived experience. Thus, beliefs that are based in language are already "false" according to the notion of an absolute standard because one side of the correspondence, the language-based belief, is already a fabrication.

Because words and concepts concentrate on similarities among things, they ignore differences for economy's sake, but they do this at the cost of any direct correspondence between them and human experience. Translating actual lived experience into any other medium, artistic or otherwise, distorts that experience, but many times language, being such an integral part of human experience, is not considered an alternate medium and thus not considered a distortion.[3] However, according to Nietzsche, truth, being dependent on language, is already conventional, distorted, and false. According to this view, truth is impossible.

But this view has its problems. If a correspondence model of language, where nature or reality is the final, perspective-neutral foundation, is rejected, how are we to read Nietzsche's remarks about the nature of language or of truth? What model of truth are we to use in deciphering his own position? If we take Nietzsche's position to be that "anything couched in language is necessarily false," we must inquire into the truth-value of such a statement. Nietzsche wants us to consider his writings to be saying something "true" about the inadequacy of the correspondence model of language, does he not? On what are we basing the truth or even the adequacy of his critique? He is using (false) language to claim that language is falsifying. It appears that Nietzsche has created his own version of the Liar's Paradox.[4] This self-referential problem may be why Nietzsche seems to have abandoned this line of attack against truth.

His subsequent line of attack criticizes any attempt to provide an objective (neutral or nonperspectival) foundation for Truth, whether that foundation is metaphysics, God, or science:

> The things of the highest value must have another *peculiar* origin—they cannot be derived from this transitory, seductive, deceptive, paltry world, from this turmoil of delusion and lust. Rather, from the lap of Being, the intransitory, the hidden god, the "thing-in-itself"—there must be their basis, and nowhere else. This way of judging constitutes the typical prejudgment and prejudice which give away the metaphysicians of all ages; this kind of valuation looms in the background of all their logical procedures; it is on account of this "faith" that they trouble themselves about "knowledge," about something that is finally baptized solemnly as "the truth." The fundamental faith of the metaphysicians is *the faith in opposite values.* It has not even occurred to the most cautious among them that one may have a doubt right here at the threshold where it was surely most necessary—even if they vowed to themselves, *"de omnibus dubitandum."* For one may doubt, first, whether there are any opposites at all, and secondly whether these popular valuations and opposite values on which the metaphysicians put their seal, are not perhaps merely foreground

estimates, only provisional perspectives, perhaps even from some nook, perhaps from below, frog perspectives, as it were, to borrow an expression painters use. For all the value that the true, the truthful, the selfless may deserve, it would still be possible that a higher and more fundamental value for life might have to be ascribed to deception, selfishness, and lust. It might even be possible that what constitutes the value of these good and revered things is precisely that they are insidiously related, tied to, and involved with these wicked, seemingly opposite things—maybe even one with them in essence. Maybe! (BGE, 2)

Die Dinge höchsten Werthes müssen einen anderen, *eigenen* Ursprung haben,—aus dieser vergänglichen verführerischen täuschenden geringen Welt, aus diesem Wirrsal von Wahn und Begierde sind sie unableitbar! Vielmehr im Schoosse des Sein's, im Unvergänglichen, im verborgenen Gotte, im "Ding-an sich"—*da* muss ihr Grund liegen, und sonst nirgendswo!—Diese Art zu urtheilen macht das typische Vorurtheil aus, an dem sich die Metaphysiker aller Zeiten wieder erkennen lassen; diese Art von Werthschätzungen steht im Hintergrunde alle ihrer logischen Prozeduren; aus diesem ihrem "Glauben" heraus bemühn sie sich um ihr "Wissen," um Etwas, das feierlich am Ende als "die Wahrheit" getauft wird. Dir Grundglaube der Metaphysiker ist *der Glaube an die Gegensätze der Werthe.* Es ist auch den Vorsichtigen unter ihnen nicht eingefallen, hier an der Schwelle bereits zu zweifeln, wo es doch am nöthigsten war: selbst wenn sie sich gelobt hatten "de Omnibus dubitandum." Man darf nämlich zweifeln, erstens, ob es Gegensätze überhaupt giebt, und zweitens, ob jene volkthümlichen Werthschätzungen und Werth-Gegensätze, auf welche die Metaphysiker ihr Siegel gedrückt haben, nicht vielleicht nur Vordergrunds-Schätzungen sind, nur vorläufige Perspektiven, vieleicht noch dazu aus einem Winkel heraus, vieleicht von Unten hinauf, Frosch-Perspektiven gleichsam, um einen Ausdruck zu borgen, der den Malern geläufig ist? Bei allem Werthe, der dem Wahren, dem Wahrhaftigen, dem Selbstlosen zukommen mag: es wäre möglich, dass dem Scheine, dem Willen zur Täuschung, dem Eigennutz und Begierde ein für alles Leben höherer und grundsätzlicher Werth zugeschrieben werden müsste. Es wäre sogar noch möglich, dass *was* den Werth jener guten und verehrten Dinge ausmacht, gerade darin bestünde, mit jenen schlimmen, scheinbar entgegesetzten Dingen auf verfängliche Weise verwandt, verknüpft, verhäkelt, vielleicht gar wesensgleich zu sein. Vielleicht! [KGW VI/2, 10–11]

According to Nietzsche, objective truth is so valuable to humans that they invent a "peculiar" origin for it—a foundation that must be permanent and unchanging, such as God, Being, or Kant's noumenal "thing-in-itself." Metaphysicians who want truth to be objective (this notion of truth will be rendered with a capital T) must ground this notion of Truth in something other than human perspective. Nietzsche, however, argues that this notion of Truth itself is perspectival, perhaps even a "frog perspective."[5] Even those who claim to "doubt everything" (and Nietzsche clearly implies Descartes) do not doubt their interpretation of Truth. Why is this interpretation of Truth valued so highly? It is the exploration of the *value* of Truth that occupies most of part 1 of *Beyond Good and Evil.*

Beyond Good and Evil begins with the now famous metaphor: "Supposing truth were a woman—what then?" The remainder of the preface is a polemic against philosophers of dogmatic Truth, whose "gruesome seriousness" cannot win the heart of the more playful, "womanly" truth. In the first aphorism of part 1 of *Beyond Good and Evil,* Nietzsche introduces what will be the overriding theme of part 1, a theme that shapes and recurs throughout *Beyond Good and Evil:*

> The will to truth which will still tempt us to many a venture, that famous truthfulness of which all philosophers so far have spoken with respect—what questions has this will to truth not laid before us! What strange, wicked, questionable questions! That is a long story even now—and yet it seems as if it had scarcely begun. Is it any wonder that we should finally become suspicious, lose patience, and turn away impatiently? that *we* should finally learn from this Sphinx to ask questions, too? *Who* is it really that puts questions to us here? *What* in us really wants "truth"? Indeed we came to a long halt at the question about the cause of this will—until we finally came to a complete stop before a still more basic question. We asked about the *value* of this will. Suppose we want truth: *why not rather* untruth? (BGE, 1)

> Der Wille zur Wahrheit, der uns noch zu manchem Wagnisse verführen wird, jene berühmte Wahrhaftigkeit, von der alle Philosophen bisher mit Ehrerbietung geredet haben: was für Fragen hast dieser Wille zur Wahrheit uns schon vorgelegt! Welche wunderlichen schlimmen fragwürdeigen Fragen! Das ist bereits eine lange Geschickte,—und doch scheint es, dass sie kaum eben angefangen hat? Was Wunder, wenn wir endlich einmal misstrauisch werden, die Geduld verlieren, uns ungeduldig umdrehn. Dass *wir* von dieser Sphinx auch unsereits das Fragen lernen? *Wer* ist das eigentlich, der uns hier Fragen stellt? *Was* in uns will eigentlich "zur Wahrheit"?—In der That, wir machten lange Halt vor der Frage nach der Ursache dieses Willens, —bis wir, zulertzt, vor einer noch grünlicheren Frage ganz und gar stehen blieben. Wir fragten nach dem *Werthe* dieses Willens. Gesetzt, wir wollen Wahrheit: *warum nicht lieber* Unwahrheit? [KGW VI/2, 9]

It is clear that Nietzsche intends to explore these questions throughout the book. The most basic question is, of course, what is the value of truth? The value of an objective, aperspectival Truth seems clear—it puts an end to certain debates. Suppose there was a question as to whether an item was red or green. We discover where in the color spectrum the color of the item falls and the question is answered "once and for all." It is no accident that this phrase has become cliché. Under a dogmatic view of Truth, Truth is absolute. Once a Truth has been established, it is eternal ("once") and universal ("for all").

Truth is eternal. The paradigm of eternal Truth is mathematical: two times two equals four in a natural number system. This was True in the time of the ancient Greeks, and it is True in the latter half of the twentieth century, and it will be True for people in the thirty-third century as well. As Dostoevsky's underground man puts it in *Notes from Underground,* "Two times two equals four and there's no sense complaining about it, it's just the way it is, and there's nothing you can do about it."[6] Given the conditions of a natural number system, two times two equals four whether or not there are actual human beings to believe it. Such eternal Truths were "out there," covered, waiting to be dis-covered by intelligent beings.

Truth is universal. The Truth of two times two equals four does not rely on how many people believe it. Truth is not determined by majority vote. If someone were to believe that two times two equals six and another were to believe that two times two equals four, the conditions of the natural numbers system would determine which belief is True. The character or condition of the believer is irrelevant. To anyone who understands numbers, multiplication, equality, and English, "two times two equals four" is a demonstrable Truth. There is only one "right" answer. People who think otherwise are "wrong" and must acquiesce to the Truth. Truth rises above differing religious, racial, cultural, or philosophical beliefs.

The attraction of absolute Truth with its twin charms of timelessness and universality is apparent. It is so appealing that many men have tried to link the nature of the external world to the nature of numbers. These attempts have an extremely old history dating back to the pre-Socratics, especially the Pythagoreans. Although this overt attempt at a one-to-one correspondence between natural numbers and natural events is currently disregarded, the desire for eternal and universal Truth continues. As we have already discussed Nietzsche's criticisms against metaphysics and God, I will focus on his critique against science as a foundation in this discussion. For Nietzsche, scientific "facts" are the current manifestation of our human desire for Truth. Scientific "facts" are supposed to be demonstrative and indisputable; they are True. They are dis-covered through impartial observation of experiments designed to isolate events of the natural world. Nietzsche spends most of part 1 of *Beyond Good and Evil* trying to convince the reader that the scare quotes around *facts* are justified.

The overriding problem with science is that it relies on what Nietzsche considers faulty underpinnings—cause and effect. As we have seen, Nietzsche criticizes causation in *The Gay Science* (aphorisms 112 and 127). Causation is one way of looking at the world but neither the only way nor, Nietzsche argues, the best way of looking at the world. Science's reliance on the notions of cause and effect as Truth is ultimately its self-deception:

> One should not wrongly reify "cause" and "effect," as the natural scientists do (and whoever, like them, now "naturalizes" in his thinking), according to the prevailing mechanical doltishness which makes the cause press and push until it "effects" its end; one should use "cause" and "effect" only as pure concepts, that is to say, as conventional fictions for the purpose of designation and communication—*not* for explanation. . . . It is *we* alone who have devised cause, sequence, for-each-other, relativity, constraint, number, law, freedom, motive, and purpose; and when we project and mix this symbol world into things as if it existed "in itself," we act once more as we have always acted—*mythologically.* (BGE, 21)

> Man soll nicht "Ursache" und "Wirkung" fehlerhaft *verdinglichen,* wie es die Naturforscher thun (und wer gleich ihnen heute im Denken naturalisirt—) gemäss der herrschenden mechanistischen Tölpelei, welche die Ursache drücken und stossen lässt, bis sie "wirkt"; man soll sich der "Ursache," der "Wirkung" eben nur als reiner

Begriffe bedienen, das heisst als conventioneller Fiktionen zum Zweck der Bezeichnung, der Verständigung, *nicht* der Erklärung. . . .*Wir* sind es, die allein die Ursachen, das Nacheinander, das Für-einander, die Relativität, den Zwang, die Zahl, das Gesetz, die Freiheit, den Grund, den Zweck erdichtet haben; und wenn wir diese Zeichen-Welt als "ans sich" in die Dinge hineindichten, hineinmischen, so treiben wir es noch einmal, wie wir es immer getrieben haben, nämlich *mythologisch.* [KGW VI/2, 29–30]

"Cause and effect" is an invention humans have devised to help them navigate in the world. Scientists have used this invention quite skillfully; NASA's space shuttle is evidence of how advanced humans have become mechanically through thinking causally. Nietzsche is not suggesting that scientists should abandon the notions of cause and effect; however, he is suggesting that they must understand that cause and effect are fictions invented by humans to successfully interact with their world. What Nietzsche is criticizing is the idea that cause and effect are "out there" in the world as Truths that scientists "discover."

For Nietzsche, the world is a continuous flux of events from which no physical laws can be inferred but only on which they can be imposed, like a musical score on a movie. To label some event as a "cause" is to make discrete some portion of the flux—to make some bit of the flux have a "beginning" and an "end" because the "cause" must stop before the "effect" can begin. Nietzsche contends that the human mind brackets out "causes" and "effects" from amid this continuous stream of events. The imposition of causal bracketing attempts to bring the continuum to a temporary standstill to emphasize one minuscule part of the entire ongoing flux. Only a limited number of things, preferably one, should be inside the bracket, thus bracketing out and ignoring great numbers of things that might be relevant to either the "cause" or the "effect." Even the "one" thing inside the "cause" bracket may not be so singular. Like "will" and "ego," it may be composed of many parts about which we do not or cannot know. Exactly where to place the brackets is, for Nietzsche, at times wholly arbitrary and at times necessitated by the needs of humans to survive in a world of becoming. But it is not the case that the events themselves determine where causal brackets go. Where humans, and especially scientists, go wrong is to think that causes and effects are "out there" in the external world rather than psychological necessities imposed by us not only for our continued survival as individuals and as a species but for our enhancement and advancement as well.

If Nietzsche does believe in a continuous flux, it would seem impossible for him to even use a word like *event* to describe activities in the world. *Event,* too, implies beginnings and endings that a view of the world as becoming would deny. Nietzsche's point seems to be not that we must abandon these kinds of concepts but that we must recognize that such designations arise from within us and not from the external world. If notions of causality, logic, numbers, substances, beauty, goodness, and truth have their origins in us and not "out there" in the world wholly independent from us, then there are grave consequences for the notion of Truth—Truth that is universal, eternal, and independent of particular humans holding it. If the origin of the notion of Truth arises from particular human beings, from perhaps their very physiology and not from any conscious decision to create it, then an independent, nonarbitrary foundation for Truth is a fiction invented by us.

What are the consequences of eliminating this long-held fascination with Truth? What would the new criteria for holding beliefs be? Nietzsche suggests an alternative in the fourth aphorism of *Beyond Good and Evil*:

> The falseness of a judgment is for us not necessarily an objection to a judgment; in this respect our new language may sound strangest. The question is to what extent it is life-promoting, life-preserving, species-preserving, perhaps even species-cultivating. And we are fundamentally inclined to claim that the falsest judgments (which include the synthetic judgments a priori) are the most indispensable for us; that without accepting the fictions of logic, without measuring reality against the purely invented world of the unconditional and self-identical, without constant falsification of the world by means of numbers, man could not live—that renouncing false judgments would mean renouncing life—that certainly means resisting accustomed value feelings in a dangerous way; and a philosophy that risks this would by that token alone place itself beyond good and evil. (BGE, 4)

> Die Falschheit eines Urtheils ist uns noch kein Einwand gegen ein Urtheil; darin klingt unsere neue Sprache vielleicht am fremdesten. Die Frage ist, wie weit es lebenfördernd, lebenerhaltend, Art-erhaltend, vielleicht gar Art-züchtend ist; und wir sind grundsätzlich geneigt zu behaupten, dass die falschesten Urtheile (zu denen die synthetischen Urtheile a priori gehören) uns die unentbehrlichsten sind, dass ohne ein Geltenlassen der logischen Fiktionen, ohne ein Messen der Wirklichkeit an der rein erfundenen Welt des Unbedingten, Sich-selbst-Gleichen, ohne eine beständige Fälschung der Welt durch die Zahl der Mensch nicht leben könnte,—dass Verzichtleisten auf falsche Urtheile ein Verzichtleisten auf Leben, eine Verneinung des Lebens wäre. Die Unwahrheit als Lebensbedingung zugestehn: das heisst freilich auf eine gefährliche Weise den gewohnten Werthgefühlen Widerstand leisten; und eine Philosophie, die das wagt, stellt sich damit allein schon jenseits von Gut und Böse. [KGW VI/2, 12]

What Nietzsche suggests in this aphorism is that for ages humans have valued Truth; yet what may have sustained our species throughout the ages was falsehood. "True" and "false" in the above aphorism must be interpreted in the historically traditional way—as a Truth (or Falsehood) that has its origin in a nonarbitrary foundation, a foundation usually derived from some kind of correlation to the "real" world—in order for this aphorism to make sense. Now Nietzsche turns this traditional interpretation on its head.

To understand how he does this, let us continue with our example of cause and effect. According to naïve empiricism, humans infer the notions of cause and effect from their visual perceptions of the world. Determining what causes which effect is accomplished by observation as well. However, for Nietzsche, being able to determine causes and effects presupposes an ordered world—a world ordered by cause and effect. But Nietzsche believes that the character of the world is in flux; there is no order. What the naïve empiricist believes he or she is "discovering" through observations is, for Nietzsche, order imposed on the world by the empiricist. The naïve empiricists "discover" what they themselves have already created and imposed on the world.

Nietzsche sees the imposition of order onto chaos as necessary for the survival of human beings, but, as he is fond of saying, the necessity of a belief does not render it True, only indispensable. It is the correlation of necessity with Truth with which Nietzsche wants to argue. Nietzsche seems to have no quarrel with the equation that necessary beliefs are valuable beliefs to have; without them we would perish as a species. The mistake is to infer that necessary beliefs are True beliefs are valuable beliefs. Truth has become an unwanted and dangerous middleman in the value equation. According to Nietzsche, the first part of this equation has become lost or ignored, so that, in the nineteenth century, the only valuable beliefs are True beliefs. But this notion of a True belief ultimately rests on a foundation that would be determined to be False if we applied the criterion of Truth to that foundation.

If "True" means that the world actually operates the way our beliefs about the world say it does, then "cause and effect" is False. But for Nietzsche, the value of a belief does not arise from the belief's Truth but, rather, from its necessity—how necessary the belief is to personal or to species preservation or enhancement. Thus, we can make good sense of what Nietzsche says at the beginning of the fourth aphorism of *Beyond Good and Evil*: "The falseness of a judgment is for us not necessarily an objection to a judgment. . . . The question is to what extent it is life-promoting, life-preserving, species-preserving, perhaps even species-cultivating."

And we can make better sense of Nietzsche's complaint against science in aphorism 22 of *Beyond Good and Evil*. As the penultimate aphorism of part 1, it ties together a number of themes before Nietzsche presents his final pronouncement of this first exploration of truth:

> Forgive me as an old philologist who cannot desist from the malice of putting his finger on bad modes of interpretation: but "Nature's conformity to law," of which you physicists talk so proudly, as though—why, it exists only owing to your interpretation and bad "philology." It is no matter of fact, no "text," but rather only a naively humanitarian emendation to and perversion of meaning, with which you make abundant concessions to the democratic instincts of the modern soul! "Everywhere equality before the law; nature is no different in that respect, no better off than we are"—a fine instance of ulterior motivation, in which the plebian antagonism to everything privileged and autocratic as well as a second and more refined atheism are disguised once more. "Neither God nor master"—that is what you, too, want; and therefore "cheers for the law of nature!"—is it not so? But as said above, that is interpretation, not text; and somebody might come along who, with opposite

intentions and modes of interpretation, could read out of the same "nature," and with regard to the same phenomena, rather the tyrannically inconsiderate and relentless enforcement of claims of power—an interpreter who would picture the unexceptional and unconditional aspects of all "will to power" so vividly that almost every word, even the word "tyranny" itself, would eventually seem unsuitable, or a weakening and attenuating metaphor—being too human—but he might, nevertheless, end by asserting the same about this world as you do, namely, that it has a "necessary" and "calculable" course, *not* because laws obtain in it, but because they are absolutely lacking, and every power draws its ultimate consequences at every moment. Supposing that this also is only interpretation—and you will be eager enough to make this objection?—well, so much the better. (BGE, 22)

Man vergebe es mir als einem alten Philologen, der von der Bosheit nicht lassen kann, auf schlechte Interpretations-Künste den Finger zu legen: aber jene "Gesetzmässigkeit der Natur," von der ihr Physiker so stolz redet, wie als ob— besteht nur Dank eurer Ausdeutung und schlechten "Philologie,"—sie ist kein Thatbestand, kein "Text," vielmehr nur eine naiv-humanitäre Zurechtmachung und Sinnverdrehung, mit der ihr den demokratischen Instinkten der modernen Seele sattsam entgegenkommt! "Überall Gleichheit ver dem Gesetz,—die Natur hat es darin nicht anders und nicht besser als wir": ein artiger Hintergedanke, in dem noch einmal die pöbelmännische Feindschaft gegen alles Bevorrechtete und Selbstherrliche, insgleichen ein zweiter und feinerer Atheismus verkleidet liegt. "Ni dieu, ni maitre"—so wollt auch ihr's; und darum "hoch das Naturgesetz"!—nicht wahr? Aber, wie gesagt, das ist interpretation, nicht Text; und es könnte Jemand kommen, der, mit der entgegengesetzen Absicht und Interpretationskunst, aus der gleichen Natur und im Hinblick auf die gleichen Erscheinungen, gerade die tyrannisch-rücksichtenlose und unerbittliche Durchsetzung von Machtansprüchen herauszulesen verstünde,—ein Interpret, der die Ausnahmslosigkeit und Unbedingtheit in allem "Willen zur Macht" dermaassen euch vor Augen stelle, dass fast jedes Wort und selbst das Wort "Tyrannei" schliesslich unbrachbar oder schon als schwächende und mildernde Metapher—als zu menschlich—erscheine; und der dennoch damit endete, das Gleiche von dieser Welt zu behaupten, was ihr behauptet, nämlich dass sie einen "nothwendigen" und "berechenbaren" Verlauf habe, aber *nicht,* weil Gesetz in ihr herrschen, sondern weil absolut die Gesetz *fehlen,* und jede Macht in jedem Augen blicke ihre letzt Consequenz zeicht. Gesetzt, dass auch dies nur Interpretation ist—und ihr werdet eifrig genug sein, dies einzuwenden?—nun, um so besser. [KGW VI/2, 31]

There are (at least!) three extremely important points made in this aphorism. First, Nietzsche says that as a philologist, a classicist, he is always concerned with interpretation. Typically, classicists pore over ancient texts looking for clues to help interpret passages. What could the writer have meant? There are better and worse methods to employ in the interpretation of texts. In the above aphorism Nietzsche accuses scientists of using bad methods of interpretation. Classicists have a text, a human artifice, to examine; yet they know they are engaged in interpretation, not in some direct apprehension of the Truth. But according to Nietzsche, scientists commit the double "errors" of treating the world as if it were a text and believing that they are apprehending the Truth and are not engaged in interpretation at all. One of the points Nietzsche wants to make in part 1 of *Beyond Good and Evil* is that all human life is engaged in interpretation. Even the act of perception is an act of interpretation. There is no such thing as "objective observation." To use Nietzsche's metaphor, if scientists think of the physical world as a text, they fail to realize that they have helped construct the text. The scientists mistakenly believe that the text is "given," simply there to be discovered, but "the given" is, for Nietzsche, a myth.

The second important aspect of this aphorism is Nietzsche's inclusion of the subject of our inquiry—will to power. This aphorism has been used to support the claim that will to power is an empirical rather than metaphysical claim about the world, and we can now see why. Nietzsche claims he can observe the same phenomena as the scientists and offer a competing description. Where the scientists "see" all sorts of natural laws (e.g., gravitational, thermodynamic, etc.) in operation in the phenomena, Nietzsche "sees" will to power operating. If one is reluctant to call gravity a metaphysical principle, then one should be reluctant to call will to power Nietzsche's metaphysics.

Now we have two competing empirical descriptions, and there can be many more interpretations. Which one is True? The scientist wants to point to the external world, but Nietzsche has already discounted this move; he can point to the world, too. What the scientist sees as a neutral external world, Nietzsche claims is already a tainted construction of the scientist. Because there is no neutral ground to which both the scientist and Nietzsche can appeal, they are left with "only interpretations."

This is the third important point. Given Nietzsche's criticism of science and "natural laws" as an interpretation and not True, the scientist can turn around and accuse Nietzsche's description of the world as will to power as being an interpretation, and not True, as well: "And you would be eager enough to make this objection?—well, so much the better." But as Nietzsche already says in the fourth aphorism, it is not an objection to a judgment that it is not True. If the scientist wants to criticize Nietzsche's interpretation of the world as will to power, it will have to be by a criterion other than Truth. But why does Nietzsche say, "well, so much the better"? I consider this such an important point because it reveals that Nietzsche is aware of the self-referential problem that is engendered when any neutral ground, any nonperspectival foundation, is eliminated.

If there are only interpretations of the world, then scientists can argue that their interpretation is no worse than Nietzsche's will to power interpretation and that Nietzsche's will to power interpretation is no better than their causal one. I believe Nietzsche's final words of aphorism 22 represent his recognition that his antifoundational stance toward Truth has this self-referential problem and that he is not overly concerned with this problem. Why he is not concerned with this problem will have to wait for just a moment. For now, Nietzsche seems content just to have the scientist recognize that the scientific enterprise is engaged in

interpretation of the world and not objective reporting or mirroring of the world. If there is any reporting or mirroring in science, it is a report of the image of the scientists. Nietzsche describes them as having "ulterior motives." He claims his interpretation of the world as will to power arises from "opposite intentions and modes of interpretation." This is why the last aphorism of part 1 of *Beyond Good and Evil,* aphorism 23, concerns psychology.

If we want to investigate the origins of interpretation, according to Nietzsche, we should look to human psychology. Science for too long has ignored the psychological role of the scientist in science. The ideal situation has the scientist as an unemotionally involved, impartial observer of the experiment or world. The scientist's gender, personality, moral beliefs, personal problems, or biases are irrelevant to the science being done. Science is to be completely divorced from the scientists themselves. As Nietzsche says in *Beyond Good and Evil* 6,

> Indeed, it is almost a matter of total indifference whether his little machine is placed at this or that spot in science, and whether the "promising" young worker turns himself into a good philologist or an expert on fungi or a chemist: it does not *characterize* him that he becomes this or that. (BGE, 6)

> [J]a es ist beinahe gleichgültig, ob seine kleine Maschine an diese oder jene Stelle der Wissenschaft gestellt wird, un ob der "hoffnungsvoll" junge Arbeiter aus sich einen guten Philologen oder Pilzekenner oder Chemiker macht:—es *bezeichnet* ihn nicht, dass er dies oder jenes wird. [KGW VI/2, 14]

Science is completely detached from the scientist in this idealized view of science. One pair of scientific observational eyes can be replaced just as easily with another pair if they are just as keen. The individual personalities behind the eyes supposedly have no impact on what they are observing.

By the last aphorism of part 1, Nietzsche will have no part of this idealized version of science. This idealized view itself is based on ulterior motives. By emphasizing only the objects of perception and rendering the perceiver almost invisible in the scientific process, science now could establish its interpretations as "above" crude opinion. Scientific data are indisputable and not open to prejudicial interpretation. By being beyond individual biases, science could set itself up as the neutral foundation for knowledge and Truth. Nietzsche realizes it would be a substantial task to make the scientific community recognize that not only are the scientific data open to interpretation but the entire foundational beliefs on which science rests, mainly the notions of cause, effect, and "objective observation," are nonneutral interpretations as well. If a scientist were willing to take Nietzsche's view that science is an elaborate interpretation seriously enough to counter with the objection that Nietzsche's will to power description, too, is an interpretation, then Nietzsche's exclamation, "well, so much the better," is understandable. It is the equivalent to, "Good, now you're starting to get it!"

If our interpretations, whether they are will to power, science, religion, morality, or what have you, are products of ulterior motives, intentions, and methods, then it would be profitable to investigate these areas. For Nietzsche, that is the province of psychology, and he says as much in the last aphorism of book 1 of *Beyond Good and Evil*. Yet he warns that psychology, too, can just as much fall prey to underlying motives and prejudices: "All psychology so far has got stuck in moral prejudices and fears; it has not dared to descend into the depths. . . . The power of moral prejudices has penetrated deeply into the most spiritual world"(BGE, 23). For Nietzsche, psychology has been afraid to plumb the depths of the human psyche, too afraid of what it might find there. Nietzsche makes a plea to psychology to go wherever its investigations lead—to go into uncharted seas. This would also lead into an investigation of physiology.

In the late twentieth century, it is commonplace to realize there is a connection between psychology and physiology, especially as it is explored in neurophysiology. Chemical imbalances in the brain are now one of the first things psychologists check in order to discover the origin of some psychological states, such as clinical depression. Nietzsche's seemingly bold assertion in *On the Genealogy of Morals* that doctors and physiologists need to be involved in the study of morality and values makes good sense within this context. People's physical makeup affects their psychological states; their psychological states affect their interpretations and values. That human values may have a nonconscious origin is an idea that Nietzsche thinks is quite dangerous to nineteenth-century European culture—and one that might be beneficial to it as well. When "wicked" human behavior is seen as the result of genetics or of chemical absences or imbalances, the moral condemnation of that behavior stops. The behavior is seen as a medical problem and not a moral weakness. For Nietzsche, much of human behavior lies in forces and physiology of which we have little or no conscious awareness. People move beyond morality when nonconscious areas of human beings are investigated. A philosophy that considers nonconscious intentions and motives would place itself "beyond good and evil" as well.

We are now in a better position from which to evaluate Nietzsche's self-referential problem. First, it is clear that Nietzsche is not simply ignorant that his epistemological antifoundationalism engenders a self-referential problem. He is aware that his position that there is no Truth, only interpretations of experience, can be used against him. Any criticism Nietzsche lodges against the traditional, foundational notion of Truth can be applied to his own, antifoundational view. Why take his interpretation on Truth to be better than the scientist's or the theologian's? After all, the scientific view of the world (what Nietzsche terms the "mechanistic" view) has resulted in consequences many people would argue are quite beneficial, from vaccines, to vehicles, to personal computers.

The main thrust of Nietzsche's complaint against science is not that it should be abandoned altogether. His emphasis is that this mechanistic way of interpreting the world is only *one* way of looking at the world. Despite its successes, it is not the best way of interpreting the world, according to Nietzsche, because it is so unartistic and passionless. However, science's methodology has become the standard for other areas of life. This is the ultimate danger of science. It sets it-self up as the highest arbitrator of other methodologies, so all other methodolo-gies are devalued. But for Nietzsche, the scientific method may be fine for sci-ence, but it is terribly lacking for other human experiences and enterprises. Science holds no exalted position. It, too, is a "frog perspective" (BGE, 2).

So this brings us around again to the self-referential problem. Nietzsche's view that everything is an interpretation is itself "just an interpretation" and need not be considered any more "true" than science or religious interpretations of the world. But what are we to make of Nietzsche's claim? Is his claim that "every-thing is interpretation" supposed to be True? If it is, then he is hoist by his own criticism against Truth, and we shake our heads at such blindness to his own words. That is why I believe aphorism 22 of *Beyond Good and Evil* becomes so important. It demonstrates quite clearly that Nietzsche was aware of this self-referential dilemma. To read aphorism 22 and still believe that Nietzsche was simply ignorant or blind to the self-referential problem his antifoundationalism produces is to pronounce Nietzsche stupid. This is a conclusion I am reluctant to draw. Thus, I must look more closely at Nietzsche's writings on Truth and truth.

For all of Nietzsche's attacks against Truth and his insistence on interpreta-tion and perspective, he is not above making pronouncements on everything from the nature of the universe to the nature of women. How are we to take these pro-nouncements? Let us briefly examine some of his remarks on women. At the end of "Our Virtues" (part 7 in *Beyond Good and Evil*), we encounter eight aphorisms devoted exclusively to Nietzsche's views on women—what Nietzsche calls his "few truths about 'woman as such.'" These aphorisms have either been ignored or criticized by scholars as embarrassments of nineteenth-century chauvinism. But the key is the aphorism that introduces this sequence on women—aphorism 231:

> Learning changes us; it does what all nourishment does which also does not merely "preserve"—as physiologists know. But at the bottom of us, really "deep down," there is, of course, something unteachable, some granite of spiritual fate, of prede-termined decision and answer to predetermined selected questions. Whenever a cardinal problem is at stake, there speaks an unchangeable "this is I"; about man and woman, for example, a thinker cannot relearn but only finish learning—only discover ultimately how this is "settled in him." At times we find certain solutions of problems that inspire strong faith in *us*; some call them henceforth *their* "con-victions." Later—we see them only as steps to self-knowledge, signposts to the prob-lems we *are*—rather, to the great stupidity we are, to our spiritual fate, to what is *unteachable* very "deep down." After this abundant civility that I have just evidenced in relation to myself I shall perhaps be permitted more readily to state a few truths about "woman as such"—assuming that it is now known from the outset how very much these are after all only—*my* truths. (BGE, 231)

> Das Lernen verwandelt uns, es thut Das, was alle Ernährung thut, die auch nicht bloss "erhält"—: wie der Physiologe weiss. Aber im Grunde von uns, ganz "da

unten," giebt es Freilich etwas Unbelehrbares, einen Granit von geistigem Fatum, von vorherbestimmter Entscheidung und Antwort auf verherbestimmte ausgelesene Fragen. Bei jedem kardinalen Probleme redet ein unwandelbares "das bin ich;" über Mann und Weib zum Beispiel kann ein Denker nicht umlernen, sondern nur auslernen,—nur zu Ende entdecken, was darüber bei ihm "feststeht." Man findet bei Zeiten gewisse Lösungen von Problemen, die gerade *uns* starken Glauben machen; vielleicht nennt man sie fürderhin seine "Überzeugungen." Später—sieht man in ihnen nur Fusstapfen zur Selbsterkenntniss, Wegweiser zum Probleme, das wir *sind,*—richtiger, zur grossen Dummheit, die wir sind, zu unserem geistigen, Fatum, zum *Unbelehrbaren* ganz "da unten."—Auf diese reichliche Artigkeit hin, wie ich sie eben gegen mich selbst begangen habe, wird es mir vielleicht eher schon gestattet sein, über das "Weib an sich" einige Wahrheiten herauszusagen: gesetzt, dass man es von vornherein nunmehr weiss, wie sehr es eben nur—*meine* Wahrheiten sind. [KGW VI/2, 176]

This transitional paragraph into Nietzsche's remarks on "woman as such" can be taken as the transitional aphorism for many, if not all, of his more blunt pronouncements about the nature of reality, women, morality, Christianity, and so on. These are *his* truths. He could even claim that these are his Truths—what he holds to be the case for everyone at all times. It would not make it any less his interpretation. According to Nietzsche's views of truth, the emphasis is no longer on truth versus Truth but, rather, on *his.* Once perspectivism has replaced the traditional notion of an absolute Truth, it no longer matters whether Nietzsche's pronouncements about the world are true or True, whether he holds a correspondence, coherence, or other theory of truth. It matters that the pronouncements are *his.*

What does this shift mean? It is Nietzsche's perspective that the world is becoming, that women should not be educated like men, and that Christianity is "Platonism for 'the people'" (BGE, "Preface"). Nietzsche could view these ideas as Truths—that is, he could think that the world is in flux for all human beings and that those who did not agree with him were wrong, *according to his perspective.* What drives readers of Nietzsche's works crazy, I think, is that Nietzsche does not feel the need to tell his readers that this is all from his perspective over and over again. Instead, we get periodic reminders, aphorism 231 being one of the most explicit, that his writings are from *his* perspective.

But aphorism 231 is splendid for another reason. Often after perspectivism is taken to heart, the reader is inclined to say, "That's only his opinion." This was particularly true for me after reading for the first time the eight aphorisms on "woman as such" that follow *Beyond Good and Evil* 231. I could simply dismiss these writings on women and hold the opposite views because, after all, these were "just Nietzsche's opinions." Once there is no independent arbitrator of opinions, my views on women are just as "legitimate" as Nietzsche's. Who could nonperspectivally judge between them?

The view that all perspectives are commensurate, have the same truth-value, is another problem that plagues an antifoundational view of truth. If everything is interpretation from a particular perspective, then how can Nietzsche criticize certain perspectives? Why isn't Christianity simply another perspective that Nietzsche does not care to share? Instead, he seems quite intent on criticizing a Christian perspective. Does Nietzsche's perspectivism engender epistemological relativism? Wouldn't we have to be tolerant of everyone else's perspectives, including Christianity?

Nietzsche's perspectivism does not logically entail that all perspectives are commensurate or that all competing perspectives must be tolerated. Rejecting the traditional notion of Truth opens up possibilities:

> *Our New "Infinite"*—How far the perspective character of existence extends or indeed whether existence has any other character than this; whether existence without interpretation, without "sense," does not become "nonsense;" whether, on the other hand, all existence is not essentially actively engaged in *interpretation*—that cannot be decided even by the most industrious and most scrupulously conscientious analysis and self-examination of the intellect; for in the course of this analysis the human intellect cannot avoid seeing itself in its own perspectives, and *only* in these. We cannot look around our own corner: it is a hopeless curiosity that wants to know what other kinds of intellects and perspectives there *might* be; for example, whether some beings might be able to experience time backward, or alternately forward and backward (which would involve another direction of life and another concept of cause and effect). But I should think that today we are at least far from the ridiculous immodesty that would be involved in decreeing from our corner that perspectives are permitted only from this corner. Rather has the world become "infinite" for us all over again, inasmuch as we cannot reject the possibility that *it may include infinite interpretations*. Once more we are seized by a great shudder; but who would feel inclined immediately to deify again after the old manner this monster of an unknown world? And to worship the unknown henceforth as *"the* Unknown One"? Alas, too many possibilities of interpretation are included in the unknown, too much devilry, stupidity, and *ungodly* foolishness of interpretation—even our own human, all too human folly, which we know. (GS, 374)

> Unser neues "Unendliches"—Wie weit der perspektivische Charakter des Daseins reicht oder gar ob es irgend einen andern Charakter noch hat, ob nicht ein Dasein ohne Auslegung, ohne "Sinn" eben zum "Unsinn" wird, ob, andrerseits, nicht alles Dasein essentiell ein *auslegendes* Dasein ist—das kann, wie billig, auch durch die fleissigste und peinlich-gewissenhafteste Analysis und Selbstprüfung des Intellekts nicht ausgemacht werden: da der menschliche Intelleckt bei dieser Analysis nicht umhin kann, sich selbst unter seinen perspektivischen Formen zu sehn und *nur* in ihnen zu sehn. Wir können nicht um unsre Ecke sehn: es ist eine hoffnunglose Neugierde, wissen zu wollen, was es noch für andre Arten Intellekt und Perspektive geben *könnte*: zum Beispiel, ob irgend welche Wesen die Zeit zurück oder abwechselnd vorwärts und rückwärts empfinden können (womit eine andre Richtung des Lebens und ein andrer Begriff von Ursache und Wirkung gegeben wäre). Aber ich denke, wir sind heute zum Mindesten ferne von der lächerlichen

Unbescheindenheit, von unsrer Ecke aus zu dekretiren, dass man nur von dieser Ecke aus Perspektiven haben *dürfe.* Die Welt ist uns vielmehr noch einmal "unendlich" geworden: insofern wir die Möglichkeit nicht abweisen können, dass sie *unendliche Interpretationen in sich schliesst.* Noch einmal fasst uns der grosse schauder—aber wer hätte wohl Lust, *dieses* Ungeheure von bekannter Welt nach alter Weise sofort wieder zu vergöttlichen? Und etwas *das* Unbekannte fürderhin als *"den* Unbekannten" anzubeten? Ach, es sind zu viele *ungöttliche* Möglichkeiten der Interpretation mit in dieses Unbekannte eingerechnet, zu viel Teufelei, Dummheit, Narrheit der Interpretation,—unsre eigne menschliche, allzumenschliche selbst, die wir kennen. [KGW V/2, 308]

This aphorism is from the fifth book of *The Gay Science,* so it was written soon after *Beyond Good and Evil.* Here we see clearly that Nietzsche is no amateur perspectivalist. He is not ignorant of the self-referential problem; yet some interpretations are "foolish" or "stupid." This indicates that Nietzsche did not think that all interpretations are equally valid. But if some interpretations are devilish, stupid, or foolish, what criteria is Nietzsche using to make these judgments? If the criterion is solely Nietzsche's individual viewpoint, nothing has been settled; we are back to square one. Nietzsche cannot deify his own viewpoint any more than he allows religion or science to become the sole evaluator of good and bad interpretations.

The above aphorism also indicates that Nietzsche was cognizant of the dangers of deifying one's own interpretation. Clearly, he was not so obtuse as to simply set his own interpretations as "God." Yet it is equally clear that he thought his interpretations on certain matters were superior to some of the prevalent views of the nineteenth century. How can Nietzsche make the case that his interpretation is better than others without resorting to the simple rider "in my opinion"?

There have been many attempts to reconcile Nietzsche's perspectivism and the self-referential and commensurability problems. One way is to recognize different meanings of truth and different levels of truth. We have already discussed the traditional model of Truth. We have capitalized its T to distinguish it as a notion that has an aperspectival frame of reference. In this model Truth consists in a correspondence between the beliefs and this objective standard. For Christianity, the objective standard is God's knowledge. For science, the absolute standard is the material world. If my beliefs correspond to God's knowledge (or, if science is my standard, to scientific facts), then my beliefs are True. Almost all of Nietzsche's polemics on truth criticize the notion of a correspondence between beliefs and an objective standard. This standard always rests on shaky metaphysical foundations that rest, ultimately, on grammar.

Nietzsche contends the foundational, metaphysical ideas of religion and science are products of grammar, explicitly, the product of subject and object. This theme runs from *The Gay Science* through *Twilight of the Idols.* Two of the passages that illustrate this best are from *On the Genealogy of Morals* and *Twilight of the Idols:*

But there is no such substratum; there is no "being" behind doing, effecting, becoming; "the doer" is merely a fiction added to the deed—the deed is everything. The popular mind in fact doubles the deed; when it sees the lightning flash, it is the deed of a deed; it posits the same event first as a cause and then a second time as its effect. Scientists do no better when they say "force moves," "force causes," and the like—all its coolness, its freedom from emotion notwithstanding, our entire science still lies under the misleading influence of language and has not disposed of that little changeling, the "subject" (the atom, for example, is such a changeling, as is the Kantian "thing-in-itself"). (GM I, 13)

Aber es giebt kein solches Substrat; es giebt kein "Sein" hinter dem Thun, Wirken, Werden; "der Thäter" ist zum Thun bloss hinzugedichtet,—das Thun ist Alles. Das Volk verdoppelt im Grunde das Thun, wenn es den Blitz leuchten lässt, das ist ein Thum-Thun: es setzt dasselbe Geschehen einmal als Ursache und dann noch einmal als deren Wirkung. Die Naturforscher machen es nicht besser, wenn sie sagen "die Kraft bewegt, die Kraft verurscht" und der gleichen,—unsre ganze Wissenschaft steht noch, trotz aller ihrer Kühle, ihrer Freiheit vom Affect, unter der Verführung der Sprache und ist die untergeschobenen Wechselbälge, die "Subjekte" nicht losgeworden (das Atom is zum Beispiel ein solcher Wechselbag, insgleichen das Kantische "Ding ans sich"). [KGW VI/2, 293–94]

Today, conversely, precisely insofar as the prejudice of reason forces us to posit unity, identity, permanence, substance, cause, thinghood, being, we see ourselves somehow caught in error, *compelled* into error. So certain are we, on the basis of rigorous examination, that *this* is where the error lies. It is no different in this case than with the movement of the sun: there our eye is the constant advocate of error, here it is our *language*. In its origin language belongs in the age of the most rudimentary form of psychology. We enter a realm of crude fetishism when we summon before consciousness the basic presuppositions of the metaphysics of language, in plain talk, the presuppositions of *reason*. Everywhere it sees a doer and doing; it believes in will as *the* cause; it believes in the ego, in the ego as being, in the ego as substance, and it *projects* this faith in the ego-substance upon all things—only thereby does it first *create* the concept of "thing." . . . I am afraid we are not rid of God because we still have faith in grammar. (TI, "Reason," 5, 482–83)

Heute umgekehrt sehen wir, genau so weit als das Vernuft-Vorurtheil uns zwingt, Einheit Identität, Dauer, Substanz, Ursache, Dinglichkeit, Sein anzusetzen, uns gewissermaassen verstrickt in den Irrthum, *necessitirt* zum Irrthum; so sicher wir auf Grund einer strengen Nachrechnung bei uns darüber sind, *dass* hier der Irrthum ist. Es steht damit nicht anders als mit den Bewegungen des grossen Gestirns: bei ihnen hat der Irrthum unser Auge, hier hat er unsre *Sprache* zum beständigen Anwalt. Die Sprache gehört ihrer Entstehung nach in die Zeit der rudimentärsten Form von Psychologie: wir kommen in ein grobes Fetischwesen hinein, wenn wir uns die Grundvor aussetzungen der Sprach-Metaphysik, auf deutsch: der *Vernunft,* zum Bewusstsein bringen. *Das* sieht überall Thäter und Thun: das glaubt an Willen als Ursache überhaupt; das glaubt an's "Ich," an's Ich als Sein, an's Ich als Substanz und *projicirt* den Glauben an die Ich-Substanz auf alle Dinge—es *schafft* erst damit den Begriff "Ding." . . . Ich fürchte, wir werden Gott nicht los, weil wir noch an die Grammatik glauben. [KGW VI/3, 71–72]

In these quotations we can see the brunt of Nietzsche's objections: it is our grammar that has infected our way of organizing the world. Because sentences must have subjects and objects, there must be subjects (egos) and objects (things) in the world. Removing the metaphysical underpinnings for religion and science removes the foundation for objective truth as well. We remain stuck in the problem posed by Nietzsche's perspectivism. Are we to take Nietzsche's views on truth as True or true? If they are only *his* truths, why should *we* believe him?

In discussing Nietzsche's writings on truth, some commentators have separated the notion of truth into different categories. These attempts to avoid the problem of perspectivism being self-referential can be divided into two camps. The first camp claims that Nietzsche's polemics against truth are only about metaphysical truths—claims about the ultimate or transcendent nature of the world. Nietzsche has a history of attacking metaphysical claims starting in *Human, All-Too-Human*. Metaphysical truths are to be distinguished from empirical truths, truths that are induced from observations of the natural world. Scientific truths are of this latter kind. The claim that water seeks its own level is true in the empirical sense, in that it is a generalization made from observing water. However, the attempt to make this observation into a "natural law" would meet with Nietzsche's criticism because it would posit the effect as the cause. This move would be another example of what Nietzsche calls "doubling of the deed" in his lightning analogy. If one were to observe that water seeks its own level and then ask why water does that, it makes no explanatory sense to Nietzsche to say it does so because water is obeying the natural law of liquid seeking its own level. Thus, the empirical observation of water seeking its own level can be called "true" by Nietzsche, but the metaphysical "law" "explaining" the observation would be criticized.

I would agree that Nietzsche is using *truth* in several different senses, which is why we find scare quotes around the word *truth* in many of his passages. But there is a danger, I think, of saying, as Walter Kaufmann does, that empirical truths are allowed by Nietzsche. This move allows Kaufmann to say that will to power is an empirical observation rather than a metaphysical principle. Because truth (and falsehood) can be applied to empirical observations, Nietzsche could say that the statement "the world is will to power" is empirically true without becoming stuck in a self-referential problem. According to Kaufmann, Nietzsche could say the world is will to power (as a result of Nietzsche's empirical observations about the world) and not be the victim of his own critique of truth because the only "truths" that Nietzsche is critical of are metaphysical truths. This tidies up some of Nietzsche's passages on truth very nicely, but it ignores those passages in which the concept of truth itself is questioned.

What seems the most confusing about Nietzsche is the fact that he writes a devastating critique on certain ideas and then continues to use those ideas in subsequent aphorisms as if he were completely unaware of his critical blow. He uses *will, self, ego,* and *soul* even after he questions whether these words have any referents at all. It is a similar story with truth. It is not just metaphysical truths that go on Nietzsche's critical chopping block. As is mentioned in chapter 2, Nietzsche uses a kind of positivistic "verification principle" in order to attack metaphysics in *Human, All-Too-Human* and employs science in the service of his polemic. But in the later works, as we have seen with *Beyond Good and Evil,* Nietzsche no longer spares science and scientific truth from his critical attacks. So a simple bifurcation of truth into metaphysical and empirical categories is not going to do justice to the subtleties of Nietzsche's thinking.

The second group that tries to rescue perspectivism from its apparent self-referential problem argues that there are two different discussions going on in Nietzsche: truths about the world and truths about truth. Truths about the world are always perspectival, always interpretations. If, for Nietzsche, attempts to characterize the world are always from a particular perspective, then even truths about the world, even Kaufmann's empirical generalizations, are "skewed." If the generalization is meant to be an accurate, objective picture of the world, it is doomed to fail. There is no world devoid of interpretation, no objective "text," with which we can compare interpretations in order to discover what is "really" the case. Therefore, "true" or "false" are inapplicable to any characterizations of the world. According to perspectivism, these characterizations are always "false" under the criteria for Truth because they are always interpretations and do not accurately capture the world before any interpretation has occurred. However, truths about truth may not be perspectival. These are "metalevel" characterizations not about the world but about the nature of truth. Perhaps we cannot apply *true* or *false* to statements or characterizations about the world, but we can apply these terms to statements about truth. That is, we can remove ourselves one position in discussing truth, so that these statements or characterizations about truth (rather than about the world) are on a theoretical rather than empirical level.

I believe this maneuver simply pushes the original problem back one level rather than circumventing or eliminating it. If we were to say that perspectivism is true, what sense of "true" is operating here—that there is a correspondence between the idea of perspectivism and how human beings actually think? Then we are back to the problems plaguing a correspondence model of truth. Certainly human beings are part of the world, and so we are back to characterizing the world—to which the terms *true* and *false* supposedly do not apply. But there are other senses of "true" besides correspondence. In saying "perspectivism is true" perhaps Nietzsche is saying that perspectivism is the most consistent idea of truth when considered with all of his other ideas. Or could Nietzsche be saying that perspectivism is the most pragmatic or useful notion of truth for human beings? While the coherence or pragmatic views of truth appear to get Nietzsche out of the self-referential problem engendered by the correspondence view of truth, there are still difficulties. On the plus side, if Nietzsche holds either a coherence or pragmatic view of truth, he can attack the correspondence notion of truth and still legitimately use *true* himself. Coherence and pragmatism also have the

Nietzschean charms of throwing truth back on the psychology of the believer rather than originating from the world. Both of these views of truth can tell us more about the believer than they do about the world. To hold a coherence view of truth is to display that one's ultimate value is coherence, consistency. Unfortunately for this view, there are passages in his writings where Nietzsche suggests that consistency is overrated and should not be the ideal or ultimate arbitrator in human affairs; it is a holdover from man's fascination with logic. To hold a pragmatic view of truth is to display that one's ultimate value is utility, usefulness. But I think this would be an odd move for Nietzsche to make. One of his chief problems with "Englanders" is that they judged everything according to its utility. Reducing everything to its usefulness strikes Nietzsche as a rather passionless way to view the world. Because Nietzsche values aesthetics over utility, I doubt that he would embrace a pragmatic notion of truth. However, coherence or pragmatic theories of truth can accommodate Nietzsche's notion of perspectivism better than a correspondence theory of truth; indeed, a common criticism of these two theories is that they lead to perspectivism and epistemological relativism. So, again, it is difficult to interpret Nietzsche's views on truth.

A helpful way to resolve this impasse might be to examine the contexts of when and how words such as *truth* are used. We could say there *are* scientific truths—but not in the sense that science thinks it has scientific truths. For Nietzsche, there *are* concepts and relationships among concepts that, given the presuppositions and limitations (the context) of science, will provide excellent consequences. The mistake science makes is to think its truths are true outside of the conceptual contexts of science. The error is not the use of the word *true* (and likewise using words like *soul, I, thing, will,* etc.); the mistake is thinking that there is a one-to-one correspondence between these words and reality. The "truth" is that these words are economies, shortcuts invented by humans to make their lived experiences manageable and communicable. We can still talk about "things" because organizing the world into the economical category of "things" is necessary for us to live in it. According to Nietzsche, and it is vitally important to remember that all this is *according to Nietzsche,* the mistake is to think that there *are* things and that they *are* the way in which we organize them.

When Nietzsche simply asserts that the world is will to power, we get confused. Is he making a metaphysical statement, an empirical statement, or a true statement about how the world really is? What we do not do and what I think Nietzsche is trying to get us to do is to think in the following way: "Nietzsche believes the world is will to power. I wonder why he sees it this way?" Nietzsche gladly tells us why he interprets the world in this way many times: seeing relationships among people and things as relationships of power consequently engenders a healthier human being.

The relationships among language, grammar, concepts, and truth are complex in Nietzsche's writings—too complex to do them complete justice in this brief chapter—but they are all tools for the human being's construction of a sensible world, a world in which the person can exist and, ideally, thrive. It is this thriving, this flourishing of humanity, or, more specifically, certain members of humanity ("great" humans), that interests Nietzsche.

Nietzsche's entire methodology seems to hinge on consequences. At first blush this would seem implausible; Nietzsche gives a scathing commentary on utilitarianism, for example, in *On the Genealogy of Morals*. But Nietzsche's criticism of utilitarianism is based not on the fact that utilitarianism looks at consequences but, rather, because utilitarianism equates "good" with "utility." How does Nietzsche attack Christianity? Of course, Christianity fails to realize that it is only one interpretation of reality among many and sets itself up as the Truth. But a large part of the criticism deals with the consequences of living under Christian ideas.

Christian morality is borne out of *ressentiment* and breeds *ressentiment*. The clichéd example is the employee who gets yelled at (unjustly from the employee's standpoint) by his boss and goes home and picks a fight with his wife. The key to *ressentiment* is that the person cannot overtly react to the seeming injustice. This may be because of sheer physical weaknesses, class differences, economic necessities, or psychological inhibitions. The person must "swallow his or her pride," thus pushing the hurt, humiliation, and anger inward, sublimating it. Eventually such feelings must be expressed, and they are expressed in various indirect and interesting ways, according to Nietzsche. In our clichéd example, the anger is expressed toward the inappropriate person. The wife cannot physically react to her husband. Her *ressentiment* may express itself by her "forgetting" to do an important errand for her husband or, in turn, getting angry at her more helpless children, who, in the cliché, finally kick the sleeping dog.

Nietzsche's genius is that he is able to see such resentment in areas that previously would not have been suspected, and he makes a plausible case that these institutions or practices are products of *ressentiment*. The institution of Christianity turns the characteristics of the herd into moral virtues—humility, modesty, meekness, compassion, charity, obedience, and so on—thereby rendering any aggression against the herd into sins. The herd thus gains moral superiority over any aggressors without having to demonstrate any physical superiority.

Nietzsche sees the consequences of Christian virtues leading to certain social and political ideas. The idea that we are all "God's children" leads to the social idea that all people are "created equal," which lends more credence to the political idea of democracy,[7] and so forth. These moral, social, and political ideas form the basis for a culture that Nietzsche thinks promotes weak human beings. The consequences of such a culture, he believes, lead to the "last man."

The last man is vividly portrayed in the preface of *Thus Spoke Zarathustra*. The last man shuns hardships and obstacles. He lives only in the temperate climates. He works only to occupy his time. His only concern is his own happiness. Everyone is "educated," but any differences of opinion are soon reconciled, for to argue with one another too long would be unpleasant. There is total equality of people; there are no classes and no rulers or subjects. Everything is done in moderation because one's health is of primary importance. This is "happiness" for the last man. Indeed, we in America have seen this vision enacted many times by retired seniors. They move to communities ("Sun City") in the warmer climates. They have "hobbies" that occupy their time. They discuss political and world events with their fellow retirees, but it is just "talk," no friendships are lost to it. They eat and exercise moderately. Many people work a whole lifetime simply in order to attain this retirement lifestyle! The last man "lives longest" because the above ideas are so deceptively agreeable. Who wouldn't want a stress-free life? In fact, it is thought that someone who disagrees with these idea(l)s would be insane: "Whoever feels different goes voluntarily into a madhouse."

Nietzsche, of course, disagrees with the ideals of the last man, but instead of going into a madhouse, he tries, through Zarathustra's speeches, to portray another kind of man who loves danger and obstacles, who is tempered by hardships, and who gives style to his own unique character rather than blend in with the herd. The consequences of Christianity for Nietzsche lead ultimately to the last man, the antithesis of Nietzsche's vision for human beings. The vast majority of humankind will be benefited and swayed by the ideals of the herd, but Nietzsche wants to create new ideals, not necessarily to persuade the herd but to leave open the possibility that those who see visions other than herd visions would not be considered mad but would be able to live their lives according to their visions: "Consequently—. Consequently. Consequently. O, do you understand me, my brothers? Do you understand this new law of ebb and flood? There is a time for us, too!" (GS, 1).

The consequences of the ideas and ideals we have are of vital interest to Nietzsche. But if looking at the consequences of holding certain beliefs is the method Nietzsche employs, we are left to ask again by what criteria Nietzsche is judging the consequences. What I want to suggest now and show in the next chapter is that the criterion Nietzsche uses is the consequence of producing and enhancing the "fully human" human being—the kind of human being who creates him- or herself with style:

Preparatory human beings.—I welcome all signs that a more virile, warlike age is about to begin, which will restore honor to courage above all. For this age shall prepare the way for one yet higher, and it shall gather the strength that this higher age will require some day—the age that will carry heroism into the search for knowledge and that will *wage wars* for the sake of ideas and their consequences. To this end we now need many preparatory human beings who cannot very well leap out of nothing, any more than out of the sand and slime of present-day civilization and metropolitanism—human beings who know how to be silent, lonely resolute, and content and constant in invisible activities; human beings who are bent in seeking in all things for what must be *overcome*; human beings distinguished as much by cheerfulness, patience, unpretentiousness, and contempt for all great vanities as by magnanimity in victory and forebearance regarding the small vanities of the vanquished. (GS, 283)

Vorbereitende Menschen.—Ich begrüsse alle Anzeichen dafür, dass ein männlicheres, ein kriegerisches Zeitalter anhebt, das vor allem die Tapferkeit wieder zu Ehren bringen wird! Denn es soll einem noch höheren Zeitalter den Weg bahnen und die Kraft einsammeln, welche jenes einmal nöthig haben wird,—jenes Zeitalter, das den Heroismus in die Erkenntniss trägt und *Kriege führt* um der Gedanken ihrer Folgen willen. Dazu bedarf es für jetzt vieler vorbereitender tapferer Menschen, welche doch nicht aus dem Nichts entspringen können—und ebensowenig aus dem Sand und Schleim der jetzigen Civilisation und Grossstadt-Bildung: Menschen, welche es verstehen, schweigend, einsam, entschlossen, in unsichtbarer Thätigkeit zufrieden und beständig zu sein: Menschen, die mit innerlichen Hange an allen Dingen nach dem suchen, was an ihnen *zu überwinden* ist: Menschen, denen Heiterkeit, Geduld, Schlichtheit und Verachtung der grossen Eitelkeiten ebenso zu eigen ist, als Grossmuth im Siege und Nachsicht gegen die kleinen Eitelkeiten all Besiegten. [KGW V/2, 206]

As the above quotation states, wars will be waged over ideas and their consequences. This is not so startlingly new; humans have been waging wars over differing views for millennia. Nietzsche's contribution to this discussion is the *kind* of ideas and consequences over which wars will be waged. It will not be over border disputes or political or economic differences but, rather, over the very visions of what it means to be a fully human human being. In this aphorism Nietzsche gives us a brief look at his vision of a fully human human being. This vision gets fleshed out in greater but not definitive detail in *Thus Spoke Zarathustra,* which he was already contemplating as he finished this fourth book of *The Gay Science.*

The ideas that do not lead to Nietzsche's vision for humankind are the ideas prevalent in nineteenth-century Europe—democracy, equality, and Christian morality, self-sacrifice, and suffering. The consequences of these ideas eventually lead to the last man—the safe, contented, homogeneous, anonymous, and serious man of the "herd." In Nietzsche's vision, fully human human beings live dangerously—take great risks, push themselves to always want more (more character, not more money or fame, although the consequences of a stylish character may be money or fame), give because they are overflowing not because they are self-sacrificing, laugh from playfulness, and are self-possessed while striving for even more from themselves. What ideas can create the groundwork for these consequences? I contend that one of the most important of them, for Nietzsche, is the idea of will to power.

This is how I see will to power joined to the will to truth. The will to truth is a psychological state. According to Nietzsche, humans have a craving for Truth. The phrase *will to truth* makes sense only if *truth* is interpreted as Truth. In *Beyond Good and Evil* Nietzsche asks us to look at a philosopher's morality if we want to find out about his (or her) metaphysics. He illustrates this with aphorism 9, chiding the Stoics for interpreting the nature of the world so that it will conform to their view of ideal human behavior. Then the Stoics turn this around and believe their morality stems from nature—the "objective" way the world really is—which is Stoic metaphysics.

It is not only metaphysics that falls into this pattern; theories of truth also are constructed to conform to morality. It is psychologically comforting for people to think that there is a universal and impartial standard for determining everything, including right from wrong. If there is a need for an objective standard for good and bad, it gets translated as well into a pronouncement of an objective standard for true and false, which again gets turned around à la the Stoics, whether this foundation is an omnipotent, omniscient God or science. In the long run, the omnipotent God or science gets turned into the primary source from which morality springs rather than vice versa. In the nineteenth century, there was a movement to create a "scientific" morality based on reason and on finding the physical and psychological causes of immoral behavior and eliminating those causes. People have the subconscious will to Truth because without Truth, traditional morality and the metaphysics on which it is based collapse. These consequences are too dire, but for Nietzsche there is more going on with the will to Truth than simply bad consequences for present-day civilization.

The will to Truth is an expression of will to power. If one has an "objective" standard to which to appeal and one's belief corresponds to that objective standard, then anyone with a differing belief is immediately and categorically wrong. This gives power to the person conforming to the objective standard. Objective Truth empowers those whose wills are slave-like. Master types are thus forced to conform to the herd's values in an indirect way. Truth is something to which all, master and slave types together, must defer, thus deflecting any wrath away from the slave type's imposition of Truth on the master type. When one sees the relationship between beliefs and truth as one of power, new insights emerge.

Beliefs empower people. According to Nietzsche, people believe certain ideas because they help people live and get around in the world, but he wonders why these helpful ideas must be called True. For Nietzsche, other adjectives are just as informative as to why we hold these beliefs, for example, *beautiful, necessary, life preserving*. What is being added by saying a belief is True? To say that a belief is useful or necessary places the locus of these adjectives within me. The beliefs are useful or necessary *to me*. To say that a belief is True is to place the locus outside of the person and onto the "real world." Thus, the Truth of a belief has nothing to do with the psychology of the individual. One looks outward to the "objective," "real world" to adjudicate differences. Again, by pretending that the Truth of beliefs originates from the world external to humans, the beliefs' alignments with these "objective facts" confer power to them and by extension to the humans who hold them.

However, if we place the locus for truth away from the "real world" and back into people, psychology becomes extremely important—as Nietzsche tells us at the end of part 1 in *Beyond Good and Evil*. As we will recall, the penultimate aphorism of part 1 charges that science's view of the world is not one of an objective discovery of the external world but, rather, an interpretation of the world—

and only one interpretation among many. Nietzsche's own interpretation of the same phenomena is that a will to power is operating. The scientist retorts that if Nietzsche is correct, then Nietzsche's view is "only interpretation." To which Nietzsche in effect replies, "Bravo!" Then the ultimate aphorism discusses psychology. This makes terrific sense because if worldviews are psychological constructions, then psychology should become prominent:

> All psychology so far has got stuck in moral prejudices and fears; it has not dared to descend into the depths. To understand it as morphology and *the doctrine of the development of the will to power,* as I do—nobody has yet come close to doing this even in thought—insofar as it is permissible to recognize in what has been written so far a symptom of what has so far been kept silent. (BGE, 23)

> Die gesammte Psychologie is bisher an moralischen Vorurtheilen und Befürchtungen hängen geblieben: sie hat sich nicht in die Tiefe gewagt. Dieselbe als Morphologie und *Entwicklungslehre des Willens zur Macht* zu fassen, wie ich sie fasse—daran hat noch Niemand in seinen Gedanken selbst gestreift: sofern es nämlich erlaubt ist, in dem, was bisher geschrieben wurde, ein Symptom von dem, was bisher verschwiegen wurde, zu erkennen. [KGW VI/2, 32]

So now we are told not only that human experience stems from our interpretations of it (our psychology) but also that our interpretations inform us about human power. This happens not only on a species level as the above aphorism suggests but on a personal level as well. Our interpretations of the world tell us about us—who we are and what we value. We hold certain beliefs because those beliefs give us a feeling of an increase in power. What we hold true (or True) tells others about our values and what gives us power. Are we leaders, followers, creative thinkers, inhibited souls, overflowing, or resentful? We cling to those interpretations that empower us. Nietzsche's beliefs tell us that seeing the world as relations of forces continually in flux, but always moving toward more power, empowers him. Interpreting the world as will to power gives him ever new and empowering ways to interpret the world. It is the way by which Nietzsche interprets the world. In chapters 2 and 3 we have already seen how interpreting the world through the lens of will to power yields insights about human behavior, especially in Nietzsche's notion of *ressentiment.*

But if will to power is "just" an interpretive tool, then Nietzsche's writings do not tell us anything about how humans or the world really are or about the nature of truth but about . . . Nietzsche. Will to power informs us about Nietzsche. We may be tempted to think that Nietzsche recommends that we all interpret the world via will to power. Wouldn't that empower all of us more than Christian or scientific interpretations do? I resist this view of Nietzsche's writings on will to power. To adopt Nietzsche's perspective is to manifest slave-like behavior. Nietzsche's recommendation is creation of one's own worldview—to choose the interpretive lens for one's own beliefs. Nietzsche has shown us that this is possible. He has done it himself by creating will to power. For the truly outstanding and enlightened individual, the task is to *re-create the process* not adopt the product.

The brilliance of Nietzsche's style of writing is that we get information not only about Nietzsche but about ourselves—our reaction to Nietzsche. Which aphorisms irritate us, with which do we identify, against which do we want to argue, which do we remember? We interpret his words in the way that makes the most sense to us, and that way, that interpretation, thereby reveals *us*. To slavishly hang on every word he writes is tantamount to hanging on every word in the Bible. It reveals us as mere worshipers, not as creators. We have a psychological need to view ourselves in the most empowering ways. Don't we want to be revealed in a good light? Don't we want our interpretations to reveal us as great human beings? What are the best interpretations to have—the ones that will enhance ourselves, give us style? What Nietzsche thinks are the answers to these questions will be investigated in the following chapter. And if you question by what standard of values Nietzsche determines "a *good* light," "*great* human beings," and "*best* interpretations"—and you are eager enough to make this objection?—so much the better!

FURTHER READING

Clark, Maudemarie. *Nietzsche on Truth and Philosophy*. New York: Cambridge University Press, 1990.

Grimm, Reudiger H. *Nietzsche's Theory of Knowledge*. New York: Walter de Gruyter, 1977.

Nehamas, Alexander. *Nietzsche: Life as Literature*. Cambridge, Mass.: Harvard University Press, 1985.

Schacht, Richard. *Nietzsche*. Boston: Routledge and Kegan Paul, 1983.

Wilcox, John. *Truth and Value in Nietzsche*. Ann Arbor: University of Michigan Press, 1974.

5

Nietzsche's Magic:
It's All Done with Mirrors

If there is no reality we could ever know apart from our own perspective of it, if everything we claim to know is a construction and product of our individual physical and psychological needs, then the question is how to orient our psychology (and at times Nietzsche suggests we change our physiology!) to produce "fully human" human beings. We have glimpses of what these humans are like. Goethe is Nietzsche's best example—someone of singular intelligence and passion, who used his great talents creatively in the arts and the sciences.

In order to produce anything, we must have a vision of what it is possible for us to do or to be. Nietzsche's description of the last man in *Thus Spoke Zarathustra* is one such vision of humanity that Nietzsche believes was the prevailing ideal in nineteenth-century Europe. The consequence of this vision, he thinks, is to lead humanity into mediocrity. Because the vast majority of the human race is mediocre, according to Nietzsche, this vision of mediocrity, supported and perpetuated by the myth of Christianity, is appealing to a great many people. Nietzsche's task, most evident in *The Gay Science* and *Thus Spoke Zarathustra*, is to present another vision, another reality, as an alternative to the one based on the notions of rationality, democracy, equality, and Christianity he sees being embraced in his time.

Nietzsche's own vision, however, consists of the major components of the *Übermensch*, eternal recurrence, and will to power and a host of other aspects, such as *amor fati,* Dionysus, masks, dancing, and play, that all intertwine with each other. How do all these components fit into each other? Unfortunately, there is no one, tidy way all these fragments fit together. Given Nietzsche's advocacy of masks and multiplicities of perspectives, the last thing that Nietzsche would want to promote is a monolithic, univocal scenario for humankind. He clearly states that his vision is not for everyone, especially not for those with weak stomachs. Nietzsche's vision is not a "kinder and gentler" society but, rather, a harder and harsher one that would overwhelm many but make the occasional successes

107

all the more glorious. To achieve success much would have to be risked. For Nietzsche, it is better to have risked all and die in a brief soaring flight than to live to old age in mediocrity.

But whatever vision Nietzsche presents in books 4 and 5 of *The Gay Science* and through Zarathustra in *Thus Spoke Zarathustra* is extremely broad in scope and awash in generalities. The reader is tempted to ask Nietzsche, "What is the exact plan? Where is the blueprint for humankind to achieve this vision? We need specifics, particulars, details!" According to my reading of Nietzsche, this temptation must be resisted. Recall that in *Thus Spoke Zarathustra* Nietzsche via Zarathustra warns us that there is no "the way"; there is only, for each of us, "my way." To ask these questions of Nietzsche is to reveal our failure to grasp his vision as *his* vision. It emphasizes the product of Nietzsche's vision rather than the process that Nietzsche is trying to teach us. My reading of Nietzsche has him promoting vision making, rather than trying to elevate his vision to God-like status. But of course he seems to want to have it both ways—to encourage those few "great" persons not to capitulate to "the norm" and to create their own visions *and* to encourage the adoption by others of his own vision. When you go to all that trouble to create a new vision, you wouldn't mind others taking it seriously. However, the fact that you can read Nietzsche either way reveals his philosophy. Do you want to adopt Nietzsche's vision? Do you crave a step-by-step manual on how to attain it? If you do, then you and your values are revealed to you. You manifest a slave-type trait. How Nietzsche can accomplish these types of revelatory moments is his real genius, and the key to it is his style of writing.

Much attention has been paid to Nietzsche's style and rightly so. Writing predominantly in aphorisms or short pieces is unusual, especially in philosophy. Many of these aphorisms are observations of European, mainly German, culture and were pronounced by analytic philosophers earlier in the twentieth century as "mere opinion" or too "literary" in style to be taken seriously by the analytic tradition. Arthur Danto's book tries to dispel this notion, but only by asking readers to ignore Nietzsche's style.[1] Others have noted Nietzsche's unique style and focused almost exclusively on Nietzsche's gift of writing in such a way that the writing undermines itself: that is, in writing that circles back around paradoxically on itself. Bernd Magnus has coined the term *self-consuming concepts* to describe these concepts—concepts that, if seriously analyzed, erode any meaning they may have had to begin with.[2] My point is not to take issue with any of these viewpoints on style or to merely reiterate them (see the list at the end of the chapter for some of them), but I think there is a dimension that has not yet been articulated in these discussions of Nietzsche's style. I call it "mirror writing."

Mirror writing is writing in such a way that the meaning of the piece the reader interprets reflects the reader's mind as much if not more than it reflects the writer's mind. In one sense, this is trivially true. In all reading of books both the writer's and the reader's interpretations are brought into play. Living 100 years after Nietzsche's lifetime has made us much more cognizant of the reader's hermeneutical role. The reader is no longer looked on as a passive sponge, merely soaking up the supposedly one, True meaning of the text. Now it is considered commonplace that the reader actively brings unique perspectives to a text and consciously and subconsciously uses her or his individual abilities and experiences to make sense of the text, selecting some lines or paragraphs as important, others as transitional, still others as insignificant. What the reader considers important is a reflection of that reader's experience.

If this were all that I mean by "mirror writing," it would not be a particularly interesting or insightful observation. But it must be remembered that this hermeneutical commonplace was not so common in Nietzsche's time, when philosophical texts were seen as having a univocal meaning and the task was to discover *the* meaning of the text in much the same way as a scientist is supposed to discover *the* cause of something. When Nietzsche was a student of philology, the profession was trying to establish a single, legitimate methodology to apply to texts in order to uncover the interpretation of them. This assumption that the text has only one meaning was not a pure fabrication on the part of the reader; the writer wrote in such a way (such as discussing metaphysical Truths) as to suggest that there was only one, right way to interpret the text. Even if the reader wants to figure out the author's intent or meaning, the reader is approaching that writer from a particular perspective—the reader's perspective. It is impossible for the reader to approach the text from the writer's perspective, only from the reader's perspective of that writer. Nietzsche's style of writing challenges the assumption that a text can have only one, true meaning. Nietzsche's style helps to controvert this assumption but not simply because it is metaphoric, suggestive, and ambiguous. Nietzsche's genius is that his style of writing is designed to reveal the sublimated prejudices and values of his readers and bring them to the fore to be (re)examined and perhaps (re)evaluated. Mirror writing is Nietzsche's deliberate effort to make the reader realize that whatever meanings the reader gleans from the writing are a reflection of her or his *values*. Certainly, any interpretation of a text reveals the reader, as I state above, but I think Nietzsche was the first writer to write specifically with the objective of revealing the sublimated, unarticulated, presuppositional values of the reader. As I argued in chapter 2, Nietzsche merely describes master-type and slave-type morality. It is *we* who jump to evaluate his descriptions prescriptively. He purposefully uses his emotionally laden language to push us to immediately reject slave-type morality in favor of master-type morality simply by naming the one type "slave." While his criticisms of past or current practices can be quite pointed and specific, his remedy for these problems involves his vision of a higher humanity that is never fully articulated. Was his vision blurry, or was he incapable of translating that vision into prose? Nietzsche is a masterful artist with the German language. His genius is that he wants to encourage others to envision a higher humanity. To fully articulate one himself would stunt the imaginations of others. Instead, this vision is written in such a clever way as to allow the reader to project her or his values onto the vision and have them revealed back.

Nietzsche's own use of the concept of mirrors spans his books and notebooks from *The Birth of Tragedy out of the Spirit of Music* through *Ecce Homo*. Throughout *Human, All-Too-Human* Nietzsche speaks of man being a mirror:

> This goal is yourself to become a necessary chain of rings of culture and from this necessity to recognize the necessity inherent in the course of culture in general. When your gaze has become strong enough to see to the bottom of the dark well of your nature and your knowledge, perhaps you will also behold in its mirror the distant constellations of future cultures. (HAH I, 292)

> Diese Ziel ist, selber eine nothwendige Kette von Cultur-Ringen zu werden und von dieser Nothwendigkeit aus auf die Nothwendigkeit im Gange der Allgemeinen Cultur zu schliessen. Wenn dein Blick stark genug geworden ist, den Grund in dem dunklen Brunnen deines Wesens und deiner Erkenntnisse zu sehen, so werden dir vielleicht auch in seinem Spiegel die fernen Sternbilder künftiger Culturen sichtbar werden. [KGW IV/2, 240–41]

In *Daybreak* Nietzsche writes of "our" intellect and the knowledge therein being a mirror of us.[3] In *The Gay Science* he includes consciousness in the mirror metaphor. While mirror imagery can be found in *Thus Spoke Zarathustra* and *On the Genealogy of Morals,* perhaps the best passage to illustrate my point can be found in *Beyond Good and Evil,* which Nietzsche himself repeats in *Ecce Homo*. Here Nietzsche is describing "the genius of the heart":

> The genius of the heart that silences all that is loud and self-satisfied, teaching it to listen; who smooths rough souls and lets them taste a new desire—to be still as a mirror, that the deep sky may mirror itself in them. (BGE, 295)

> [D]as Genie des Herzens, das alles Laute und Selbstgefällige verstummen macht und horchen lehrt, das die rauhen Seelen glättet und ihnen ein neues Verlangen zu kosten giebt,—still zu liegen wie ein Spiegel, dass sich der tiefe Himmel auf ihnen spiegele. [KGW VI/2, 247]

In *Beyond Good and Evil* this aphorism is situated as the penultimate aphorism of the book, placing it under the ninth chapter, entitled "What Is Noble." This is a vaunted position, especially because the last aphorism has Nietzsche lamenting (still) whether he has been understood rather than clarifying his position. This leaves *Beyond Good and Evil* 295 as the final description of what is noble according to Nietzsche, and part of that description involves the mirror metaphor. In *Ecce Homo,* "Good Books," 6, Nietzsche reiterates this passage and leaves little doubt that he considers himself to be a genius of the heart, even though he ironically tells readers not to speculate about whom he is describing.[4] It is Nietzsche's genius to be a mirror—to be able to reflect to others themselves. It is even greater genius to teach others (through Zarathustra and his teaching of eternal recurrence) to be able to reflect themselves to themselves.

The *Nachlass* material echoes this theme. We have already seen that when Nietzsche responds to his own query about what the world is, he responds that he will show it to us in his mirror. Clearly this suggests that what is to follow will be a reflection of him more than a reflection of the world. Soon after Nietzsche wrote this entry (WP, 1067; KGW VII/3, 38[12]) in the summer of 1885, he began a series of possible book titles or chapters with the word *mirror (Spiegel)*. The first is simply called *The Mirror*. Then subtitles begin appearing with it, including "Philosophy of the Forbidden Knowledge" and "An Opportunity for Self-Reflection for Europeans." "The Mirror" became a chapter heading for a book entitled *Gai Saber* (*Joyful Wisdom* in Italian). In the brief lines of a supposedly new foreword to *Human, All-Too-Human,* Nietzsche writes that *Human, All-Too-Human* is a mirror that will reveal the "good European's" vanity. While in the middle of writing *Ecce Homo* (October–November 1888), Nietzsche again puts *The Mirror* as a book title, with "Attempt at a Self-Evaluation" as the subtitle. This theme of mirrors, while not occupying a predominant portion of Nietzsche's writings, occurs enough in the published and *Nachlass* material to convince me that he was consciously attempting to incorporate it into his own style. Both the published material and the *Nachlass* entries center around the theme of his writings providing people with an occasion for self-reflection.

Not everything Nietzsche wrote is in the style of mirror writing, and sometimes he has other goals for his writing, but I believe that the central themes to his vision of a higher humanity are written in this style. Nietzsche's concepts of the *Übermensch,* eternal recurrence, and will to power are examples of mirror writing, especially as these concepts are presented in *Thus Spoke Zarathustra.* They are designed to reveal your values to you.

First, let us examine Nietzsche's notion of the *Übermensch.* In the prologue of *Thus Spoke Zarathustra,* Zarathustra presents the *Übermensch* in a metaphor— man is a rope suspended between the ape and the *Übermensch,* suggesting that man is to the *Übermensch* what the ape is to man. This is interesting in two ways. First, this metaphor suggests that the *Übermensch* is a different *species* than human, not just a "bigger and better" model. Humans do not consider themselves simply a bigger and better model of the ape but, rather, a different, albeit related, kind. Second, it suggests that we cannot have much insight into what an *Übermensch* might be like. Can the ape imagine the human? The *Übermensch* as a distant goal is certainly an obscure being. The best that we can do now, suggests Zarathustra, is to provide fertile ground for "cultivating" this goal. Although some readers believe that Zarathustra himself is a *Übermensch* by the end of book 4, I tend to take Nietzsche seriously when he writes that Zarathustra is the *teacher* of the *Übermensch.*

Zarathustra also says that there is not one path, one blueprint, to *Übermenschlichkeit*:

> "This is *my* way; where is yours?"—thus I answered those who asked me "the way." For *the* way—that does not exist. (TSZ, 307)

> "Das—ist nun *mein* Weg,—wo ist eure?" so antwortete ich Denen, welche mich "nach dem Wege" fragten. *Den* Weg nämlich—den giebt es nicht! [KGW VI/1, 241]

Not only is this a parody of the Christian notion that the only way is through Christ (John 4:16), but it also makes illegitimate and unnecessary any attempt to blueprint the way to *Übermenschlichkeit*. Instead, the vagueness of the *Übermensch* allows each of us individually to imagine for ourselves who and what this grand being might be. Whatever image arises, it cannot be compared with anything present; it is at present only a future possibility. The image can only inform us about ourselves—our values: what being we think is grand, beautiful, and good. In that way our individual conceptions of the *Übermensch* are mirrors to our individual values and selves.

Nietzsche, however, gives us another gauge for assessing our values and our-selves (the two are nearly identical in Nietzsche, for humans cannot escape valu-ing any more than we can escape willing or breathing). He gives us the concept of eternal recurrence. Eternal recurrence has always been a particularly thorny concept for me. I think Nietzsche believes that anyone who understands eternal recurrence would experience something life altering, something akin to his "epiphany" he describes as having when the idea came to him on the shores of Lake Silvaplana.[5] But none of the "traditional" interpretations of eternal recur-rence seems so revolutionary. As a description of how the world operates, it seems at worst contradictory and at best irrelevant to my life. If eternal recurrence is a description of how the cosmos actually operates (the cosmological interpretation), then it fails on several levels. First, in a *Nachlass* note (WP, 1066; KGW VIII/3, 14[188]), Nietzsche claims that given finite space and matter and infinite time, even random chance would result in repetition of events. We have already dis-cussed the scholarly problems of basing interpretations solely on *Nachlass* ma-terial. But we could also argue with Nietzsche's "given" that space or matter are finite; they both could be infinite, and only one of them being infinite, as space might be, is sufficient to ruin Nietzsche's probability calculus.

Also, if we view time as linear, then eternal recurrence of the same is concep-tually problematic. Let us suppose our sequence of events that will recur is A, B, and C. ABC occurs on our time line at t_1. Farther along on the time line ABC occurs at t_{1+52}. Now there is a difference between the two occurrences of ABC. We can distinguish them by ascribing them their time line designations, t_1 and t_{53}. Their different places on the time line distinguish them as different; there-fore, they are not the same sequence. This problem may be the reason that Nietzsche (elsewhere than in WP, 1066) proclaims that time is circular. But this maneuver does not solve the problem. If ABC occurs at one point of the circle and time curves around to reconnect with that point, we still have a way to dis-tinguish between ABC occurrences. That is, we can still say that this occurrence is the second, third, or 3,000th time around the circle.

The last objection to the cosmological view is that it has no practical conse-quences for us. Let us suppose that the cosmological interpretation is true—we relive our lives over and over again (although we have no memory of past oc-currences). Given that time *is* infinite, my life as I am currently living it must have occurred before, so I am simply reliving it, complete with thinking that I have free will and that I only will live once. I can only alter these opinions if I altered them in my previous (re)occurrences; otherwise, this life would not be a recurrence of *the same life* of my previous lives. If eternal recurrence is supposed to be such a life-altering idea, the cosmological interpretation robs it of its impact because no practical consequences arise from it. Because I am "fated" to relive this life, anything I do must also be "fated," even my ideas of free will and causality. I cannot make better choices this time around because that would violate the notion of "recurrence of the *same.*" So, practically, it seems, I just continue to live my life, presumably with the added knowledge (if I had gotten it in a previous go 'round) that I cannot change my fate. Because I do not know what my fate is, there is little point in concerning myself with the entire concept.

If this sounds a bit familiar, it is because it is a problem that the Stoics had with their concept of a predetermined cosmos: if the cosmos is predetermined to be dissolved by fire and reconstructed again in a certain, unalterable way, what sense does it make to say that people "ought" to live in a certain way? The concept of fate, the Stoics believed, would lead one to the practical state of equanimity or "unperturbedness." Events occurred in a preestablished cosmos in which one's actions were also preprescribed, so the reasonable approach to such determination was simply to "go with the flow" in as unflappable a manner as possible. But being "unperturbed" about one's fate is not logically entailed by the supposed "fact" that the universe is predetermined. Arguments against the union of the notions of a fated universe and human free will were well known. Surely Nietzsche, a classicist, was familiar with these arguments. Eternal recurrence resurrects the idea of a fated universe, and Nietzsche inherits all the problems inherent in the concept. I believe Nietzsche must have had something different in mind with eternal recurrence than simply reviving the Stoic controversy.

Eternal recurrence need not be interpreted only cosmologically. Some people interpret it as a normative principle, but it fares no better as a principle for guiding action than as a description of how the cosmos operates. One attraction of the normative interpretation is that it relies on text from *The Gay Science* rather than from the *Nachlass* notes. In *The Gay Science* a demon who has approached you in your "loneliest loneliness" asks you whether you would be willing to live the life you are now living over and over again for eternity. Nietzsche writes,

If this thought gained possession of you, it would change you as you are or perhaps crush you. The question in each and every thing, "Do you desire this once more and innumerable times more?" would lie upon your actions as the greatest weight. Or how well disposed would you have to become to yourself and to life *to crave nothing more fervently* than this ultimate eternal confirmation and seal? (GS, 341)

Wenn jener Gedanke über dich Gewalt bekäme, er würde dich, wie du bist, verwandeln und vielleicht zermalmen; die Frage bei Allem und Jedem "willst du diess noch einmal und noch unzählige Male?" würde als grösste Schwergewicht auf deinem Handeln liegen! Oder wie müsstest du dir selber und dem Leben gut werden, um nach Nichts *mehr zu verlangen,* als nach dieser letzten ewigen Bestätigung und Besiegelung? [KGW V/2, 250]

Eternal recurrence, then, asks you to consider whether you would be willing to choose your course of action not just this once but for eternity. But I believe interpreting eternal recurrence in this normative way is ultimately untenable because it is subject to too many problems. While relying on this lone aphorism from *The Gay Science,* the normative interpretation must ignore much of what is presented on eternal recurrence in *Thus Spoke Zarathustra.*

Second, as Magnus notes, either one must accept the cosmological interpretation along with the normative one (one must choose one's actions *as if* eternal recurrence is the case because it is the case) or one must pretend that the cosmological interpretation is true (one must choose one's actions *as if* eternal recurrence is the case even though it is not). To believe the former is to inherit the problems inherent in the cosmological interpretation. To believe the latter is to eviscerate eternal recurrence of its powerful impact: Choose as if the choice is going to be relived over and over even though it is not. However, if we are not really going to relive the choice, why bother pretending that we will? In other words, if there are no grounds for believing that one will live again, why bother with Nietzsche's normative principle rather than Kant's or Mill's? It could be argued that as Nietzsche argues against there being one, genuine and universal foundation for morality, the eternal recurrence "pretending" is just as valid as Kant's pretense of the Categorical Imperative or any other "supreme moral principle." Then we could just flip a coin in order to adopt one normative theory over others.

However, if we were to look at the consequences of adopting one normative principle over another, eternal recurrence as a normative guide seems to pale in comparison. If we did accept eternal recurrence as a principle for guiding action, it seems less helpful for determining the right act than Kant's Categorical Imperative or Mill's utility calculation. Interpreting eternal recurrence as Nietzsche's normative principle—"Do that act whereby you could will it again and again for all eternity"—does not seem to have sufficient content to be a very helpful guide for action. There are many times when I could live with and repeat eternally several of my alternatives for action, just as there are those devilish dilemmas in which several of my best choices are still ones that I would not want to choose among even once. Eternal recurrence cannot help me choose my course of action in these situations. Although there might be situations in which such a normative principle might be helpful, as a regular "rule of thumb," I believe it lacks sufficient content to be of much use.

There is also something unsettling about Nietzsche proposing anything like a "supreme moral principle" after his criticisms against Kant's ethical theory. Nietzsche's critiques of morality suggest that offering a new first principle for morality is not his project. His problems with Kant's Categorical Imperative or utilitarianism's principle of utility run deeper than their content. He does not criticize them because they say the wrong thing and he says the right thing. The problem with them is that they propose to be *universal* moral principles, applying to any and all human beings. Universal moral principles imply moral equality among humans, an equality Nietzsche denies. The "un-Nietzschean" character of the normative interpretation is the most persuasive aspect against it.

Bernd Magnus's interpretation that eternal recurrence as a description of an *Übermensch's* attitude toward time and life seems more appealing than the other two. Magnus claims that eternal recurrence "is emblematic of the attitude of *Übermenschlichkeit* and is the being-in-the-world of *Übermenschen.*"[6] How this gets fleshed out is somewhat complex, but the most important point for me is that eternal recurrence's role in Nietzsche's philosophy, according to Magnus, is descriptive. Eternal recurrence describes a way of interpreting the world that is life affirming rather than nihilistic, celebratory rather than plaintive, and playful rather than in the spirit of gravity. Magnus claims that the doctrine of eternal recurrence invites us to seek out "what is worthy of infinity in our lives."[7] The focus is not on the choices that we make (the product) but on the affirming (the process). Affirming aspects of our lives renders them, in a way, "infinite." While I am very sympathetic to eternal recurrence being descriptive rather than normative or cosmological, how Magnus plays this out strikes me as only partially satisfying. What is discovered or revealed by eternal recurrence, according to Magnus, is *Übermenschlichkeit*. Exactly how does all this affect human beings? Are we supposed to emulate this attitude or get as close as we can to it, even though at present we are a rope between ape and *Übermensch*? What would be the point of that? Magnus's interpretation, though inventive and not subject to the other interpretations' problems, leaves eternal recurrence incapable of affecting humanity in any meaningful way. What I believe is revealed by eternal recurrence, if someone is possessed by the idea, is that person's values.

As the notion of Nietzsche's "mirror writing" developed, it seemed to lend an interesting and hopefully revealing perspective on eternal recurrence, too. Eternal recurrence is an ideal that enables you to see yourself. As a mirror reflects your physical body, eternal recurrence reveals your values. This perspective emerged as I reread "The Convalescent" in *Thus Spoke Zarathustra*. If we read "The Convalescent" as the culmination of Nietzsche's presentation of eternal recurrence in *Thus Spoke Zarathustra,* the connection between eternal recurrence and will to power becomes more clearly reflected.

In "The Convalescent" Zarathustra is stricken with a thought and falls down as if dead. He remains in this comatose state for seven days. What makes Zarathustra so sick? The easy answer is, of course, the thought of eternal recurrence. But Nietzsche rarely gives us easy answers. It cannot be the thought of eternal recurrence that makes Zarathustra ill. He has thought of eternal recurrence previously in the book. Why is it only in "The Convalescent" that he becomes sick from the thought of it?

Except for some allusions to circles in earlier speeches, Zarathustra first speaks of eternal recurrence to a hunchback in "On Redemption." The title immediately invites a comparison with the Christian notion of redemption. According to Nietzsche's interpretation of Christianity, redemption is attained by the grace of

God through Christ. From what does God redeem us? Humans are stained by the sin of Adam and Eve. Original sin has rendered present humans impotent because no acts humans have done have caused the sin. Simply being descendants of Adam and Eve renders humans sinful, so no present acts of will by humans can redeem that sin. Thus, it is only the grace of God through Christ that can redeem us. Zarathustra provides another interpretation of redemption:

> To redeem those who lived in the past and to re(-)create all "it was" into a "thus I willed it"—that alone should I call redemption. (TSZ, 251)

> Die Vergangen zu erlösen und alles "Es war" umzuschaffen in ein "So wollte ich es!"—das hiesse mir erst Erlösung! [KGW VI/1, 175]

Thinking that the past is unchangeable and immutable is the curse of linear time. Christianity needs time to be linear. It needs the sinful act by Adam and Eve to be wholly unaffected by the actions of present human beings in order for God's grace, and not human will, to be redemptive. But rendering the human will impotent has terrible consequences for humans. When the will realizes that it is constrained by the past, the "it was," of a linear model of time, the will rages against the constraint and finds resentful ways to continue to will. As Nietzsche says in *On the Genealogy of Morals*, the human will "will rather will *nothingness* than *not* will."[8] This hapless revenge against the "it was" reduces humans to what Zarathustra calls fragments of humanity and inverse cripples.

Without explicitly referring to eternal recurrence, Zarathustra remarks that will, which is always a creator, must create a will that can say, "Thus I will it; thus shall I will it." The idea of eternal recurrence challenges the idea of linear time. If events eternally recur, then "past" events are "future" events and vice versa. Notions of backward, forward, past, and future lack an adequate reference point.

Both Laurence Lampert and Kathleen Higgins cite the pivotal role this speech has for the entire book. Lampert states, "In the language of philosophy, the connection between will to power and eternal return is the connection between fact and value."[9] The will realizes that preceding moments are facts but also that the meaning and value of this past are open to total creativity. Thus, "it was" is something to be embraced rather than tolerated because it is the media from which the will paints its interpretive art. For Lampert this "redeems" the revengeful will that is resentful of the "it was" of time into the will that is so joyful at the task of freely interpreting the "it was" that it proclaims, "Thus I willed it." This is the lesson Zarathustra is supposed to be teaching through eternal recurrence.

Higgins's perspective is similar to Lampert's:

> On [a nonlinear] model of time, the self of the present, far from being constituted by the past, has a kind of power over it. The present self, in acting, can modify the significance of what the self in the past has been. Our wills are not capriciously free to abolish the forces that lead to the present, or to make ourselves into different persons on whom the past has had no real influence. Our wills are able to reformu-

late the spectrum of materials that our past bequeaths us by focusing them into patterns of aspiration. . . . This potential of the will allows the will to "redeem" its past—and the historical past that influences it.[10]

If the will is no longer stymied by the seemingly impenetrable past, it can "modify the significance" of the self and "reformulate the spectrum of materials." This sounds remarkably similar to Lampert's independent interpretation of the will's freedom to attach meaning and value to the past. If time is not linear, there is no point of reference from which to say "backward" or "forward," leaving only moment to moment—and who is to say whether the subsequent moment is forward or backward? "Thus I willed it," "thus I will it," and "thus I shall will it" become the same.

In "The Convalescent," Zarathustra falls sick from the idea of eternal recurrence. What is it about eternal recurrence that would produce such sickness in Zarathustra? When he recovers, he claims his nausea was caused by his disgust with man:

> Naked I had once seen them both, the greatest man and the smallest man: all-too-similar to each other, even the greatest all-too-human. All-too-small, the greatest!—that was my disgust with man. And the eternal recurrence of even of the smallest—that was my disgust with all existence. Alas! Nausea! Nausea! Nausea! (TSZ, 331)

> Nackt hatte ich einst Beide gesehn, den grössten Menschen und den kleinsten Menschen: allzuähnlich einander,—allzumenschlich auch den Grössten noch! Allzuklein der Grösste!—Das war mein Überdruss am Menschen! Und ewige Wiederkunft auch des Kleinsten!—Dass war mein Überdruss an allem Dasein! Ach, Ekel! Ekel! Ekel! [KGW VI/1, 270–71]

It is not the past historical events of mankind but man himself that makes Zarathustra sick. Why? Because he saw that the greatest man was not so great. The key to understanding this passage is to remember that Zarathustra is not a being on the outside looking in at all this. He is not a disinterested third party studying humans in a scientifically "objective" way. For example, humans can study gorillas scientifically. We may decide that Koko, the gorilla who reportedly uses language, is the greatest gorilla. However, when compared with humans, Koko is not so great; most human four year olds have her mastery of language and more. But Zarathustra is studying humans and *is* a human. Even if he is the greatest human, he is all too similar to the smallest man, all too human, all too small. Zarathustra himself has been revealed by the thought of eternal recurrence.

Eternal recurrence is the instrument by which you are revealed. The thought of eternal recurrence is like a mirror held up to your body. A mirror simply reflects your outward appearance. Allow me to develop this analogy from my own experience with mirrors. I have a mirror opposite my shower door. When I step out of the shower, there I am in full view of my mirror. Most of the time I am not too keen on what I see. I start thinking I should exercise more, eat better, get in better shape. I could say that my mirror tells me this, but of course it does not—it just reflects the image of my body. I am the one who is nauseated by what I see. But my nausea is based on my standard of values. My body is unacceptable if based on the Madison Avenue media and fashion values of creaseless, waif-thin, but preferably big-breasted female bodies. If I adopt a new value standard, one that values wrinkles, pregnancy stretch marks, and cellulite, I'm beautiful! But the *mirror* tells me neither that I am ugly nor that I am beautiful. I place those values on myself according to what standard for beauty I have chosen, either by adoption or by creation, for myself.

Analogously, the notion of eternal recurrence is a kind of mirror. It simply reveals to me the state of my will to power. Am I crushed by the thought of it? nauseated? empowered by the notion? It is descriptive; it simply reveals you by your reaction to the notion. However, it must be more than just an intellectual exercise. After all, Zarathustra has *thought* about eternal recurrence before his collapse in "The Convalescent."

There is foreshadowing from metaphors of rings and circles that informs us that Zarathustra has thought about eternal recurrence. He later talks to the hunchback about willing backwards in "On Redemption." He converses with the dwarf-mole about the nature of time and presents his views of the primacy of the Moment in his dream in "The Vision and the Riddle." Clearly, Zarathustra has had the thought of eternal recurrence before. But it is not until "The Convalescent" that the idea "gains possession" of him. When it does, the thought finally forces him to see himself. Why is it so sickening that he lies comatose for seven days? It is because *he* is in the revelation. *He* is revealed by this thought, and he is revealed as puny. When you are overweight or misshapen, you don't want to look in that mirror! Sometimes the image revealed there makes you sick.

On the other hand, this eternal recurrence idea is a very handy device (like mirrors) for finding out about yourself. Again, eternal recurrence is purely descriptive—this is what you think of yourself. But it can also goad you into taking action about yourself like a mirror can goad me into exercising. What action you take depends on what standard for actions you have, and eternal recurrence highlights the underlying value standards. A mirror can remind me of how youth-oriented this society is. But the *mirror* does not tell me anything I "should" do; only my will can do that.

Interpreting eternal recurrence as a mirror sheds new light on "The Convalescent," as well as on the aphorism in *The Gay Science*. Aphorism 341 of *The Gay Science* begins with a hypothetical "what if" story. A demon sneaks up on you at your lowest point, your "loneliest loneliness," to ask whether you could endure living your life over again an infinite number of times. At first you might be glad—you get to live again, make up for all your past mistakes, do things right the second time around, and so on. But the demon throws in a wrench—you must live this same life over again, thus making the same mistakes. No improvements can be made in your life as your life recurs. Because you are at your lowest point in your life, you may not be able to answer yes to the demon's proposition. Nietzsche asks whether you have experienced a "tremendous moment," which even at your lowest hour would make all the problems and risks worth taking again. Would the thought of eternal recurrence crush you, or would you fall down on your knees and call the demon a god? Finally Nietzsche asks,

> Or how well disposed would you have to become to yourself and to life *to crave nothing more fervently* than this ultimate eternal confirmation and seal? (GS, 341)

> Oder wie müsstest du dir selber und dem Leben gut werden, um nach Nichts *mehr zu verlangen,* als nach dieser letzten ewigen Bestätigung und Besiegelung? [KGW V/2, 250]

He leaves the reader with this question unanswered.

In this aphorism, Nietzsche writes as if there were only two possible reactions to the demon's scenario. Either it would be a great weight and crush you, or you would proclaim the notion divine and crave that eternal recurrence to actually be the case. But this hypothetical event is not an either/or situation. Between this crushing weight and craving is a whole slew of in-between reactions—from lukewarm against through lukewarm toward to actually craving that eternal recurrence was indeed the case. Surely Nietzsche recognized that "slightly inclined to the idea" was a possible response, even though it makes for much better reading to present the two extreme views.

The key to this aphorism, I believe, is the last line: "Or how well disposed would you have to become to yourself and to life *to crave nothing more fervently* than this ultimate eternal confirmation and seal?" Nietzsche uses the word *become (werden)* rather than *be (sind).* This is telling because it denotes a continuing process rather than a one-shot trial that either you fail by having the thought crush you or you pass by proclaiming the thought of eternal recurrence divine. A process suggests that it is possible to move through a series of responses to the demon's question. If the past can be redeemed by the notion of eternal recurrence, then we can be redeemed as well. We can reformulate ourselves (and our values) as well as history.

This is what happens during Zarathustra's seven-day affliction. At the beginning of "The Convalescent" the thought of eternal recurrence gains possession of him, not just as an intellectual exercise but as an idea that, like a mirror, is a reflection of him, warts and all. It means his triumphs and his atrocities are not as large as his ego may want them to be. This seems to be a point at which Zarathustra is at his "loneliest loneliness." He is at his lowest point, and he reacts with nausea to the idea of the small man, and himself as one, eternally recurring. This idea sits upon him as the greatest weight.

But Zarathustra does not stay in his afflicted state. After seven days he awakens and takes great pleasure in simply smelling an apple. Clearly, being possessed by the thought of eternal recurrence has not crushed him for all time; he has been able to reconcile himself with the thought of the smallest man eternally recurring. How? If we return to *The Gay Science,* Zarathustra must have become "well disposed" to himself and to life. But how has he accomplished that? How has he redeemed himself?

Being a man, Zarathustra must be part of the humanity that he says is all too human and all too small. In other words, eternal recurrence has shown him to himself much like my bathroom mirror shows my body to me. We are both struck nauseous. How well disposed would I have to become toward my body/myself to crave nothing more fervently than to live in it eternally? Pretty damn well disposed! How can I, looking at myself in the mirror, not be constantly reminded of the value standard created for females in this society? Intellectually, I know that the value standard has been created by a fashion industry that wants women to resemble hangers and by cameras that add ten pounds to a person. I know that only 5 percent of females naturally fall into this narrow construal of beauty. I also know that according to a different standard of value, say, the standard of being able to produce more human beings, I have a splendid body. But my daily dejection upon seeing my image in the mirror informs me of how well I have internalized the former value standard. I have been trying for twenty years to rid myself of this society's value standard for female beauty, and I have not succeeded yet. It is no easy task to reevaluate your values.

This is what the idea of eternal recurrence does to human beings if we are some of the few humans capable of being possessed by it. It tells us about ourselves and our value standards. Eternal recurrence is Nietzsche's mirror for the revaluation of all values. It shows Zarathustra that he is a puny person—his highs are not so high, his lows are not so low. The revelation of himself makes him nauseous. It takes him some time to reconcile himself with the image of himself that eternal recurrence has forced him to look at. It is no coincidence that it takes him seven days to emerge from his sickness. He is (re-)creating himself and his world into "thus I have willed and shall will it." Zarathustra has become the god of creation—not the creation of the physical universe, as the biblical God, but the creator of his interpretative/evaluative reality. Through the seven days he *becomes* well disposed to himself and to life; he creates himself and his world. He revalues all his values.

Now let us remember Nietzsche's first mention of will to power: that a people's tablet of values is an expression of their will to power. All our beliefs are expressions of will to power, from the ascetic priest to the teacher of eternal recurrence. All our beliefs, all our interpretations of what is going on, reveal *us,* are mirrors for *us.* We remake ourselves if we revamp our values, for our values shape our interpretations of "reality." Revalued values would reconstitute realities for us.

Being possessed by the thought of eternal recurrence reflects the magnitude of one's will to power. Hopefully, the consequence of this revelation will be redemptive: one will become well disposed to oneself as Zarathustra becomes well disposed to himself. But the risk is grave. There is the possibility of a diminished self—to the point of being crushed once and for all by its weight.

We can simply ignore this thought of eternal recurrence, and of course the vast majority of people do, but recall that Nietzsche has written that the more perspectives we have of something, the more complete our understanding of that something. If this is so, then knowing our magnitude of will to power is another "eye," another perspective toward understanding ourselves. And for Nietzsche, seeing the world from the perspective of relations of power is an extremely informative and empowering perspective. Of course, viewing certain relationships from this perspective could result in a lessening of potency. Even viewing oneself from the perspective of power can also result in a loss of self-esteem, self-empowerment. This is the risk of any perspective, although it may not be so apparent or so forceful in some perspectives. Mechanistic (scientific) perspectives can lead to very useful devices, but as has been written by many observers, including Heidegger, it also leads to a decrease of spirituality or turning away from the "question of Being." This diminution goes unnoticed much of the time, but it is no less a potentially devastating "down side" of that perspective. Any perspective has the potential for disaster; any revaluation of values has the potential to heighten those aspects Nietzsche finds unacceptable.

But couldn't a revaluation result in a worsening for humanity, a "lower" humanity? A revaluation would reflect new goals; could we be sure those goals would be better than those goals of today's values—equality, democracy, compassion for others? In what sense do we use *better*? And we have once again arrived at Nietzsche's conundrum. But is it such a conundrum as it first seemed?

If our beliefs, languages, interpretations, actions, reactions, and so forth reveal us, then Nietzsche's writings reveal him more than they tell us about the "objective" nature of the world. And indeed that is the case. Nietzsche's writings certainly tell us about his values. But values are not objective, absolute, and fixed; Nietzsche's values are *his* values. Why should we take Nietzsche's values to heart more than Kant's, or Christ's, or Hitler's?

Again, the answer, according to my interpretation of Nietzsche, lies in the consequences he sees for holding such values. The consequences of Kantian-*cum*-Christian values lead to the last man and mediocrity. What this ultimately leads to for Nietzsche is a diminishing of power. Christian-based ethics that stress sin, guilt, and hell diminish a human's capacity to freely explore and express will—the conscious and subconscious inner drives that constitute the individual. This free exploration has its down side. There may be more suffering in the world. But Nietzsche sees suffering as a value-neutral "fact" of the world. It can be interpreted as a terrible fate for humankind or, as Nietzsche suggests, a challenge to be met and possibly overcome. But challenges need to be overcome, not avoided, if humans are to excel and not just exist. Power seeks not just to maintain itself but to increase. Nietzsche criticizes Schopenhauer's "will to life," for one must be already living in order to even have a "will." Thus, Schopenhauer's phrase is redundant or trivial. Nor is simple preservation an adequate explanation for life, for Nietzsche argues that everywhere life is absurdly more prolific than mere preservation requires. *Will to power* becomes a better phrase for Nietzsche than *will to life* or *will to survive*—not better in the sense of being more True but in the sense of providing a more informative perspective of the world. Interpreting the world through the lens of will to power engenders a more passionate and aesthetic view of the world.

Yet it is also so broad that it does not provide a blueprint for any one way for humankind to act or think. Power is expressed in a multitude of ways, some beneficial, some neutral, and some harmful to humans. And remember that his values include the value of individuality, solitude, and *not* doing what everyone else is doing, so a collective effort to embody his values would not lead to a monolithic value system.

Nietzsche has no idea of the actual consequences of someone, much less an entire society, adopting his values. He has only predictions or visions of what a will to power perspective might engender. One of the last descriptions of what kind of human being might emerge from such revalued values is in *Ecce Homo*:

What is it, fundamentally, that allows us to recognize *who has turned out well*? That a well-turned-out person pleases our senses, that he is carved from wood that is hard, delicate, and at the same time smells good. He has a taste only for what is good for him; his pleasure, his delight cease where the measure of what is good for him is transgressed. He guesses what remedies avail against what is harmful; he exploits bad accidents to his advantage; what does not kill him makes him stronger. Instinctively, he collects from everything he sees, hears, lives through, *his* sum: he is a principle of selection, he discards much. He is always in his own company, whether he associates with books, human beings, or landscapes; he honors by *choosing,* by *admitting,* by *trusting.* He reacts slowly to all kinds of stimuli, with that slowness which long caution and deliberate pride have bred in him: he examines the stimulus that approaches him, he is far from meeting it halfway. He believes neither in "misfortune" nor in "guilt": he comes to terms with himself, with others; he knows how to *forget*—he is strong enough; hence everything *must* turn out for his best. (EH, "Wise," 2)

Und woran erkennt man im Grunde die *Wohlgerathenheit*! Dass ein wohlgerathner Mensch unsern Sinnen wohlthut: dass er aus einem Holze geschnitzt ist, das hart, zart und wohlriechend zugleich ist. Ihm schmeckt nur, was ihm zuträglich ist; sein Gefallen, seine Lust hört auf, wo das Maass des Zuträglichen überschritten wird. Er erräth Heilmittel gegen Schädigungen, er nützt schlimme Zufälle zu seinem Vortheil aus; was ihn nicht umbringt, macht ihn stärker. Er sammelt instinktiv aus Allem, was er sieht, hört, erlebt, *seine* Summe: er ist ein auswählendes Princip, er lässt Viel durchfallen. Er ist immer in *seiner* Gesellschaft, ob er mit Büchern, Menschen oder Landschaften verkehrt: er ehrt, indem er *wählt,* indem er *zulässt,* indem er *vertraut.* Er reagirt auf alle Art Reize langsam, mit jener Langsamkeit, die eine lange Vorsicht und ein gewollter Stolz ihm angezüchtet haben,—er prüft den Reiz, der herankommt, er ist fern davon, ihm entgegenzugehn. Er glaubt weder an "Unglück," noch an "Schuld": er wird fertig, mit sich, mit Anderen, er weiss zu *vergessen,*—er ist stark genug, dass ihm Alles zum Besten gereichen *muss.* [KGW VI/3, 265]

This is one of Nietzsche's descriptions of the "higher," nondecadent person. And he unabashedly admits that it is a description of him: "Well then, I am the *opposite* of a decadent, for I have just described *myself.*" True, *Ecce Homo* is one of Nietzsche's last books, and some would argue that his illness may have been giving him delusions of grandeur; however, I think it illustrates the most revealing aspect of Nietzsche's philosophy—that the philosophy cannot help but be a mirror of the philosopher. It is not just a grandiose statement; it is an example of his writings:

(Philosophy) always creates the world in its own image; it cannot do otherwise. Philosophy is this tyrannical drive itself, the most spiritual will to power, to the "creation of the world," to the *causa prima.* (BGE, 9)

[Philosophie] schafft immer die Welt nach ihrem Bilde, sie kann nicht anders; Philosophie ist dieser tyrannische Trieb selbst, der geistigste Wille zur Macht, zur "Schaffung der Welt," zur causa prima. [KGW VI/2, 16]

There is no value system applicable to everyone that Nietzsche wants to or can establish, if he is to remain consistent. Even his own value system is not etched in stone; it can be reevaluated at any moment. It is subject to infinite interpretations, eternally revisited. This is the fate of humankind's ability to question and interpret their experiences. We must learn to love this fate.

Nietzsche's use of the term *amor fati* occurs only nine times in his entire writings and in only two books he authorized for publication—*The Gay Science* and *Ecce Homo. Amor fati*—love of fate—is usually interpreted as loving eternal recurrence. This interpretation defines our fate as having to live our lives over and over again, as the demon in *The Gay Science* proposes. We must learn to love this fate by, presumably, falling down on our knees and proclaiming the demon holy. But this interpretation of *amor fati* relies on the cosmological interpretation of eternal recurrence, and I have tried to demonstrate that the cosmological interpretation is not a particularly good one. However, if eternal recurrence is the mirror to our values and our selves, as I have suggested, then *amor fati* has more to do with loving our ability to interpret and reinterpret our reality and values than with embracing a vast, fixed cosmology.

Let us look at the first (and only) occurrence of *amor fati* in *The Gay Science.* It appears in the first aphorism of book 4, written on 1 January 1882:

For the new year.—I still live, I still think: I still have to live, for I still have to think. Sum, ergo cogito; cogito, ergo sum. Today everybody permits himself the expression of his wish and his dearest thought; hence, I, too, shall say what it is that I wish from myself today, and what was the first thought to run across my heart this year—what thought shall be for me the reason, warranty, and sweetness of my life henceforth. I want to learn more and more to see as beautiful what is necessary in things; then I shall be one of those who makes things beautiful. Amor fati: let this be my love henceforth! I do not want to wage war against what is ugly. I do not want to accuse; I do not even want to accuse those who accuse. *Looking away* shall be my only negation. And all in all and on the whole: some day I wish to be only a Yes-sayer. (GS, 276)

Zum neuen Jahre.—Noch lebe ich, noch denke ich: ich muss noch leben, denn ich muss noch denken. Sum, ergo cogito: cogito ergo sum. Heute erlaubt sich Jedermann seinen Wunsch und liebsten Gedanken auszusprechen: nun, so will auch Ich sagen, was ich mir heute von mir selber wünschte und welcher Gedanke mir dieses Jahr zuerst über das Herz lief,—welcher Gedanke mir Grund, Bürgschaft und Süssigkeit alles weiteren Lebens sein soll! Ich will immer mehr lernen, das Nothwendige an den Dingen als das Schöne sehen:—so werde ich Einer von Denen sein, welche die Dinge schön machen. Amor fati: das sei von nun an meine Liebe! Ich will keinen Krieg gegen das Hässliche führen. Ich will nicht anklagen, ich will nicht einmal die Ankläger anklagen. *Wegsehen* zei meine einzige Verneinung! Und, Alles in Allem und Grossen: ich will irgendwann einmal nur noch ein Ja-sagender sein! [KGW V/ 2, 201]

Amor fati is Nietzsche's New Year's resolution of 1882. But what is the resolution? Nietzsche wants to see "what is necessary in things" as beautiful to the point at which someday he becomes a "Yes-sayer." Although the phrase *amor fati* never appears in *Thus Spoke Zarathustra,* being a "Yes-sayer" and "affirming life" are prominent themes in the book. But what are we to make of "what is necessary in things"? It could be inferred that the cosmological interpretation of eternal recurrence is "what is necessary" and that Nietzsche is suggesting that we declare holy the fact that we will live this same life over and over again for all eternity. But I have offered a competing interpretation of eternal recurrence, one that takes as its "necessity" not a cosmological outlook but a heuristic one. According to my interpretation, humanity is "fated" to interpretation, to never know the "ultimate reality," the True nature of the universe. Because we are doomed to this "necessity" (to necessarily interpret our experiences and place values on them), Nietzsche wants the interpretation to be positive; he wants to become a yes-sayer. However, as the remainder of book 4 in *The Gay Science* wants to show, this yes-saying is not merely a Pollyanna attitude toward life. Life is harsh. Suffering abounds. The "Christian" interpretation of harshness and suffering as evils leads to the "solution" of making life softer and of eliminating suffering. Nietzsche suggests a revaluation of these values. Harshness and suffering are not seen as evils but, rather, as opportunities for testing one's mettle (one's "power-constellation" of will to power). Remember that the notions of "ego," "soul," "cause and effect," and so on are also "necessary" in Nietzsche's view. They are all "errors" according to the correspondence theory of truth, but they are necessary for the survival and flourishing of the human species. These notions, too, must be interpreted as aesthetically beautiful creations of humankind, although they are not exempt from reinterpretation or revaluation.

"Great" human beings desire nothing more or less than the "stuff" of their interpretations: the physical, psychological, historical, socioeconomical factors that activate their interpretive powers. While their individual will to power can affect and effect some of these factors only marginally, their ability to reevaluate them is limitless. "Great" human beings not only must love their ability to reinterpret and reevaluate but must also love the content of their interpretations and valuations:

> My formula for greatness in a human being is *amor fati*: that one wants nothing to be different, not forward, not backward, not in all eternity. Not merely bear what is necessary, still less conceal it—all idealism is mendaciousness in the face of what is necessary—but *love* it. (EH, "Clever," 10)

> Meine formel für die Grösse am Menschen ist *amor fati*: dass man Nichts anders haben will, vorwärts nicht, rückwärts nicht, in alle Ewigkeit nicht. Das Nothwendige nicht bloss ertragen, noch weniger verhehlen—, aller Idealismus ist Verlogenhelt vor dem Nothwendigen—, sondern *lieben*. [KGW VI/3, 295]

This passage from *Ecce Homo* seems to support the interpretation that eternal recurrence is what Nietzsche means by "necessary," particularly because it mentions all eternity and *forward* and *backward,* words used in his writings on eternal recurrence. But let us reinterpret it in light of the interpretation of eternal recurrence as a kind of mirror of values.

How I interpret/value certain episodes of my life informs others about me, not about those events of my life. What I must learn to love, by my reading of Nietzsche, is the necessity of interpreting these events. It is my "fate" to have been born into the "baby boomer" generation; it is also my "fate" that I can reinterpret and reevaluate that "fate" into a life-affirming "yes-saying."

One of Nietzsche's primary goals is to question the value of the value standards of the age. He believes that the Judeo-Christian value standard leads to weak, resentful human beings and ultimately to the last man. Eternal recurrence, then, as part of a larger myth that includes the notions of will to power and the *Übermensch,* is an instrument that enables you to more clearly see your standard of value for evaluating yourself. A mirror gives me a new and different perspective from which to see myself. Eternal recurrence provides a new and different perspective as well—one that lets the prevailing value standard be seen more clearly. That is why it must be taught, so that others will have this instrument of revelation, too.

So is Nietzsche's myth "just another story" to be piled with Homer or Aesop, Dante or Michener? We could do that. But some stories seem to strike us as better than others. They are more enduring, perhaps because they help us see ourselves or our world in interesting and beautiful ways. There is a power to myths, and Nietzsche hoped that the one he presents in *Thus Spoke Zarathustra* might become as powerful as the New Testament. But if Nietzsche sees resentment and powerlessness as the legacy of the myth of Christianity and passionless expediency and utility as the consequences of science, he sees the legacy of Zarathustra as "healthier" than that—it would enable a human will to fully realize its artistry. At this point, it is all speculation whether human beings would be improved, and in what sense "improved," operating under the myth of eternal recurrence. We need not adopt Nietzsche's notion of health as our own. But even the act of investigating Nietzsche's values versus other values, especially Christian ones, would mean an improvement in humanity. It would mean that some of humanity would realize that values are not external to humans, objective, absolute, and to be obeyed without question. It would mean that some of humanity would be actively engaged in evaluating values, an activity discouraged by those who benefit from the existing values:

> *Revaluation of all values*: that is my formula for an act of supreme *self-examination* on the part of humanity. (EH, "Destiny," 1, emphasis added)

> *Umwerthung aller Werthe*: das ist meine Formel für einen Akt höchster *Selbstbesinnung* der Menschheit. [KGW VI/3, 363]

What the consequence to humanity may be of such an evaluation is difficult to predict. Nietzsche saw any change from the complacent, Christian dogma–dominated society as an improvement. We have had an additional 100 years of human experience and perspectives. There are still those who benefit from continuing the status quo. Whether Nietzsche's myth will ever become as powerful as Christianity remains to be seen. He suggests that a first step is to see values as expressions of power relations and to reevaluate those power structures. It will be humanity that is revealed.

FURTHER READING

About eternal recurrence, see the following:

Higgins, Kathleen. *Nietzsche's Zarathustra*. Philadelphia: Temple University Press, 1987.
Lampert, Laurence. *Nietzsche's Teaching*. New Haven: Yale University Press, 1986.
Magnus, Bernd. *Nietzsche's Existential Imperative*. Bloomington: Indiana University Press, 1978.
Rosen, Stanley. *The Mask of Enlightenment: Nietzsche's "Zarathustra."* New York: Cambridge University Press, 1995.

About Nietzsche's style and "play," see the following:

Allison, David. *The New Nietzsche*. New York: Dell Publishing Co., 1977.
Derrida, Jacques. *Spurs*. Trans. Barbara Harlow. Chicago: University of Chicago Press, 1978.
Irigaray, Luce. *Marine Lover of Friedrich Nietzsche*. Trans. Gilliam C. Gill. New York: Columbia University Press, 1991.
Koelb, Clayton, ed. *Nietzsche as Postmodernist: Essays Pro and Contra*. Albany: State University of New York Press, 1990.

Kofman, Sarah. *Nietzsche and Metaphor.* Trans. Duncan Large. Stanford: Stanford University Press, 1993.

Schrift, Alan. *Nietzsche and the Question of Interpretation.* New York: Routledge, 1990.

Winchester, James. *Nietzsche's Aesthetic Turn: Reading Nietzsche after Heidegger, Deleuze, Derrida.* Albany: State University of New York Press, 1994.

Afterword

What is will to power? We began this investigation with this question, and I hope I have demonstrated why this simple question is so difficult to answer simply. One of the most prominent reasons why there are different answers to this question is that it depends mightily on whether one decides to treat the notes from the *Nachlass* as equivalent to those from the writings Nietzsche published or authorized for publication before his illness struck. As I hoped to show in chapter 3, the *Nachlass* notes that contain the phrase *will to power* are quite different from those aphorisms in the published works. Commentaries on Nietzsche's writings also vary in their analyses of will to power according to whether the commentator considers the *Nachlass* notes. Interpretations that have will to power as Nietzsche's metaphysical principle rely almost exclusively on the *Nachlass* notes as their textual support.

Although interpretations of will to power either as a cosmological or an onto-logical principle fare better, they too heavily imply objective, nonperspectival standpoints, not just "otherworldly" ones. Interpreting will to power as Nietzsche's empirical principle to which all experience can be reduced or inter-preting will to power as Nietzsche's science have the benefit of being in this world, but in my view they suffer from the implication that will to power some-how transcends Nietzsche's perspectivism.

I have proposed that will to power is his lens through which he interprets the world—his shorthand way of suggesting that experience be viewed as differing struggles for superiority among humans and other things, especially among hu-mans and other humans. Thus, human physiology and psychology can be seen as the interaction of power relations. According to a will to power interpretation of experience (as opposed to a Christian or a mechanistic/scientific interpreta-tion), human interaction, whether it be with other humans or with things, whether it be physically or psychologically, is interpreted as a struggle between compet-ing forces for superiority. Ways of interpreting the world—and particularly human relations—also increase or decrease power. Ultimately, Nietzsche suggests that the fullest expression of power can be attained through interpreting the world as will to power. Will to power, then, is a consciously created slant on the world that, according to Nietzsche, allows certain humans to flourish better than the mythic worldviews of Christianity or science.

But more importantly, viewing will to power as a consciously chosen perspective from which to interpret the world eliminates any need to argue about whether will to power is metaphysical, cosmological, or ontological. My reading of Nietzsche's views has Nietzsche unconcerned with this kind of debate. As I read Nietzsche, the primary question becomes, "What are the consequences of holding certain worldviews?" The consequences of holding an "otherworldly" view (e.g., Christianity) are the perpetuation of mediocrity and humans who are guilty, sinful, shameful, and resentful. The consequences of holding a scientific view are humans who are stripped of their passions and reduced to mere causally determined entities. Nietzsche sees the consequences of holding a will to power view constitute the grounds for the possibility of "great" beings who are passionate, self-controlled, and creative. Their creativity is boundless in the sense that it can be in the arts, in spiritual matters, or in "science."[1]

But after all the negative attacks on Christian and scientific worldviews and the values they engender, what about Nietzsche's vision of the consequences of holding a will to power worldview? Unfortunately, because the creation of *individual* values and realities is the very foundation of his vision, he cannot offer anything close to a "blueprint" for the betterment of humanity. That would be wholly contradictory to his vision. "Great" individuals must find their own ways. I am not convinced that Nietzsche would claim that will to power is "the best" worldview for all humans to have. I think *he* thinks it is better than Christianity and science, but in the works he authorized for publication, Nietzsche often offers will to power as *an* alternative rather than *the* alternative to them. When he champions a multiperspectival view in *Beyond Good and Evil,* Nietzsche must allow for other perspectives to be consistent. Again, the biggest difficulty Nietzsche has with science is it becoming too dominant a perspective to the point at which it forgets it *is* a perspective and starts considering itself as aperspectival, objective Truth. Nietzsche's stance, as I read him, is not to eliminate the scientific perspective but, rather, to remind it that it *is* perspectival. In order to do this, Nietzsche attempts to explain the same phenomena science claims to explain and offer another explanation of it. Will to power serves as that alternative explanation.

According to Nietzsche's perspective, viewing relations among humans through the lens of will to power would lead to creating a climate in which certain "great" humans could possibly emerge and flourish. According to Nietzsche's interpretation of Christianity, Christianity demands equality and conformity based on humility and servility. Nonhumble and nonservile people are seen as "sinners" and "evil." A will to power interpretation of the world allows and acknowledges that people have different capabilities, that everyone is not equal, and that the strong dominate. Just who "the strong" are, however, is not immediately discernable. Sheer physical strength, an obvious candidate for "strong," is, according to Nietzsche, the "lowest" form of power.[2] Strength of character, having a character with "style," is, for Nietzsche, a higher, if not the highest, form of power. Physical strength, though, is not ruled out. Neither are military or political powers; however, they are not very interesting forms of power for Nietzsche. But because Nietzsche does not explicitly condemn sheer might, many readers have criticized him for promoting traditionally "bad" actions.

Nietzsche does not rule out "bad" actions because he sees a connection between the capacity to do great things and the capacity to do terrible things. His metaphor for this is that a tall tree must have deep roots. That is why he sees the elimination of the possibility of terrible things as also the eradication of the possibility of great things. Cut the roots from the trees and they die. Because Nietzsche desires the flourishing of great human beings, he must allow for the possibility of great suffering as well. And Nietzsche is prepared to accept any suffering that may be necessary for the flourishing of great humans. This is no consolation for an actual person concerned that he or she may be on the receiving end of a "great" person's expression of power, which the actual person perceives as harmful, but to be fair to Nietzsche, it is only these "capabilities" for terrible acts that Nietzsche sees as necessary, not the actual manifestation of them.[3]

However, humanity would probably suffer through "wannabe *Übermenschen*" who would make the herd suffer but not produce much of interest culturally or historically. But the emergence of truly great *Übermenschen* would somehow be worth whatever price was paid. It is this last claim that deservedly has raised criticisms.[4] The most charitable reading of it can be analogous to someone beginning a fitness program. It will take a lot of effort, sweat, and pain to get in shape, but the rewards are worth it. But it could also be interpreted as suggesting that one keep hitting one's head against the wall because it will feel so good when one stops. In the first interpretation, the individual seems heroic and praiseworthy; in the second, the person would be viewed as a fool. It is not clear that Nietzsche's position would not result in our banging our heads against the wall. The fact that Nietzsche encourages rather than discourages the possibility of life getting much harsher (and "worse" according to herd values) without the guarantee that it will ultimately be wonderful makes his philosophy difficult for many to accept wholeheartedly. Nietzsche recognized this, as his frequent references to writing to the "few" or the "free spirits" attest.

Perhaps interpreting all relationships through the lens of will to power will not lead to the cultural renaissance of which Nietzsche was so enamored in his youth, but we could never know this until we try it. We have experienced life through the interpretive lenses of Christianity and of science. Both worldviews lead, at best, to human mediocrity, according to Nietzsche. Why not try interpreting the world as will to power?

But is my interpretation that will to power is an interpretative tool the right one? Given what I say in chapter 4, this question is a peculiar one to ask. If we take Nietzsche's perspectivism seriously, we cannot answer this question, for "the right one" presupposes that there is only one interpretation that corresponds to Nietzsche's notion of will to power. In setting out to "get will to power right," I have discovered a paradox. If I have "got Nietzsche right," then I must acknowledge Nietzsche's skepticism regarding this whole project. "Getting Nietzsche right" undermines my entire project, for if I got Nietzsche right, then I should realize that "getting Nietzsche right" is, in some sense, impossible to do. I can always reinterpret my interpretation of will to power at any time.

Paradoxes come into play in many other areas of Nietzsche's writings. Nietzsche's views on truth spring immediately to mind. In trying to "get Nietzsche right" on truth, we encounter a self-referential problem. Should Nietzsche's contention that truth is perspectival be taken as nonperspectivally true? Nietzsche seems to enjoy the conundrum rather than work feverishly to eliminate it. This suggests to me that Nietzsche was not very bothered by such inconsistencies; they only reveal our will to Truth.

Another paradox I see in Nietzsche writings is the relation of eternal recurrence and time. Nietzsche's desire to set humans free from the straightjacket of linear time (and the unhealthy consequences of guilt and shame that result from such belief) culminates in his notion of eternal recurrence, whereby he attempts to dislodge us from our conventional, linear perspective of time. What exactly is the alternative perspective is, I think, unclear, but it involves more than simply thinking that time is circular, if we are to take *Thus Spoke Zarathustra* seriously. The paradox may be in living as if time were linear but interpreting it as "eternity in every moment."

The tension and interplay between living in flux and interpreting that flux bring Nietzsche to his notions of style and "play." In the end, everything we humans take so seriously—values, morality, truth, science, God—boils down to questions of taste. Experimentation with different and new spices and seasonings, quantities and combinations of ideas, leads to more diverse and healthier human beings. What you eat reveals your taste in foods; how you live reveals your taste in values. There is no "true" way to live; Nietzsche invites us to "play" with the paradoxical world in which we live.

Thus my foray into "getting will to power right" reveals as much if not more about me than it does about Nietzsche's phrase *will to power*. First, it reveals that I value (perhaps overvalue?) Nietzsche's texts. It reveals that I read these texts rather straightforwardly and perhaps not as playfully as some (or Nietzsche) might like.[5] It reveals me as a "scholarly laborer,"[6] slavishly poring over Nietzsche's texts, rather than a "philosopher," artistically creating a philosophy in my own image that will effect change. It also mirrors back to me my preoccupation with making Nietzsche consistent, even though I have written an article questioning whether Nietzsche himself would hold this value.[7] In addition, I seem to take great pains to make Nietzsche's ideas appear reasonable and palatable, although hopefully not too Pollyanna-ish, to the average person, even though Nietzsche does not seem at all interested in the average person's comprehension or acceptance of him. Most of all, this book mirrors back to me my training in analytic philosophy—it is an analysis of will to power, which basically begins and ends with Nietzsche's texts. I am not so naïve, however, as to think that the text has only one, "true" interpretation, that I have uncovered that interpretation, and that all other interpretations are thus rendered wrong or inadequate. If I am "right," competing interpretations or criticisms tell me as much about the interpreter/critic as they might about Nietzsche. These considerations start to make me realize the attraction to the view that one should forget about textual analysis altogether and just play as one wishes with Nietzsche; even the author's interpretation of his own work should not be privileged over any others' (*Ecce Homo* be damned!).

Although I understand this view (and sometimes am quite sympathetic to it), I know of no better place to begin playing with will to power than by trying to make sense of the passages in which the idea occurs, with special emphasis on those passages in the books Nietzsche published himself or authorized for publication before his collapse. It is this process that I find so rewarding. There is always the possibility that I could change my interpretation of will to power in the future. After all, if I follow my own reading of Nietzsche, I will interpret and reinterpret the world "eternally." Interpretation is my fate. By reading and rereading Nietzsche, I am learning to love that fate. If this book is a successful introduction to the topic of will to power, you will be inspired to begin your own interpretive journey.

Notes

CHAPTER 1

1. See, for example, the cover of the 8 June 1981 issue of *Der Spiegel,* where it states, "Nietzsche thinker, Hitler doer."

2. See Steven Aschheim's *The Nietzsche Legacy in Germany, 1890–1990* (Berkeley: University of California Press, 1992).

3. Even talking about being faithful to a text or making Nietzsche internally consistent is problematic and is dependent on dubious presuppositions; see my "On Making Nietzsche Consistent," *The Southern Journal of Philosophy* 31, no. 1 (spring 1993).

4. See GS, 13; KGW V/2, 58–60.

5. WP, 1067; KGW VII/3, 38[12], 338–39.

6. See particularly R. J. Hollingdale's *Nietzsche* (Boston: Routledge and Kegan Paul, 1973) and Harold Alderman's *Nietzsche's Gift* (Athens: Ohio University Press, 1977).

7. See Walter Kaufmann's introduction to his translation of *The Will to Power* (New York: Random House, 1968, xvi) and his *Nietzsche: Philosopher, Psychologist, Antichrist* (New York: World Publishing Co., 1966).

8. Both Hollingdale and Alderman come to this conclusion.

9. See especially "On Truth and Lie in the Extramoral Sense," *The Gay Science,* 354; *Beyond Good and Evil,* 17; and *On the Genealogy of Morals* I, 13. There are, of course, many other places where Nietzsche talks about the limitations of language.

10. I first encountered this division in Kaufmann's *Nietzsche: Philosopher, Psychologist, Antichrist.* These divisions have some rhyme and reason to them, although I think there are some "transition" books that make the breaks between periods not as distinct as Kaufmann suggests they are.

11. See Bernd Magnus's *Nietzsche's Existential Imperative* (Bloomington: Indiana University Press, 1978), especially chapter 2.

12. See, especially, D, 432; KGW V/1, 270.

13. Kaufmann, *Nietzsche,* 153.

14. See Linda L. Williams's "Will to Power in Nietzsche's Published Works and the *Nachlass,*" *The Journal of the History of Ideas* (July 1996), 447–63.

15. The idea that science rests on cause and effect comes from Schopenhauer. See Schopenhauer's *The World as Will and Representation,* trans. and ed. E. F. J. Payne (New York: Dover Publications, Inc., 1969), 28–29.

CHAPTER 2

1. See BGE, 260; KGW VI/2, 218.

2. See AC, 24; KGW VI/3, 189–91.

3. GM, preface, 6; KGW VI/2, 264–65.

4. See GM I, 5; KGW VI/2, 263–64.

5. See BGE, 32; KGW VI/2, 46–47.

6. Kaufmann states that *ressentiment* should not be translated into the English "resentment," but it is not clear why it should not be. The only reason I can find that Kaufmann provides is that *ressentiment* now is a fairly technical term in psychology. But "resentment" (albeit sublimated) seems to adequately capture the meaning of Nietzsche's *ressentiment.* See Kaufmann's "Editor's Introduction" to his translation of *On the Genealogy of Morals* for his discussion.

7. Gilles Deleuze makes a similar claim about will to power being both active and reactive in his *Nietzsche and Philosophy.* Trans. Hugh Tomlinson (New York: Columbia University Press, 1983). I independently came to this conclusion in my doctoral dissertation, "Nietzsche's Doctrines of Will to Power: Some Recent Anglo-American Approaches" (University of California at Riverside, 1983).

8. See BGE, 263; KGW VI/2, 227–28.

9. Of course it could be argued that when the acts these words describe are directed toward or involve humans, then the acts are immoral or evil. Ore is one thing; human beings are another. That might be why Nietzsche eventually tinkers with a theory that attempts to eliminate the distinction between animate and inanimate objects in some of the *Nachlass* entries.

10. For another interpretation of will to power being active and reactive, see Deleuze's *Nietzsche and Philosophy.*

11. This "bulk" consists of approximately thirty aphorisms out of the thousands Nietzsche authorized for publication. More on this subject will be presented in chapter 3.

12. Note that the tarantula is a metaphor for *ressentimient* in *Thus Spoke Zarathustra.*

13. See Maudemarie Clark's interesting article, "Nietzsche's Doctrines of the Will to Power," *Nietzsche-Studien* 11 (1982), 458–68.

14. See BGE, 16–17; KGW VI/2, 23–25.

15. See David Hume, *A Treatise on Human Nature* (London: Oxford University Press,1975), especially part 3.

16. See Maudemarie Clark's discussion of *Beyond Good and Evil* 36 in *Nietzsche on Truth and Philosophy* (Cambridge: Cambridge University Press, 1990), 212–20.

17. George Stack comes to a similar conclusion from a different analysis of *Beyond Good and Evil* 36 in *Man, Knowledge, and Will to Power* (Durango, Colo.: Hollowbrook Press, 1994), especially 271–74.

CHAPTER 3

1. See George Stack, *Lange and Nietzsche* (New York: Walter de Gruyter, 1983).

2. Stack makes a similar claim in his book *Man, Knowledge, and Will to Power* (Durango, Colo.: Hollowbrook, 1994); see especially chapter 8.

3. WP, 715; KGW VIII/2, 11(73).

4. See Larry Wright, *Teleological Explanations* (Berkeley: University of California Press, 1976).

5. See GS, 344; KGW V/2, 259. See also WP, 1048; KGW VIII/1, 2(186), 157–58.

6. R. J. Hollingdale, *Nietzsche* (Boston: Routledge and Kegan Paul, 1973).

7. See KGW VIII/3, 19(8), 347.

8. Bernd Magnus, "The Use and Abuse of *The Will to Power*," in *Reading Nietzsche,* ed. Robert Solomon and Kathleen M. Higgins (New York: Oxford University Press, 1988).

9. Ibid., 220–21.

10. Martin Heidegger, *Nietzsche,* trans. David Krell (New York: Harper and Row, 1979), 8–9.

11. Stanley Rosen makes a similar claim in *The Question of Being: A Reversal of Heidegger* (New Haven: Yale University Press, 1993); see especially chapter 6.

12. Wolfgang Müller-Lauter, "Nietzsches Lehre vom Willen zur Macht," *Nietzsche-Studien* 3 (1974), 1–60.

13. See WP, 693; KGW VIII/3, 14(80), 52.

14. Clark, *Nietzsche on Truth and Philosophy* (Cambridge: Cambridge University Press, 1990), 210.

15. See KSA XI, 724–26.

CHAPTER 4

1. See Maudemarie Clark, *Nietzsche on Truth and Philosophy*; Alexander Nehamas, *Nietzsche: Life as Literature*; and Reudiger H. Grimm, *Nietzsche's Theory of Knowledge.*

2. For the purposes of this introductory discussion, I will not engage in the more technical philosophical discussion over the fine distinctions among sentences, statements, and propositions. I use *sentences* and *statements* interchangeably, but I could also say *propositions.*

3. Maurice Merleau-Ponty accuses Descartes of such an oversight when Descartes neglects to doubt language in *Meditations on the First Philosophy*; see Merleau-Ponty, *The Phenomenology of Perception,* trans. Colin Smith (New York: Routledge and Kegan Paul,1962), part 3, chapter 1.

4. The Liar's Paradox, most succinctly put, begins with me saying that everything I tell you is a lie. I then say that I'm lying. If everything I say is a lie, then my telling you I'm lying must be a lie, but then I am saying something true—I'm (truly) lying. This would be impossible if everything I say is a lie.

5. See BGE, 2; KGW VI/2, 10.

6. Fyodor Dostoevsky, *Notes from Underground,* trans. Serge Shishkoff (New York: Thomas Crowell Co., 1969), 12.

7. Laurence Hatab argues that democracy does not entail equality in *A Nietzschean Defense of Democracy* (Chicago: Open Court Publishing, 1995).

CHAPTER 5

1. Arthur Danto, *Nietzsche as Philosopher* (New York: Columbia University Press, 1980).

2. Bernd Magnus, "Self-Consuming Concepts," *International Studies in Philosophy* 21, no. 2, 1989.

3. See especially D, 121, 243, 263, 481; KGW V/1, 113, 204–05, 212, 289–90.

4. Walter Kaufmann surmises that Nietzsche could be talking about Socrates in the *Beyond Good and Evil* aphorism but that, by *Ecce Homo,* Nietzsche is talking about himself.

5. See *Ecce Homo,* "Thus Spoke Zarathustra," 1; KGW VI/3, 333–35.

6. Bernd Magnus, *Nietzsche's Existential Imperative* (Bloomington: Indiana University Press, 1978), 142.

7. Ibid., 143.

8. GM III, 28; KGW VI/2, 430.

9. Laurence Lampert, *Nietzsche's Teaching* (New Haven: Yale University Press, 1986), 149.

10. Kathleen Higgins, *Nietzsche's Zarathustra* (Philadelphia: Temple University Press, 1987), 187.

AFTERWORD

1. I put *science* in scare quotes because the great human being recognizes that science is also a creative, artistic endeavor in the first place, unlike the typical nineteenth- and twentieth-century scientist, who believes he or she is discovering Truths about the nature of reality.

2. See GS, 13; KGW V/2, 58–60.

3. Of course, there are no objectively "terrible" acts. In Nietzsche's view, acts are good or bad not according to the act itself but only according to who performs the act, and this is not "objectively" determined.

4. See Erik Parens, "From Philosophy to Politics: On Nietzsche's Ironic Metaphysics of Will to Power," *Man and World* 24 (1991), 169–80.

5. I am thinking that some deconstructionists, like Jacques Derrida, would have a more playful time with interpreting will to power. See Derrida, *Spurs,* trans. Barbara Harlow (Chicago: University of Chicago Press, 1978). Another way to play with Nietzsche is presented by Luce Irigaray in *Marine Lover of Friedrich Nietzsche,* trans. Gilliam C. Gill (New York: Columbia University Press, 1991).

6. See BGE, 211; KGW VI/2, 148–49.

7. See my "On Making Nietzsche Consistent," *The Southern Journal of Philosophy* 31, no. 1 (spring 1993).

Relevant Bibliography

SELECTED BOOKS BY FRIEDRICH NIETZSCHE

Nietzsche, Friedrich. *Werke, Kritische Gesamtausgabe.* 8 vols. Ed. Giorgio Colli and Mazzino Montinari. New York: Walter de Gruyter and Co., 1967–71.

———. *Sämtliche Briefe.* 3 vols. Ed. Giorgio Colli and Mazzino Montinari. New York: Walter de Gruyter and Co., 1980.

———. *Sämtliche Werke, Kritische Studienausgabe.* 15 vols. Ed. Giorgio Colli and Mazzino Montinari. New York: Walter de Gruyter and Co, 1980.

———. *Werke in drei Banden.* Ed. Karl Schlecta. Munich: Hanser, 1959–61.

———. *The Antichrist.* In *The Portable Nietzsche.* Trans. Walter Kaufmann. New York: Viking Press, 1982.

———. *Beyond Good and Evil.* Trans. Walter Kaufmann. New York: Random House, 1966.

———. *Daybreak.* Trans. R. J. Hollingdale. Cambridge: Cambridge University Press, 1982.

———. *Ecce Homo.* Trans. Walter Kaufmann. New York: Random House, 1969.

———. *Human, All-Too-Human.* Trans. R. J. Hollingdale. Cambridge: Cambridge University Press, 1986.

———. *On the Genealogy of Morals.* Trans. Walter Kaufmann. New York: Random House, 1969.

———. *Philosophy and Truth: Selections from Nietzsche's Notebooks of the Early 1870's.* Trans. and ed. Daniel Breazeale. Atlantic Highlands, N.J.: Humanities Press International, 1979.

———. *Thus Spoke Zarathustra.* In *The Portable Nietzsche.* Trans. Walter Kaufmann. New York: Viking Press, 1968.

———. *Twilight of the Idols.* In *The Portable Nietzsche.* Trans. Walter Kaufmann. New York: Viking Press, 1968.

———. *Untimely Meditations.* Trans. R. J. Hollingdale. Cambridge: Cambridge University Press, 1983.

———. *The Will to Power*. Trans. Walter Kaufmann and R. J. Hollingdale. New York: Random House, 1967.

SELECTED RECENT BOOKS ON NIETZSCHE

Ackermann, Robert. *Nietzsche: A Frenzied Look*. Amherst: University of Massachusetts Press, 1990.

Ahern, Daniel. *Nietzsche as Cultural Physician*. University Park: Pennsylvania State University Press, 1995.

Alderman, Harold. *Nietzsche's Gift*. Athens: Ohio University Press, 1977.

Allison, David. *The New Nietzsche*. New York: Dell Publishing Co., 1977.

Ansell-Pearson, Keith. *An Introduction to Nietzsche as Political Thinker*. Cambridge: Cambridge University Press, 1994.

———, ed. *Nietzsche and Modern German Thought*. New York: Routledge, 1991.

Aschheim, Steven. *The Nietzsche Legacy in Germany*. Berkeley: University of California Press, 1992.

Berkowitz, Peter. *Nietzsche*. Cambridge, Mass.: Harvard University Press, 1995.

Blondel, Eric. *Nietzsche, the Body, and Culture: Philosophy as a Philological Genealogy*. Trans. Seán Hand. Stanford: Stanford University Press, 1991.

Brandes, Georg. *Friedrich Nietzsche*. New York: Haskell House Publishers Ltd., 1977.

Clark, Maudemarie. *Nietzsche on Truth and Philosophy*. New York: Cambridge University Press, 1990.

Conway, Daniel, and Peter Groff, eds. *Nietzsche: Critical Assessments*. New York: Routledge, 1998.

Copleston, Frederick. *Friedrich Nietzsche, Philosopher of Culture*. London: Burns, Oates, and Washbourne, 1942.

———. *A History of Philosophy*. Garden City, N.Y.: Doubleday and Co., 1963.

Crawford, Claudia. *The Beginnings of Nietzsche's Theory of Language*. New York: Walter de Gruyter, 1988.

Danto, Arthur. *Nietzsche as Philosopher*. New York: Columbia University Press, 1980.

Deleuze, Gilles. *Nietzsche and Philosophy*. Trans. Hugh Tomlinson. New York: Columbia University Press, 1983.

Derrida, Jacques. *Spurs*. Trans. Barbara Harlow. Chicago: University of Chicago Press, 1978.

Elsner, Gary. *Nietzsche: A Philosophical Biography*. Lanham, Md.: University Press of America, 1992.

Gillespie, Michael Allen, and Tracy B. Strong, eds. *Nietzsche's New Seas*. Chicago: University of Chicago Press, 1988.

Golomb, Jacob. *Nietzsche's Enticing Psychology of Power*. Ames: Iowa State University Press, 1989.

Graybeal, Jean. *Language and the Feminine in Nietzsche and Heidegger*. Bloomington: Indiana University Press, 1990.

Grimm, Ruediger H. *Nietzsche's Theory of Knowledge*. New York: Walter de Gruyter, 1977.

Hatab, Lawrence J. *Nietzsche and Eternal Recurrence: The Redemption of Time and Becoming.* Lanham, Md.: University Press of America, 1978.

————. *A Nietzschean Defense of Democracy.* Chicago: Open Court Publishing, 1995.

Havas, Randall. *Nietzsche's Genealogy: Nihilism and the Will to Knowledge.* Ithaca, N.Y.: Cornell University Press, 1995.

Hayman, Ronald. *Nietzsche: A Critical Life.* London: Weidenfeld and Nicolson, 1980.

Heidegger, Martin. *Nietzsche.* 4 vols. Trans. David Krell. New York: Harper and Row, 1979.

Heller, Erich. *The Importance of Nietzsche.* Chicago: University of Chicago Press, 1988.

Higgins, Kathleen. *Nietzsche's Zarathustra.* Philadelphia: Temple University Press, 1987.

Hollingdale, R. J. *Nietzsche.* Boston: Routledge and Kegan Paul, 1973.

Houlgate, Stephen. *Hegel, Nietzsche, and the Critique of Metaphysics.* New York: Cambridge University Press, 1986.

Hunt, Lester. *Nietzsche and the Origin of Virtue.* New York: Routledge, 1991.

Jaspers, Karl. *Nietzsche.* Trans. Charles Wallraff and Frederick Schmitz. Baltimore: Johns Hopkins University Press, 1997.

Kaufmann, Walter. *Nietzsche: Philosopher, Psychologist, Antichrist.* New York: World Publishing Co., 1966.

Klein, Wayne. *Nietzsche and the Promise of Philosophy.* Albany: State University of New York Press, 1997.

Koelb, Clayton, ed. *Nietzsche as Postmodernist: Essays Pro and Contra.* Albany: State University of New York Press, 1990.

Kofman, Sarah. *Nietzsche and Metaphor.* Trans. Duncan Large. Stanford: Stanford University Press, 1993.

Krell, David, and David Wood, eds. *Exceedingly Nietzsche: Aspects of Contemporary Nietzsche Interpretation.* New York: Routledge, 1988.

Lampert, Laurence. *Nietzsche's Teaching.* New Haven: Yale University Press, 1986.

Magnus, Bernd. *Heidegger's Metahistory of Philosophy.* The Hague: Martinus Nijhoff, 1970.

————. *Nietzsche's Existential Imperative.* Bloomington: Indiana University Press, 1978.

Magnus, Bernd, and Kathleen Higgins, eds. *The Cambridge Companion to Nietzsche.* New York: Cambridge University Press, 1996.

Magnus, Bernd, Stanley Stewart, and Jean-Pierre Mileur, eds. *Nietzsche's Case: Philosophy as/and Literature.* New York: Routledge, 1993.

Müller-Lauter, Wolfgang. *Nietzsche: His Philosophy of Contradictions and the Contradictions of His Philosophy.* Trans. David Parent. Urbana: University of Illinois Press, 1999.

Nehamas, Alexander. *Nietzsche: Life as Literature.* Cambridge, Mass.: Harvard University Press, 1985.

O'Flaherty, James. *Studies in Nietzsche and the Classical Tradition.* Chapel Hill: University of North Carolina Press, 1976.

O'Hara, Daniel T., ed. *Why Nietzsche Now?* Bloomington: Indiana University Press, 1985.

Oliver, Kelly, and Marilyn Pearsall, eds. *Feminist Interpretations of Friedrich Nietzsche.* University Park: Pennsylvania State University Press, 1998.

Parkes, Graham. *Composing the Soul.* Chicago: University of Chicago Press, 1994.

Patton, Paul, ed. *Nietzsche, Feminine, and Political Theory.* New York: Routledge, 1993.

Pletsch, Carl. *Young Nietzsche.* New York: The Free Press, 1991.

Poellner, Peter. *Nietzsche and Metaphysics.* Oxford: Clarendon Press, 1995.

Richardson, John. *Nietzsche's System.* New York: Oxford University Press, 1996.

Rosen, Stanley. *The Mask of Enlightenment: Nietzsche's "Zarathustra."* New York: Cambridge University Press, 1995.

———. *The Question of Being: A Reversal of Heidegger.* New Haven: Yale University Press, 1993.

Sadler, Ted. *Nietzsche. Truth and Redemption: Critique of the Postmodern Nietzsche.* Atlantic Highlands, N.J.: Athone Press, 1995.

Schacht, Richard. *Making Sense of Nietzsche.* Urbana: University of Illinois Press, 1995.

———. *Nietzsche.* Boston: Routledge and Kegan Paul, 1983.

———, ed. *Nietzsche, Genealogy, Morality.* Berkeley: University of California Press, 1994.

Schrift, Alan. *Nietzsche and the Question of Interpretation.* New York: Routledge, 1990.

Schutte, Ofelia. *Beyond Nihilism: Nietzsche without Masks.* Chicago: University of Chicago Press, 1984.

Scott, Charles E. *The Question of Ethics: Nietzsche, Foucault, Heidegger.* Bloomington: Indiana University Press, 1990.

Sedgewick, Peter, ed. *Nietzsche: A Critical Reader.* New York: Blackwell Press, 1995.

Shapiro, Alan. *Alcyone: Nietzsche on Gifts, Noise, and Women.* Albany: State University of New York Press, 1991.

———. *Nietzschean Narratives.* Bloomington: Indiana University Press, 1989.

Sleinis, E. E. *Nietzsche's Revaluation of Values: A Study in Strategies.* Urbana: University of Illinois Press, 1994.

Smith, Gregory. *Nietzsche, Heidegger, and the Transition to Postmodernity.* Chicago: University of Chicago Press, 1996.

Solomon, Robert. *Nietzsche.* New York: Doubleday, 1973.

Solomon, Robert, and Kathleen M. Higgins, eds. *Reading Nietzsche.* New York: Oxford University Press, 1988.

Stack, George. *Lange and Nietzsche.* New York: Walter de Gruyter, 1983.

———. *Man, Knowledge, and Will to Power.* Durango, Colo.: Hollowbrook, 1994.

Stambaugh, Joan. *Nietzsche's Thought of Eternal Return.* Lanham, Md.: University Press of America, 1988.

———. *The Other Nietzsche.* Albany: State University of New York Press, 1994.

———. *The Problem of Time in Nietzsche.* Philadelphia: Bucknell University Press, 1987.

Staten, Henry. *Nietzsche's Voice.* Ithaca, N.Y.: Cornell University Press, 1990.

Stern, J. P. *Nietzsche.* Cambridge: Cambridge University Press, 1981.

Strong, Tracy. *Nietzsche and the Politics of Transfiguration.* Los Angeles: University of California Press, 1975.

Tanner, Michael. *Nietzsche.* New York: Oxford University Press, 1994.

Thiele, Leslie. *Friedrich Nietzsche and the Politics of the Soul: A Study of Heroic Individualism.* Princeton: Princeton University Press, 1990.

Warren, Mark. *Nietzsche and Political Thought.* Cambridge, Mass.: MIT Press, 1988.

White, Alan. *Within Nietzsche's Labyrinth.* New York: Routledge, 1990.

Wilcox, John. *Truth and Value in Nietzsche.* Ann Arbor: University of Michigan Press, 1974.

Winchester, James. *Nietzsche's Aesthetic Turn: Reading Nietzsche after Heidegger, Deleuze, Derrida.* Albany: State University of New York Press, 1994.

Yovel, Yirmiyahu, ed. *Nietzsche as Affirmative Thinker.* Boston: Nijhoff Press, 1986.

Zeitlin, Irving. *Nietzsche: A Re-Examination.* Cambridge, Mass.: Polity Press, 1994.

Index

About the Author

Linda L. Williams is associate professor in the Department of Philosophy at Kent State University. She is the author of numerous articles, including "On Making Nietzsche Consistent," "The Development of Will to Power in Nietzsche's Published Works and the *Nachlass*," "What Makes Zarathustra Sick?" and "A Feminist Interview with Friedrich Nietzsche." Her areas of specialization are ethics and nineteenth to mid-twentieth century continental philosophy, and she is a member of the North American Nietzsche Society.